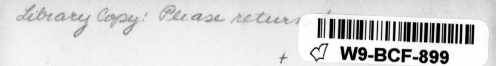

PÈRE JACQUES

THE MACMILLAN COMPANY
NEW YORK · CHICAGO
DALLAS · ATLANTA · SAN FRANCISCO
LONDON · MANILA
IN CANADA
BRETT-MACMILLAN LTD.
GALT, ONTARIO

PÈRE JACQUES

by Michel Carrouges

translated by
Salvator Attanasio

NEW YORK
THE MACMILLAN COMPANY
1961

❖❖❖

Nihil obstat: John A. Goodwine, J.C.D.
                     CENSOR LIBRORUM

Imprimatur: ✠ Francis Cardinal Spellman
                     ARCHBISHOP OF
                     NEW YORK
                     March 10, 1961

The nihil obstat and imprimatur are official declarations that a book or pamphlet is free of doctrinal or moral error. No implication is contained therein that those who have granted the nihil obstat and imprimatur agree with the contents, opinons or statements expressed.

First Printing

French edition, Le Père Jacques, © 1958 Éditions du Seuil

The Macmillan Company, New York
Brett-Macmillan Ltd., Galt, Ontario

Printed in the United States of America

Library of Congress catalog card number: 61-10025

Contents

I
IN THE SEINE VALLEY
❖❖❖

1   The Bunel Brothers

From the moment we entered, they were laughing. Every time we crossed the threshold of their small red brick houses with their tiny gardens, the same unanimous, solid, good-humored wave of laughter burst out. Although they were all well past fifty they feigned mock blows and teased each other like youngsters. Some brothers seem to interact upon one another. Among themselves they are aware of too many of their past capers and antics not to feel like laughing. The Bunel brothers did not deny themselves this pleasure.

During the tumult of our arrival, Lucien's name was quickly brought up at the first opportunity while chairs were still being arranged around the oilcloth-covered tables. Immediately the Bunels' expressions changed. Something incredibly tender and solemn spread through the little house. After a moment's pause, their recollections of him multiplied and gave rise to fresh oubursts of laughter in which enjoyment, nostalgia, and admiration mingled.

We had shown up among them suddenly, like intruders, but they were not in the least embarrassed by our presence. They behaved as usual, just being their natural selves, letting their memories flow freely, like veterans who stand on no ceremony when instructing raw recruits. During our tour of Normandy and the Paris region, every time we brought Lucien's name into the conversation we had met a peculiar reaction. The tone of the response was not always the same.

In some cases we had detected a slight irony, annoyance, or even disapproval at the memory of certain scarcely conformist fancies, reservations, however, which did not exclude a high regard

3

for the rest. In the majority of cases, the regard rose to admiration but it did not prevent a smile or even uncontrollable laughter. Now here, among the Bunel brothers, we met the same mixed reaction and it was all the more astonishing.

This buoyancy, this zest for life, this quick transition from the serious to an easy cordiality, this tone of good will despite trials and bad times, these teasing gestures despite the brothers' years, was the mark common to all of them. And it sprang from the same source as did Lucien's character. When they began to talk about him, one sensed in the air of the little house much more than a faithful reflection of the old days, something which had the glitter of native gold, extracted from the same vein of ore. As we met them one after another, Gaston, André, Maurice, and their sister Madeleine—while waiting to meet René—we came very close to the hidden secret of one of their number. Their gestures, voices, eyes all spoke intimately to us of their two brothers—alike and different as are all brothers— Alfred, the eldest, who was killed in World War I, and Lucien, Père Jacques.

Ordinarily families do not like to disclose the secrets of their origins. In a confusion of fear and modesty, they hide or disguise them. They do not willingly admit that one of them appears to be exceptional, unless, of course, he is cast in the form of a statue. But the Bunel brothers, their wives, their sister, and their brother-in-law—speaking with that marvelous openness of the people—talked most freely and frankly about Lucien in our presence. And what they said was truer than the most authentic document. He was there, very close to us, indisputably alive in the mirror of their common past.

What people discern exceeds in an unimaginable way the limited circle in which we see them live out their daily routine. Through the great rear window looking out on the past an infinite series of horizons stretches beyond the horizon of the moment. We asked the Bunels what they had seen, heard, felt, and understood about their brother. It was enough to pronounce his name. In an instant the image of Lucien was there, overflowing with life, but only for them, reflected in the look that came into their faces, in the vast blue country of remembrance intimate to them, but inaccessible to us.

Let us admire, if we will, the scholars who think they can reconstruct everything from a great distance: the psychology of Isaiah, the motives of the Apostles, the logic underlying wars or palace revolutions, as if all this were not like the sieve of the Danaides, as if the sap of life did not escape freely through the slim bindings of historical documents. To be sure, account must be taken of them, for on their bridge to the past we always find some valuable pointers, traces, fingerprints, remains, which unquestionably attest to certain facts. Yet they are but fragments and vestiges. The movement of life is elusive. Still we were asking very little from the Bunel brothers! We were simply on the track of a man dead less than fifteen years, their own brother, a man who had lived among them in that region between Havre and Rouen, in the place where at that moment we were all gathered. We could draw plentifully on their recollections. They were full of them and offered them to us wholeheartedly. As we watched and listened we seemed to find Père Jacques laughing and talking again in their midst. But there remained a subtle difference which the Bunels were the first to proclaim with humble vehemence, a difference which had existed from the beginning and had continued to grow. How could it be grasped? Although they did all they could to be of help to us, we felt to what an extent it is nearly impossible to imagine another man's secret. The Bunels themselves knew quite well that they had been able to get a glimpse of him only from the outside. No man is exactly like another. Each individual alone knows himself from the inside, despite the most ingenious traps set to catch him.

As they talked something came through in their gestures, words, and looks that was like a signal one could not ignore—an arrow of remembrance, from far away, from the inaccessible horizons of their pasts.

Thus I was acting like the Havre schoolboys, who, not satisfied with having seen Abbé Bunel a hundred times a day at will—even in his room—would take it into their heads to scramble up upon the roof of a pavilion. From here they would spy on him stealthily through the large open window to find out what he was up to, what the secret of his life could be as it might disclose itself when he believed that he was alone. Meanwhile, I was at André Bunel's with our friends. A rosary hung on the wall directly in front of me. It was not one of those rosaries used by fashionable ladies, so small that you wonder how they manage to count the beads, no matter how delicate their hands. Nor was it one of those monumental apparatuses, as solid-looking as tools, that you see hanging from monastic robes. No it was a very ordinary, average-sized rosary whose beads were made of simple boxwood. This was Père Jacques' rosary. Only the cross was missing. It was the most precious memento in the house, a family relic.

How could the little Lucien with whom they had played together have become Abbé Bunel, a teacher at the School of St. Joseph in Havre, Père Jacques, the Carmelite of Fontainebleau, and then Père Jacques the indomitable prisoner of the concentration camps? How grasp such a series of metamorphoses? There was a host of luminous landmarks from the night of the past in the mass of documents collected by the Carmelites, and in the testimonies which all those who had known Père Jacques had entrusted to their care. But how could one find the living silhouette of the man along the way?

2   The Mills Below the Viaduct

As the train rolled along between Le Havre and Rouen, all we saw for miles was an interminable suburb. Huge smokestacks pierced the sky. The train skirted an uninterrupted series of small valleys, filled with factories and red-brick workers' houses, surrounded by green hills.

Here the Bunel brothers had grown up. Their father, Alfred, the same name bequeathed to his eldest son, was a spinner by trade. He had spent his life working in the mills, or looking for work, and frequently moving from one place to another in order to be nearer to the job opportunities in these localities—industrial at their cores, rural on their peripheries—which dot the landscape west of Rouen for a radius of fifteen miles in the immediate proximity of the railroad. Without the kindness of Gaston Bunel who gave us two days of his time, constantly driving us around in an automobile, we would have never been able to make such a complete tour of the Bunel brothers' childhood realm. An austere realm indeed. It had already been crammed with factories at the time when they were still small children, that is to say, at the beginning of the century. Lucien, who was the fourth of the eight children brought into the world by Pauline Bunel, was born on January 29, 1900, at Barentin which is about ten miles from Rouen. He was brought back there at the age of five, after the family had ended its sojourn in Pavilly a little more than a mile farther down. At the age of twelve he left Barentin for the Petit Séminaire at Rouen, three years before the Bunels definitely settled down in Maromme. Hence it was Barentin that Lucien knew best during his childhood. It is also the most easily recognizable locality

7

because all the trains overlook it when they cross the 1500-foot viaduct that spans it.

For that matter the three towns, Barentin, Pavilly, and Maromme,
are but three links of the same industrial complex. They abound in
textiles. Everywhere there are spinning mills, factories for weaving
linen and cotton, textile plants for printed cotton goods and calico.
Add to this the dye works, the factories making chemical products,
and the metallurgical establishments which work for Rouen and Le
Havre. The workers' houses look alike here: tiny four- or five-room
bungalows built of red brick, which can be spotted from the windows
of the express.

As he drove his car through the very center of this labyrinth, along
a road which meandered in all directions, Gaston Bunel pointed out
the house on Rue Bennetot in Barentin, and then the one on Rue de
la République in Maromme. He no longer remembered the others
exactly, but who would be surprised at this after so many moves, and
after so many years? Besides we were not trying to proceed along the
lines of an archeological reconstruction, but simply to see with our
own eyes this little universe that Lucien had seen with his, and in
which his entire childhood has been steeped. Also this uncertainty
and this monotonous resemblance of the interchangeable and drab
cottages made us feel, and most forcefully, the monotony and uncertainty of the life of a working-class family. This childhood kingdom
had nothing to do with fairy tales. But harsh as it was, it was nevertheless delightful in comparison to the hell of Mauthausen.

At the turn of the century people were fascinated by the Exposition
Universelle, the political drama of the Panama scandal, the beauty of
the actress Polaire, or the commanding performances of Sarah Bern-
hardt. It was also the glorious age of the pioneers in aviation, of Ader,
Lilienthal, and the Wright brothers. But who had built this platform
crowded with wonders and scandals if not the toiling millions under
their smoke-filled skies, by their hard, grueling labor through long,
tedious years? In 1900, when Lucien Bunel was born, the first line of
the Paris subway was opened; it was also the year of one of the first
great trade-union victories—the establishment of the ten-hour day.

It was a far cry, however, from the trade-union victories of our day. Alfred Bunel père rose and went out at five every morning and returned after seven in the evening. There was no such thing as a half day on Saturdays, or dismissal pay, of course, but instead the fatiguing job of having to clean out the factory every Sunday morning. Nor was the wage picture much brighter. From an ordinary spinner, Alfred Bunel had become a foreman by dint of hard work. At the time of Lucien's birth, he was making about three francs fifty centimes a day. Nor was there any question of allowances for large and growing families. And in addition to a little girl, who died young, the Bunels had Alfred and André, then Lucien, followed by Madeleine, Gaston, Maurice, and René.

The mother of the Bunels, whose maiden name was Pauline Pontif, was no better off than her husband; for she was the daughter of a shepherd. Both were so poor at the time of their marriage that they had to buy on credit the few sticks of furniture with which to furnish their first home. It took a long time and many privations to pay off this debt, penny by penny. Madame Bunel herself worked in a factory during the first years of her marriage, until André was born. During working hours she left her first babies with neighbors, rather than place them in a public day nursery, for fear that one day her children might be mistakenly exchanged for others.

One year, despite the very serious risks he was running as the father of a family, Alfred Bunel became a dedicated, militant union leader and led an active campaign for higher wages and better working conditions. It was not long before he was fired. People at the top find it quite normal to organize to defend their interests, but they find it almost impossible to understand that the people at the bottom also should organize to protect their interests. No, high wages and trade-union freedom did not come about all at once.

The only material fortune that ever came Alfred Bunel's way in his whole life was when he inherited a small sum from an uncle. It nearly made up for the lack of family allowances. René Bunel described what this lack meant with a precision that needs no comment:

"I remember the normal, almost invariable menu. At noon: *pot au feu* on Sunday, stew on Tuesday, outside of that, vegetables without cream sauce. We did not know what beefsteak was in our house, it was too dear. I do not remember any butter on the table, since my mother bought only one pound a week. In the evening, watered soup. At the age of ten or eleven, and later, I used to make it myself. Instead of cream, I would pour a fourth of a quart of milk into it just before serving. Under the pretext of rinsing the pitcher my mother would pour a pint of water into a quart and a half of milk which allowed her to keep up appearances. In the summer, after the soup, a bite of gray radish, a salad, or a small piece of cheese, and off to bed! In winter, half a smoked herring or a penny meat pie. On rare occasions we got to taste a slice of bread and cream smeared with powdered sugar, but these were feast days in our house. More often we got a slice of bread with a little piece of chocolate. Mother cut a bar (about an ounce and a half) into four pieces."

His sister Madeleine, now Madame Clatot, added:

"My parents had figured that the money saved on sugar and coffee would make up the rent. Papa never drank coffee, brandy, or wine."

It goes without saying that after such workdays and such meager meals there was little thought of staying up late, much less of going out in the evening.

And at Barentin or at Pavilly, in one cottage or another, it was always the same red bricks and the same living conditions among all the working families.

"And yet we lived happily," René Bunel recalled with astonishing good humor. "Because if Papa worked all day, Mama looked after his little children, all of whom very soon learned to pray, sitting in her lap. At the table we had to wait for Mama to serve us and ask very politely for anything we might need. Before sending us out on a shopping errand, my mother always cautioned us to say, 'Good day, sir, and good day, madame; thank you, sir, and good-by, sir.' And we'd be in for a good drubbing if by chance we ever forgot to carry out this protocol! If Mama called us while we were playing we came on the double, otherwise we got spanked, or still worse were sent to bed without any supper! In the mornings there was no nonsense, the door opened, and a resounding 'Les gosses!' was enough to have everybody jump out of bed at once. On Sunday mornings we could lie in bed—until eight o'clock. The respect due to parents was not a mere fable to us. It was something so sacred that looking back I always see my mother as a person with whom one did not argue and before whom one bowed without wincing, even though she was very thin and tiny. How many spankings! How many nights in bed without supper! Yet what memories of Papa and Mama, what affection between our parents and us children!"

In effect, all of them told the same story with a smile. Materially it was a harsh life; their upbringing was strict. Madame Bunel was an imperious woman who loved to command and whose own life was hard. At any rate she was not afraid, and with good cause, that she would instill any complexes in the children she was raising. In fact the Bunel brothers seemed hardly to be burdened with any today. Above all else they have retained a deep memory of love and of the happiness of life around the family hearth.

Having arrived at this point they would have been hard put to be more explicit, for these are things lived which cannot be related in detail. They are beyond words.

"Poor but honest!" André Bunel put it, as he and Gaston burst into laughter.

3   Crusade in the Rain

As we sat there unwinding the skein of memory, the trains roared by at full speed. The indifferent faces of the passengers could be seen in a flash, looking down from the heights of the viaduct without showing the slightest compassion for the immobile heap of identical-looking cottages in Barentin. What could happen here other than the eternal day in, day out struggle of a colony of human ants? But are not beautiful houses necessary for beauty to flower? And journeys in order to make adventures possible? Before I myself plunged into the streets of Lucien Bunel's childhood, I had imagined them as scattering in all directions like the simple villages in the middle of the pasture lands of Normandy. I had not yet confirmed with my own eyes that they were continuous, or almost so, crammed against the railroad to form a linear industrial suburb. Of course to lovers of the picturesque all this could appear to be a simple setting, without importance for the rediscovery of the future Père Jacques, hero of the purest kind of resistance movement, hero of hope and charity in the concentration camps. But not believing in the wave of a magic wand, I could not suppose that Lucien Bunel had by chance or miracle suddenly become the hero that he showed himself to be in the face of hell on earth.

How grasp the life of his childhood? How glimpse what was already its hidden power, the apprenticeship of a terrifying adventure? Was he not like all saintly souls who have always lived piously, and imperturbaby followed the straight line, apart from trifling slips more in the nature of peccadilloes than true evil, until the coming of their hour of trial and the assured mystical triumph? Had not little

Lucien been born in a "poor but honest" family, of a pious mother who had fervently taught him his first prayers? And the father— punctilious, hard-working, drinking water only, entirely devoted to his large family and faithful to the prescriptions of Holy Mother Church—this father, no less punctilious in assisting at communion, who secretly said his rosary by counting the beads in his pocket on his way to work, was he not a model of the Christian worker of former times? A model, moreover, that made his neighbors in Barentin smile, for his friends and acquaintances fell very much short of sharing the same religious climate. Disbelief had spread widely in Barentin. From this point of view the Bunels were also set apart because the two brothers of the paternal grandfather had been priests. Both of them had been pastors in the vicinity, one in Saint-Jacques-sur-Darnetal, the other in Saint-Ouen-du-Breuil. One was remembered for his perfect conduct and great piety, the other was reputed to be so good and generous that on the day of his death no shirt could be found; he had given away, it was said, his last one.

After all this, then, should it be surprising that one at least of the Bunel youngsters was a model child and had a vocation, one of those pious fatalities adored by hagiographers and which bore the reader in inverse ratio? And if to this one adds that, with the help of charitable persons, Lucien was able to enter the Petit Séminaire and then the Grand Séminaire, and that he became a proctor and a teacher in a private school, it makes one despair of any hope of surprise. Nothing of that all too human tumult of soul, none of those dramatic events that make the lives of the great converts so exciting. Only the distant hope of coming to the moment when Lucien Bunel, abandoning teaching, became a Carmelite. There is a double attraction about this. To give up the priest's cassock for the habit of the monk is at last the index of a metamorphosis. To be a curé here or there, with robes of one color or another, should amount to the same thing, but the fact is that the monk has always excited the imagination of believers and unbelievers in an altogether special way: the monk cannot be a man who compromises, more or less strictly, with the world; he is either one or the other. The obese monk, ribald, completely perverted, or the absolute ascetic, a kind of spirit in flesh and bone, are the two types who have always triumphed in stories. The author has merely to produce the stereotype, and the reader follows happily.

Simple honesty compels me to say that I myself was discouraged by the early life of Père Jacques. I had heard too many stories about ersatz little curés of Ars and little Thérèses of Lisieux. From a distance it is always the gray tints, necessarily, that stand out in the fog of ignorance and vague generalities; up close, one can discover something altogether different. It is like the factory where the ugly surroundings, the throbbing of the machinery, the lives measured by time clocks seem to crush everything. But in the hours when the strong wind of workmen's brotherhood begins to blow, one rightly feels that there is something more there than a testimony of indomitable hope, more than a will for future changes. Suddenly there is the revelation of a faith in life, personal and collective. It is like love when the dreariest streets, the dullest hallways glisten like the countryside after a sudden shower, if they lead toward the person one loves with all his heart. Thus what mattered in the Bunel family was not the black cassocks of the great-uncles, nor the rosary in the foreman's pocket, nor the respectful observances that could have been a moral highway code, all of which in an instant could spill over into fetishism or a hollow morality, gnawed away at by termites. What matters is the life that was really lived, true love, the true track of blue above the everyday drabness of the street. But how grasp what brotherhood, human love, and divine love can be, without plunging into it oneself in the living flesh? How discover the inner place in the little labyrinth of the petty, insignificant scenes of Lucien's childhood, perhaps small but full of life, sun, and movement?

Life? Indeed it was a question of life from the very start. Alfred and Pauline had trembled for Lucien when he was barely a year old. He became so ill that the doctor had no hope for his recovery. All the neighbors were sympathetic, but they did not know what to do. One of them, a devout believer, recommended a novena and a pilgrimage to Saint-Germain.

South of the railroad and the workmen's gardens, on the other side of the bordering hills, along the twists of the Seine in open country among cows and apple trees, there lies an ancient region filled with memories of saints. Here rise ancient and splendid abbeys of the Middle Ages, partially ruined and partially restored, like Saint-Wandrille, Saint-Martin-de-Boscherville, and Jumièges. They are Benedictine structures, almost a thousand years old, whose arches still gleam white through great trees. Germain had no such architectural honors paid to him. His shrine is not far from Saint-Wandrille, on the little road to Fréville, and one can pass it a thousand times without ever noticing it. Near a crucifix, if I remember correctly, one turns down a dirt road and comes upon a shallow pond. This is the shrine. It is nothing but a rough shaft with a statuette and some wild flowers, protected by an ordinary grille. It is there, that is all.

It is not hard to make a novena, and what would one not do to save a child in danger of death, if a few prayers suffice to give one at least a little hope, or no more than courage? Madame Bunel did not fail to appear at the shrine. It is easy to drive out from Barentin to this holy place in the open air of the heights. But this is no more than the semblance of a pilgrimage. For the Bunels, burning with anxiety and hope, it was a quite different matter.

"My mother had faith," René recalled. "Accompanied by my father, she took the baby there one Sunday morning. The weather was awful. It was raining very hard, and a stormy wind was blowing. The neighbors said it was not a very sensible thing for her to do, since she was expecting another baby which she had been carrying for five months. Nevertheless, she went. You had to walk two and a half hours, I think, to get to the shrine."

"It's seven miles from Barentin," Madeleine broke in.

"My father and mother recited their rosary as they pushed the baby carriage. They arrived exhausted and dripping wet. Then they knelt before the little statue of the saint and Mama offered her little one with words heard a thousand times since: 'My God, leave him to me until he is twenty, then take him if he belongs to Thee. But give me the joy of offering him to Thee when he is grown up.'

In the carriage the dying baby immediately began to stir. My father and mother lifted the blanket cautiously: he was smiling. Enraptured, my parents again fell to their knees to thank God. Then they went to a nearby farmhouse and tried to give the baby some milk. He drank it, gurgling with joy.

"When they returned home, the unbelieving neighbors could not get over it. Mère Marie, the midwife, exclaimed, 'Yes, truly, there is something above us.'"

At a distance nothing is more simple than to be coldly reserved, to suppose a coincidence, an exaggerated diagnosis, or whatever else one wishes, rather than a miracle, mere suppositions among which only God can unveil the true one. But what is not supposition is this long march of desperate hope, this poor crusade in the rain, cold and mud-splashed, without trumpets and the clashing of armor, this faint murmur of the rosary and the rattling of the little carriage, this march of anxiety and supplication. The father and mother trembled to see this baby menaced by death. From the depths of the Normandy countryside love called out wildly to the resurrected Crucified whose cross remains an eternal promise of hope in the history of humanity for as long as all the tombs shall not have been opened, as was His, by the physical and divine violence of the Resurrection. Would He who had multiplied not the marvels of magic but the compassionate healings of body and heart now have less power and less love?

Little Lucien's father and mother did not entertain such a doubt for one second. They walked for miles on foot with their child, just as had those who had come running along the road trod by Jesus of Nazareth to address the same petitions to Him. What madness, said the wise neighbors! But the secret of this madness depends only on the fact that for these two pilgrims, as for all Christians, nothing had changed. It was certainly not the pond in the meadow, or the old rough shaft, or even the statuette and the memory of an old St. Germain, whose origins could be traced only by scholars, which mattered to the two pilgrims in the rain. But it was a meeting place, as formerly in Palestine, where one knew one would meet the Master passing by on such and such a day. It was this same Man they wanted to meet, the rest was only circumstance. Those supplicants of former times did not yet know that Jesus was more than the carpenter of Nazareth, and those of our time no longer think that the Lord of the Gospels was first, visibly, a man living like the others, and in a like manner living today. He is hidden, but He is there, and if the father prayed in silence, the mother talked to Christ as did all the mothers in the Gospels. At this moment, more than at any other time in her life, there was an encounter between herself and Christ. She never forgot it and this encounter illuminated the entire life of her son. When Père Jacques later confided to some intimate friends that he hardly thought he would live beyond forty, one could psycho-analyze him at bargain rates and attribute some morbid death wish to him, or believe, as he himself said, that the war would come and carry him off. One can also consider a sermon he delivered at Easter in which he spoke of death with enthusiasm. About death? Quite the contrary, about life after death.

"To see God," he said, "just think of it!" But at the same time was it not true that he considered his life to be a long reprieve ac-corded to him in order to give him a greater range in this life and in the other life? He knew by heart everything that had taken place during that dramatic day of his childhood. And Pauline Bunel was also to remember it with all her soul on that summer day of 1945 when René came to break the news of Lucien's death. "Without saying a word she took a photograph of Père Jacques, and placed it openly on the little sideboard next to that of my brother who was lost in the other war. Then she went to look for some white flowers which she placed in a glass next to the photographs and she knelt down. 'My God,' she said, 'I promised him to Thee. Thou hast left him to me longer than I could have hoped. Thy will be done!'"

4 "We Should Have Been Jealous"

When Lucien posed the great question of his life, his father and mother said "no." They had known of his desire for a long time and they had dreaded this moment. For years he had made allusions to it, at first childishly, then in a more and more clear and serious way. On this April day of 1912 he was only twelve years old, but he raised the same question in an earnest and urgent manner. We all know what fanciful, laughable, sublime, or absurd projects children can invent and how the parental tactics consists in putting everything off indefinitely with the timeworn formula, "When you grow up," from which moment life itself takes charge of trampling upon the dream. But Lucien's parents sensed the seriousness of this demand so well that they answered "no" in order to cut it short once and for all.

That Lucien should desire to become a priest and that this desire had grown greater came as no surprise to his parents. They had too much faith in their hearts for that. Between the two dramatic prayers overflowing with evangelical faith—the day when the mother had trembled for her baby's life and the day when she had learned of the death of Père Jacques—a great interval of time, of doubts, of trying to find the way, of wearisome life had intervened. Faith is a beacon, but a beacon in the night. It has nothing about it of the character of the seemingly solid, actually tangible beam of light that one imagines from afar.

Faith would not be faith if it were evidence, repose, security, comfort. The first thing that it has to deal with is money. As faithful attendants at Sunday Mass in the Barentin church, the Bunels knew enough of the Gospel to realize that money is the greatest enemy of

18

divine love, as long as the heart of man has not learned to desire avidly this latter love so that the passion for money is crushed under a more violent passion. Money was the first obstacle to Lucien's desire. There were ways of getting around it, or in any case they could have been found, but the Bunels wanted to set them aside for a determining reason.

This reason, moving and profound, was justice. For Lucien was not an only child. He was but one of their many children, one of a small and growing group of seven—six boys and a girl—who sat around their table, who slept under their roof and who forged ahead with them along life's stony road. They all lived together under the iron law of a livelihood that had to be laboriously earned day by day, without respite, from one end of the year to the other. The two eldest boys, Alfred and André, had gone to work the year before, immediately upon getting their school certificates, the former at the age of twelve, the latter at the age of eleven and a half, in order to keep the household going with extra money.

"By what right," said Pauline Bunel, "should one of the children be privileged while the others work in a factory to earn their living?" She was so intractable on this score that in order to test Lucien one day she said to him, "It's laziness that drives you not to want to work like the others. There's no reason why your brothers should work for you while you go gallivanting about!" She knew very well that the two great-uncles had not spent their lives gallivanting about. Indeed she knew everything that could be said on this subject, and that the privations and hard work of some are not those of others. But it was this very difference that raised the moral obstacle. Lucien's project would lead to his escape from the common fate, toiling to be sure, but over books, toiling to evangelize a parish, but this would not be the same kind of toil. It would be the realization of a dream and the taking possession of a wider horizon. Lucien could impose on himself all the hardships he pleased, but he would do it freely while his brothers would never be finished coming and going like slaves from the house to the factory, from the factory to the house, indefinitely until their last breath, save by extraordinary luck.

Lucien's parents could certainly have gone to see Abbé Ternon, the pastor of Barentin. Unhesitatingly, he would have answered them with the sanctioned formula: that to let their son follow this call of a priestly vocation was simply to give him to God, to realize in a way both pious and gentle the prayer with which, on their knees, they had implored the Lord for Lucien. But the difficulty did not lie there; it was not their intention to refuse anything to the will of the Lord; they simply asked themselves whether it was really His will. Could this will be contrary to what seemed to them a law of justice and mutual support among them all?

It is true that Lucien had always held a place apart in the family circle. He was much admired by his sister Madeleine, eighteen months younger than he. Lucien belonged to the poetic and resourceful type of children who can make up marvelous games out of pieces of thread, stones, and bits of wood. They spent hours together in the tiny garden baptizing dolls. To be sure it was Lucien who always played the curé, the more so because he was never at a loss to invent a sermon to which his sister listened, all ears. Lucien's prestige was all the greater because he also knew how to give in as well as how to lead, a rather rare quality.

"He was much calmer than I," said Madeleine, "and he readily let me play with his toys." Perhaps she was generalizing, but she had no difficulty in remembering one of those little incidents that inscribe themselves on a child's heart: "One year Father Christmas brought him a puppet with cymbals on its hands. It made me envious, and Lucien gave it to me at once. On the other hand, he never failed to reproach me if I did or said something bad."

Lucien not only preached by example, he preached only that way, as a little girl plays at being a mother with a shred of ribbon, or little boys play chauffeur with a string attached to a stone, pulling it along as if it were an automobile. He must have been pretty intolerable when he played at being spiritual director in this way, but he put so much gentleness and sincerity in it that the others agreed to play along with him, and not only Madeleine.

"One evening, it must have been during the month of May," René recounted, "it was very warm and beautiful and there was an evening service with hymns to the Blessed Virgin. Lucien took me there. I must have been about six, and he twelve. I was eager to go inside the church, to tell God that I loved Him with all my heart, that I would not lie any more, that I would kiss Mama and Papa, and that I would never do any harm to others. This impression of supernatural happiness experienced by contact with my older brother Lucien has remained so clearly with me that, while writing these lines, I again feel a child's soul within myself."

Aside from the family his old friend Dessanaux recalled that Lucien had always told him, "When you're worried, take your rosary and say all of it. When you're finished, you won't think about your worries any more." Hence what the curé of Barentin said about Lucien is not surprising: "He loved the services and received Communion from time to time, a little more often than was customary there. He loved to go to church and to pray by himself, quietly and for a long time. From childhood, his prayer was contemplative, a surprising thing at his age."

It is impossible to say from whence this ardor, this feeling for the religious life came, just when it had been born in him, but the fact is that he had it in his very blood. At the age of five, at the time when Alfred was entering the public school, Lucien had suddenly told his mother, "You know, maman, when I grow up, I shan't go to Alfred's school."

"And where will you go?"

"To Monsieur le Curé's school, because I'm going to be a big Monsieur le Curé."

Was this just a passing fancy? If so it certainly passed through his mind very often. From the time he began to assist Sunday Mass regularly and joined the children's choir, he organized processions, with Madeleine and René at their head, which were as comical in character as they were sincere in intention. In short, he was training himself and had only that single idea in his head. One day he was found in the attic alone, delivering a sermon to an imaginary audience. He was not embarrassed at being surprised and, when asked what he was doing, replied with the utmost naturalness, "I must learn how to speak to people." At home he was usually called "the little curé." And the pastor of Barentin, delighted to find him a model choirboy, the star pupil of the catechism class, and a kindly aide with the small fry, was convinced of Lucien's vocation. He prayed for its fulfillment. Young Bunel came to serve Mass at six-thirty in the morning, although getting up at this hour was not easy on anyone else in the house. Madame Bunel did not approve of his early departure, especially on cold mornings. She tried to forbid it, but with none too firm a tone, and Lucien asked for nothing more than permission to continue.

At the risk of making Lucien out to be a little saint of rose-colored wax, which he was not, we must admit that he was studious and often first in his class, but at the same time quite a scoffer. He did not restrain himself from making cruel fun of the failings of his teacher, M. Beaudet, and even roared with laughter one day when the unhappy man tripped on the stairs and sprained his ankle.

An unusual incident impressed the Bunels deeply. It took place on Rue Bennetot in Barentin in 1909.

"On this day we were playing in the garden, my brothers, my sister, and myself," René recalled. "It must have been about four o'clock in the afternoon and it was surely a Thursday or a holiday. Suddenly a beggar pushed open the front gate and came toward us. I still see this venerable old man with his long beard, leaning on a cane and carrying a bundle on his back. Frightened, we ran to Mother's side. The beggar asked for alms, were it but a piece of bread. My mother showed him her children, saying that she was too poor, that she had nothing to give, that he should go to the houses of the rich. Meanwhile, Lucien had opened the sideboard and cut off a big piece of bread on which he had laid some cheese; then going up to the old man he presented it to him. The beggar, placing his hand on Lucien's head, said: 'I knew, my little one, that you would give me some bread; I thank you but I don't need it. May the good God protect you!' Since my brother insisted that he take it, the old man said, 'No, thank you, little one, your gesture is enough.' Angry because the beggar had deceived her little Lucien whom she loved so much, my mother spoke rather harshly to the visitor and accompanied him to the end of the walk in the garden, telling him not to return. Alerted, the neighbors ran out to ask what the commotion was all about. Maman pointed out the old man who was going into the kindergarten and described the scene that had just taken place."

The excitement of the neighbors reached its height when they noticed that the old man did not come out of the kindergarten. They entered and were still more astonished. The school had only one door, but the washerwoman and the teachers swore that they had seen nobody enter. All searches were fruitless and one of the neighbors began to cry "miracle" as fast as one could also cry "hoax." It would be simpler to suppose that there had been some mistake in the direction taken by the old man. This kind of thing happens every day without miracle or hoax.

The wonderful thing was the encounter between the child and the old man, in the full light of the garden within sight and sound of all, the spontaneous movement of the little boy, then the reply of the old man who declined the food, not out of disdain, but to signify that all he wished to retain of that day was the pure remembrance of a generous gesture. Whether this old man was, like St. Benedict Labre, a beggar of a former time who had appeared by a miracle, or just another of God's vagabonds, the significance of the encounter is exactly the same. It is the encounter of love.

Père Jacques, for whom this day was unforgettable, told one of his friends that he had also offered the old man a glass of water which he had touched to his lips without drinking a drop. This real glass of water and this real piece of bread, real in the most positive sense of earthly life, are the water and the bread offered to the Lord Himself in the person of the first-comer of the poor. It is the bread and the water on which God affirms that He will judge men. "Your gesture is enough," the old man had said. The beggar had had the last word, the masterly word of the day. Why deprive him of his human truth by supposing him to be an apparition of a saint rather than a saint in flesh and blood?

A day was to come when Lucien Bunel at the age of forty-four was to repeat and multiply the same gift like a gesture of heaven in the midst of the hell of deportation. This profound call of divine love in the heart of a child, at an age when adults are sometimes tempted to say that he is too young to understand religious questions, is the true secret of Lucien Bunel. The little boy of Barentin had a heart filled with divine love like the little boys of Palestine who pushed their way through the crowds to come closer to Christ. The reasonable disciples wanted to chase them away because they judged them to be too small and incapable of understanding and behaving properly. But the Lord protested. "Suffer the little children to come unto me," He said to the disciples. Lucien did just that.

Among all the Bunels someone undoubtedly was able to understand better than any of the others just what was going on in Lucien's heart. This was his oldest brother, Alfred. This brother, who was to be killed in the war of 1914, was a young worker at that time. At the age of twelve and a half he had already begun to contribute his wages to the household. Whenever he had a free moment, he would dream of doing big things and would study the world around him. He drew sketches of airplane motors (it was the heroic age of the Wright brothers and Blériot), but life had already clamped him in too harsh a vise for him ever to realize the dreams that haunted him. At five o'clock in the morning, he would be up, usually the first in the family to rise. He would go to Mass and then for a walk in the woods before reporting to the spinning mill.

Why give to the younger and not the eldest the freedom to realize a childhood dream, and to escape from this jumble of red-brick cottages clustered around the textile factories? And there was something still harder to do: Lucien would have to stretch forth a supplicant hand as the mendicant had stretched forth his.

The days passed. Everybody in the house saw that Lucien was painfully eating his heart out in silence. There was something, however, that could make his parents come to a decision; and this something was disclosed by his brother René in a single remark.

"Lucien? There was never any reason for him to be spanked. He was cited as an example to us. We should have been jealous. But on the contrary, we respected him like a great person, so much was there of gentleness in his manners and character."

One smiles at the formula when one finds it in the life of a saint. When it is the brother of a hero who speaks, the same statement takes on another meaning. It could in no way have been a question of affected nobility or manners. Adults are easily taken in by artificial airs, but nothing escapes the criticism of brothers. They observe each other with a naked eye. There is no question here of confusing the sugariness of a "mama's boy" with the virtue of sweetness, that is to say with the power of true sweetness. Moreover, René signed this testimony, so to speak, with the admirable phrase, "We should have been jealous of him. But on the contrary. . . ." Who finds it agreeable to see his brother cited as an example? Who finds it agreeable to see him endlessly escape from the punishments that are meted out to the others? Lucien's special treatment was entirely justified merely by the fact that it was accepted.

His brothers were not only not jealous—they admired him. They were all more than ready to countersign Lucien's right to freedom so that he could realize his dream. Only God knew that this dream would lead him to a terrestrial hell alongside which life in Barentin was heaven, a hell in which Lucien would be a thousand times poorer, more humiliated, and hungrier than the old beggar in the garden.

5   Distinguished People

Lucien rang the bell and waited, his heart beating violently. He had not told a soul, not even his family, but it was impossible to do otherwise; he had resolved to gamble his all. To be sure he had never been inside such a beautiful house. It must be full of tapestries, carpets, old pieces of waxed furniture, beautiful rooms for receptions, and above all the solemn silence of lordly manors broken only by the faint ring of silver, or of muffled footsteps—a mansion in elegant taste. The door opened at last and the first miracle was that Lucien was admitted and asked to be patient for a few minutes.

Only a few days before, the Bunels had surrendered. Dressed in his best, Bunel père had gone on Sunday to visit the pastor of Barentin, Abbé Ternon, and had told him their decision. Although Abbé Ternon had known of Lucien's desire for a long time, he was delighted by this news of the parent's consent. No doubt about it, he said to himself, this boy must enter the Petit Séminaire. There remained the ominous question of money. The Bunels did not have a cent to pay for his board. A scholarship? Seminaries do accept scholarship students, but seminaries are almost as poor as their recruits, a great number of whom come from the poor, so requests for scholarships are not encouraged too much. Abbé Ternon thought it best to advise M. Bunel to ask for assistance from his employer. "Though poor, my father was proud," exclaimed René Bunel. "He could not tolerate the idea of begging for charity. To work, yes, but to beg, that was too much!" Days went by and M. Bunel could not make up his mind to take such a step. Lucien sensed this at once, and for this reason had taken the matter into his own hands.

26

Without telling a soul, he went to beg like the old mendicant who had blessed him a few years earlier.

In the beautiful house, Madame appeared, escorted by her daughter. Very embarrassed, Lucien timidly explained the purpose of his visit. Madame made a show of politeness, deigning to listen patiently. After which she took out her purse, removed a coin, and invited her daughter to do the same. Outside Lucien found that he was holding two twenty-centime pieces in his hand. The matter was closed. "He left disoriented, disheartened," René told us. "Everything was topsy-turvy. Fashionable society had suddenly and brutally appeared to him in its true light, with all its hypocrisy. Where to go? To whom complain, if not his mother? And he broke into tears in Mama's arms, letting the two coins they had donated for his subsistence for one year in a seminary drop to the floor."

It was not the only incident of this period. While Abbé Ternon was giving him his first lessons in Latin and undoubtedly doing his best to obtain a scholarship for the boy, Lucien tried to earn a little money to defray at least part of the expenses. He and one of his brothers spent their Sunday afternoons on the tennis courts retrieving stray balls. The rate was fifty centimes. The young employers who lured Lucien and his brother did not place this money in their hands. They were such distinguished people that they threw it on the ground. After all, the Bunel boys spent the afternoons picking up tennis balls while the others played; so they could just as well bend over to pick up their money.

Later Père Jacques, past forty, a Carmelite and headmaster of a school, was to confess that he could not recall incidents of this kind without sadness.

Other arrows, moreover, were aimed at him in his own neighborhood of the red-brick cottages, when news of his approaching departure for the seminary got around.

"One more fellow who doesn't want to tire himself out. He just doesn't want to get his hands dirty."

Upon leaving the station Lucien had only to turn to the left. He was in Rouen, on the opening day of the school term, in October, 1912. Among the streets that rise above the tunnel, the one called Champ des Oiseaux brings one in a few minutes to a huge ramshackle building, the Grand Séminaire, surrounded by foliage filled with the chirpings of sparrows, reminding him of the church in Barentin.

Although Lucien did not stop, it was here that he hoped he would come some day, but what trials he would first have to undergo! Seven years of study from the first class, the "sixième," to philosophy in his last year. He went on his way, made another left turn, and there he was before the ancient fir trees that guard the entrance to the Petit Séminaire. "Petit" it was with respect to the age of its beginning recruits, but quite impressive in the size of its buildings.

Inside was a whole new world, especially when one has known only the cottages of Pavilly and Barentin. There were endless hallways; formal reception rooms that dampened any desire to confide secrets; staircases which, like the corridors, were permeated with the smell peculiar to educational, ecclesiastical, and military establishments; classrooms whose desks and lecterns were ritually painted black. Let us not linger on the classically cold refectories, or the dormitories with their endless rows of iron beds with whitish or grayish coverlets, their towel racks, the ancient washstands with faucets sticking out of the wall over zinc drains. There was nothing to attract a casual visitor, yet this was the place where Lucien wanted passionately to be.

His dream had led him to the Petit Séminaire, but it had proved to be no dream. Everywhere in this new world into which he had plunged, within himself and without, Lucien found both help and hindrance, springs of enthusiasm and revolt. There may be calm boys whose lives unfold like a parade of seminarians, hands joined, in cathedral processions. But this was not the case with Lucien, nor with all the seminarians. Moreover, he was indignant to see how some of them behaved.

At the moment Lucien was only another newcomer who was

entering the first year. His reaction was turbulent. He was still the gentle Lucien described by his sister and his brothers, but he was at the age of great inner changes and these changes coincided with his entry into the world of the boarding school. If birth is the first battle of life, the second is the formation of character.

"Lucien Bunel was my pupil during his first year at the Petit Séminaire," recalled Abbé Bance. "His was a strong will, almost fierce. His energetic traits, his direct manner, his quick movements immediately compelled recognition from his classmates. His intelligence was lively and his application to work remarkable. He aimed at success and achieved it in everything, even in recreation. Lucien, in fact, led all his classmates in play, sometimes even in certain sudden disturbances in class. His voice was already so clear and so powerful that he soon became our master reader. He was endowed with a rich nature, but he needed long and painful efforts to control those faults of disposition, pride and obstinacy, that threatened to be his undoing. But he prayed so well and was so quick to accept advice that I never had any doubts about him, not even during the troublesome times of adolescence."

At the core of his being was an unshakable desire to become worthy of the vocation that called him. The struggle was a long one, lasting several years. One observer recalled that in his preseminary years Lucien was at once timid and touchy, even cantankerous, despite his piety. One of his classmates put it more gently—Lucien was a wag, something of a Montmartre type, a mocker, a tease, whose eyes sparkled with mischief, but who would unexpectedly leave the playground and go to the chapel alone. Left to himself, this classmate added, Lucien might have easily become a street-corner tough.

At any rate he was stubborn. One year the seminarians were dissatisfied with one of their teachers. All they wished for was his departure from the school, and they had made up their minds, despite the custom, not to offer him birthday congratulations. The Superior called Lucien into his office.

"Bunel! You will deliver a congratulatory address!"

"No, Monsieur le Supérieur, the students don't want it."

"Bunel, I order you to deliver one!"

"Very well, Monsieur le Supérieur, I shall do so."

Lucien wrote the little speech and presented it to the Superior for censure. The Superior looked at it and read, "Monsieur le Supérieur having formally ordered me to compose a congratulatory . . ."

"Bunel, you have a head as hard as a wall!"

"A wall has its own grandeur," replied Lucien.

Remarkably intelligent and willful, Lucien was not one of those who indifferently accept the views of their teachers. He was as ardent in protesting against what appeared unjust to him as he was in following the counsel of those whom he respected. When he rebelled, it was not against the seminary but for the seminary. For him the seminary was neither the cold machine one imagines it to be from the outside, nor that monument of unchallengeable wisdom that pious persons credit it to be. It was an environment ablaze with life in which his own life was feeling its way. He knew where he was going, and on this score he had no hesitation, although his progress alternated between advances and setbacks. Undiscouraged he pushed on.

But new dangers loomed, perhaps at the moment when he most needed to feel how very strongly he was attached to this place.

Alongside the dormitory was a large terrace from which he could look down upon a vast panorama. Beyond a thicket of trees below he could see the entire city of Rouen, the station, the spires of churches, the tower of Jeanne d'Arc, and still farther off, the mass of factories and workers' suburbs that stretched as far as the horizon. The Pavilly and Barentin side was hidden by the hills to his right, but he often thought of it with deep anxiety. War had begun. His eldest brother had left for the front; his father, despite his large family, had been mobilized; André too was waiting to be called up. His mother struggled in black poverty with the four children left at home. If this continued Lucien would have to return to Barentin and take a job in a factory in order to keep the family alive. The seminary itself was in a state of confusion; it was to become a military hospital and the students were to be evacuated to a temporary establishment at Ernemont near Rouen.

The war dragged on and terrible news came from the front: André was taken prisoner at the battle of Verdun; Alfred was killed in the prime of his youth at Bouchavesne in 1917. In the interval, Providence intervened for Lucien: after several months in uniform his father had been demobilized and the situation in Barentin had become more normal. But this was not enough. Then came the intervention of Sister Marthe, a religious belonging to a small congregation in Ernemont. She knew Lucien well, having helped him get together his school outfit, and felt a maternal affection for him. Since she had connections in the town, she got in touch with M. Badin who was M. Bunel's new employer. This time the response was altogether different from that which Lucien might have feared. To this day the Bunels gratefully acknowledge that without M. Badin's assistance Lucien would not have been able to remain in the seminary. Nor did M. Badin content himself with emergency aid at a bad moment. His wife, his daughter Alice, and he himself watched over their protégé until he was ordained. It was they who presented him with his vestments for his first Mass.

A sheet of paper has been found on which Père Jacques, after becoming a subdeacon, had made a note always to pray for the Badin family, as for his own, while saying his office.

During his last years in the Petit Séminaire, Lucien had changed. He guarded and confirmed his gift of contemplative prayer that the pastor of Barentin had noticed, and one of his fellow-students told us: "I admired his devotion. He liked to pray without distraction. When the bell sounded the end of recreation, he never added a word to the conversation which had suddenly been interrupted. If necessary, he unceremoniously preached silence by placing his index finger on his lips. When he became a Carmelite, I was not at all surprised, since he had such a meditative and quiet spirit during his adolescence. . . . He put his whole soul into whatever he did. I can still see him, with his cropped hair, his head slightly bowed, praying, praying without distraction."

Reports indicate that Lucien was noted for excellent conduct and was among the first in his class, obtaining his bachelor's degree without difficulty. The Superior, Canon Haly, still had reservations:

"Hard on himself and also on others, he has more than once shown himself to be severe in his judgments. His teachers have always appreciated his zeal for work, but much less his fretful and distrustful character. But he is virtuous and will be able to correct himself."

In October, 1919, Lucien left the Petit Séminaire for the Grand Séminaire. There again he became impatient with what did not please him. He was dissatisfied with the disciplinary counsel which primarily concerned itself with such trivia as bits of paper dropped in the washbasins, dissatisfied with the philosophy classes where one talked endlessly in order to demonstrate that the admirable instinct of bees is not the same thing as intelligence, and dissatisfied with a course on Holy Scripture in which erudition put rigid plaster casts on the prophets of the Lord. All this seemed fusty and ineffectual to him, especially when he returned on vacation to the milieu of the workers' world in Maromme where his family had moved after leaving Barentin.

His vacation did not last long, however, for he was called up for military service. Six months later he was assigned to the 82nd Regiment of heavy artillery at Fort Montlignon near Paris.

6   "I Longed for Solitude"

To Lucien, the barracks were a great shock, not because of the harsh life and the discipline to which he was already accustomed, but from a moral point of view. During his childhood he had known only an exemplary family life, and he had spent his adolescence in the shelter of the seminary where even the crudest pranks were basically kindly. The faults of some of his professors appeared insignificant to him now that he was thrown among the mass of conscripts. He was horrified to see the unbelief, the demoralization that was spread out before him. But he had too much energy and too sympathetic a personality to let himself be intimidated. With the help of two old comrades he began to counter the current.

In the barracks, as at the seminary and at home, Lucien was a leader. On Palm Sunday when the recruits were asked whether any of them wished to attend Mass, twenty-one young soldiers out of a unit of a hundred raised their hands. Lucien was the first to give the signal. In the regiment, as elsewhere, he drove himself relentlessly. He was "bucking" for a promotion, said his comrades, and he did indeed become a noncommissioned officer. But the men did not complain about this because from the day Lucien was made mess sergeant the rank and file never had it so good. He sent packing all the suppliers who thought they had to offer him a refund against overpriced rations; he also managed to get hold of a cow and some pigs to feed the soldiers better, and he let himself be hauled over the coals by an officer who could not understand how he did it. To this dressing-down Lucien merely replied, "I am allotted funds to feed my men and not to go on a spree."

33

Lucien was insatiably active. With the help of the curé of
Montlignon, one of his closest comrades, and of the Leroy family, he
organized a study group for the soldiers. On Sunday afternoons he
took the members of the parish boys' club for hikes through the
forests of Montmorency. In the evening, after supper, he worked
on his Greek and Latin in a room which the Leroy family had
graciously put at his disposal. Here he made himself completely at
home, and became the adopted son of the house. With Madame
Chalot, the grandmother, he went on a pilgrimage to Ars and to
Paray-le-Monial.

Never before had he been so active, but never before had he felt
so deeply his thirst for contemplation. Sometimes he would suddenly drop whatever he was doing and lose himself in the forest.

"It is in the fullness of nature," he wrote one day in 1921, "it is in
the most hidden and peaceful corners that one best opens out, that
one most easily finds what constitutes our being—there, under the
eye of God, whose goodness, magnificence, and infiniteness we adore.
It is there, when one is rightly united with Him, that one feels all
the force of the ties that attach you to those you love. Try to do
what I myself have often done: receive Communion in the morning, after a good preparation the night before, and go to make your
act of thanksgiving in the solitude of the woods."

Several months later he returned to this theme. "I have found
a restful consolation in the quiet of the woods, in the murmur of
trees, in the prayer of birds. How near one feels the presence of
God in the fullness of nature. It is there, far from the cities where
evil festers, that He is best pleased. If only we were able to love
Him above all to console Him for the rebuffs He receives and to
bind up His poor heart so cruelly torn! But alas! Do we give Him
even one hour a day? And out of that hour do we really love Him
for a quarter of the time?"

One can feel his heartbreak in these fragments of letters. He knew
very well that Christ, on whom he meditated so ardently whenever
he pondered the suffering of God, had not lived in the woods, but
in the towns and villages of Palestine. The image of Francis of

Assisi preaching to the birds is an exquisite one, but Christ did not come to speak to birds. He would not have been the Christ if he had not come, as He Himself said, first of all for the lost sheep. Where the suffering of the Lord is, there also is His greatest love for all the prodigal sons and the laborers of the eleventh hour, for all those who have fled from Him or who still await the moment to turn back to Him. After the Resurrection His disciples were to do the same, establishing themselves in Jerusalem, Antioch, and even in Rome, "the city of perdition," to bring the Lord's message into the very heart of the people. Thus Lucien felt a great call to apostolic action, but at the same time a strong desire for solitude. One day, while walking through a Rouen suburb with his brother Gaston, he said to him with all the bitterness of impotence, "There are so many falls from grace!" Another time while he was wandering around Paris in uniform a girl accosted him on the sidewalk. "Poor unhappy wretch!" he said to her. And he spent a night praying for her in Montmartre.

During his two years of military service, one image never ceased to grow within him, the image of the Trappists. How different the outer man from the inner man! While Lucien roamed through the barracks in his uniform, for moments as brief and as quick as lightning flashes, he saw himself dressed in the white cowl and the brown scapular of the Trappists. It had been a very long time ago that the idea of joining the Trappists had first occurred to him. It was in 1916, when Lucien had come to spend his vacation with Abbé Michel who had succeeded Abbé Ternon as the curé of Barentin. One day he had run an errand to the cousins of Abbé Michel, the Bourys, farmers in the vicinity of Barentin. He had been instructed to tell Madame Boury that her eldest son was in a rest area in the Somme. It was good news, and Lucien was welcomed with enthusiasm. He was sixteen, the youngest son of the Bourys was eighteen; they liked each other at once and became close friends. Lucien spent the evening with the curé's cousins and stayed the night. The following morning he returned to Barentin on his bicycle for the early Mass, but the Bourys had invited him to come again. So every morning he went off again to Mass, then immediately returned to the Boury farm where he helped milk the cows and worked in the fields. In the evening, sitting sociably around the oilcloth-covered table, they talked for a long time. Lucien spoke of the seminary and about what he did in Barentin during the summer: he organized a club for children on vacation. "Even then he wanted to win souls and the children he sought out were those who are called 'the toughs,' " said his young friend Boury. But almost at the same moment, as if driven to an intimate confidence, Lucien confided that he would like to become a Trappist. "You, Lucien, who would make such an excellent parish priest!" exclaimed Madame Boury. "I would do far more good by giving myself fully," the young man had replied.

Thus they whiled away their evenings talking about the future, and when Lucien left the farm everybody missed these pleasant gatherings. "We felt his absence," said his friend. The two had enjoyed working together and playing practical jokes on each other as well as discussing the religious life. A seminarian is not necessarily steeped in piety any more than a worker is reduced to a robot without a soul. To Lucien, who was overflowing with life, all the ways in which life can be seized were eagerly experienced. During Abbé Ternon's tenure, when Lucien visited the curé, he would wash the dishes instead of letting the old housekeeper do them, stopping an instant later to fill up the pastor's gluepot with oil. Inevitably a large spot would appear on the papers that the pastor wanted to glue together, and in consequence Lucien would have his ears boxed. "So you've been at it again!" would shout the same curé who had discovered the boy in contemplative prayer.

All these tendencies developed at the same time in Lucien. His taste for work intensified. He had become a sergeant, in the same way he had passed the examination for his degree, out of love of learning and a sense of duty well done, even though he considered it a duty of the moment. As a professor he was not to be like those who do nothing when they are not teaching or correcting papers. Nor did he ever lose his taste for practical jokes, for he particularly enjoyed upsetting traditional discipline. When he was assistant proctor at the Petit Séminaire, he cheerfully authorized his companions to go out secretly to scrounge for supplementary rations during a time of shortage. As a sergeant he took the place of a comrade who had been confined to the barracks—by what subterfuge is not known—but the fact was confirmed by a responsible noncommissioned officer, Antoine Thouvenin. And when he became a teacher and even the director of a school, Père Jacques was to play more than one of these tricks against established authority.

More singular still was the contrast between his overflowing dynamism, sympathy, and charm, and his taste for solitude and silence. It was a native taste, bred in the bone, which was an organic part of his most intimate self. He wrote of it one day in 1928 in a letter:

"I have a burning thirst to serve God, to possess Him forever, to feed on Him, to live in a profound and constant intimacy with Him.

"Thus, always, I have desired solitude, and, since my second year, la Trappe. I am so profoundly drawn to the hidden cloister of the Trappists! There one is poor, one suffers lovingly for God; one finds God there and watches Him always in silence and meditation."

Why so great a love? And how could it have been born so early and have grown so intensely in Lucien's heart? Love can never be explained. One can try hard to cage it in theories, but love makes sport of their abstract bars. It is the reality itself that is most ungraspable. And it is the same for divine love as for human love. There is no need to resort to hallucination to create a sort of wax museum of mysticism. For men God is, first of all, absent. Faith would not be faith without this absence, it would be an evident fact, like the light of the sun. The presence of God can be grasped only in the depths of this absence. The presence of God at the heart of absence is like that of all those who love each other, who have faith in each other, and who are far apart, separated by space, the night, the sea, mountains, walls, frontiers, and barbed wire, whether they are lovers, mothers and their children, or comrades who have fought together. Materially everything separates them, but if they love each other, if they keep faith in their mutual fidelity, if they struggle, if they have sworn to win and to meet again no matter what, then they remain united despite separation, present from afar, regardless of absence, in thought, action, love, and fraternity. The union of Christ and His disciples is similar. Christ is life itself and what unites Him to His disciples is the sharing of a same life, at once human and divine, simple and mysterious, like that of Jesus among the people of Palestine.

Lucien had only one desire: to share this same life himself. But how? As a priest among men or as a monk in solitude? Was he to follow the path of the Apostle who brought the message of the Word, or that of the Virgin and the Desert Fathers who lived in silent contemplation? It was on this point that his heart was divided. He loved mental prayer and solitude, but at the same time he had many friends whom he thirsted to speak to of Christ. The road of the seminary would lead directly to a parish, barring the unexpected. But now the call of Trappist solitude moved him for the first time. Perhaps it was born of an overwhelming desire for the interior life, but perhaps also it stemmed from a certain discouragement induced by military service which had brought him face to face with the mass of men who did not know Christianity, or who reduced it to the rules of minimum morality and certain reassuring rites with respect to eternity. He dreamed, as he had told his young friend Boury, of "conquering souls." He may have been slightly taken in by this bizarre expression, banal, half military, half spiritual, which hardly resembles the language of Christ. The Gospel speaks only of giving or serving, not of conquering. It addresses itself to men and not to "souls." The purpose of saints is anything but conquest. Their true role is that of reflection. They are the windows that filter the rays of divine love into the world, insofar as they conform to God's will. This was what Lucien was looking for. But before the search was over, he was to need years to find his true place and to know what he was capable of—years of patience, of love, of struggles, and of fidelity.

For the moment, he thought of la Trappe as the road he must take. The call of solitude seemed to be taking precedence over the need of the multitudes.

Throughout 1921, Lucien was stirred by this desire for the contemplative life. After his pilgrimage to Ars with Madame Chalot, he
wrote to his mother without any warning that he wanted to go off
to la Trappe. Madame Bunel reacted violently. She immediately
caught a train and rushed off to Montlignon to Madame Chalot with
whom Lucien now stayed when he was on leave. With one son
dead and a second married, Madame Bunel could not tolerate the
idea of a third son locking himself up forever in a cloister. She
implored him to give up this plan. At least he should remain in
the secular clergy! He would then live in the diocese and she could
still see him. Lucien protested that he could not give up this plan.
Madame Bunel lost her temper and answered that unless he gave
it up then and there, he would no longer set foot in her house.
Lucien too became heated. He turned to Madame Chalot, who was
present and who vainly tried to calm them down, and asked whether
she, at least, would continue to receive him. This time Madame
Chalot replied with a grandmotherly smile: "What's the good of all
this? You are not ready to go; your military service is not yet ended.
If God wants you, He will guide you." Her smile and her words
were oil on troubled waters and the evening ended peacefully.

But the affair was far from settled. In May, while on leave at
Maromme, Lucien again spoke about his plan and his parents reiterated their opposition. Lucien, however, had just come from visiting one of his seminarian friends who was very ill and probably on
the verge of death, and this so affected Lucien that he vowed he
would enter the Trappist order if his friend recovered. He also discussed it with his director and with the Superior of the seminary.
The latter two had not appeared unfavorable to the idea, Lucien
wrote Madame Chalot. They knew the obstacles in the way of such
a change of direction. Perhaps they were simply skeptical and
thought it preferable to wait until Lucien himself changed his mind
rather than oppose him head-on. However that may have been,
Lucien took advantage of his last leave to make a retreat at the
Trappist monastery at Soligny, in lower Normandy, about eight or
nine miles from Mortagne.

Lucien shivered constantly during those three days of retreat at

Soligny. November is a very cold month in these parts and there was only one heated room in the monastery, and that heated only at certain hours.

"Terrible cold," he wrote. . . . "I had dreamed of doing great penances, of sufferings inflicted and endured, and here I was incapable of standing the cold for the space of one day."

He was one, at least, who no longer dared believe that the ascetic life comes naturally to man. But he did not read with less passion the *Life of the Curé of Ars*, especially the pages on penance and mortification. Nor for that matter did he draw any definitively discouraging conclusions from his experience, but on the contrary voted the chief impression made on him by the life of Abbé Vianney: "The inner and practical knowledge of his nothingness did not discourage him, for discouragement is only hurt pride. It is born in weak souls of an excess of confidence in their own powers and a lack of confidence in God. The curé of Ars trusted in himself for nothing and awaited all from God. He gave himself up to devotion with all the more ardor, convinced that without it the most beautiful gifts of nature are useless and that, even without any one of these gifts, piety by itself performs prodigies." This was the secret of the curé of Ars, but it is also the secret of all the saints. It is hardly credible that one could define it with fearless clarity at twenty-one. But this was no longer the young seminarian; it was already Père Jacques speaking.

Four months later, in March, 1922, he got his final discharge papers from the army. The shy lover of Trappist solitudes was now in his soutane, perched precariously on a cart, and escorted by his comrades who wanted to accompany him to the station to show their friendship and their regret over his departure. The soldiers had decided that this little seminarian was a "real priest."

7 "I Open My Secret Soul to You"

Once again Lucien walked up the Rue de Champ des Oiseaux. It was March, 1922. The two-year military interlude now over, life at the Grand Séminaire was resumed in earnest. Although it was the same Bunel who had come back, still industrious and lively, and as quick as before in his enthusiasms, confrontation with life had matured him greatly. Once through the entry gate and across the adjoining lawn, he entered the huge red-brick building and then went down the inner corridor which owes its cloistral charm to its arcaded gallery. Farther along in the large enclosed garden, he liked to go up the old stone steps, in the open air amid the greenery to the statue of the Virgin sheltered by two immense cedars. He went there to pray each morning for a few minutes after Mass.

Life of a seminary cannot be understood by a glance at the high walls, the study halls, the young men in cassocks, or a whiff of soup from the kitchen. Lucien knew well all the warmth and power concealed in this simple-appearing life. It takes everything together to make a seminary: money, food, furniture, books, students, and professors. But none of this could hold together for a second if it did not have God as its support and its goal. Even if the classical statuary is mass-produced, even if the pages of the theology books may seem arid, God is life and the evangelical source is never tainted. At every morning Mass in the seminary chapel, as in all the churches of the world, it is the repast of Christ that goes on without end. As on the evening of the Last Supper, the disciples are gathered and the bread of Christ is consecrated and shared. One day all these men will depart in their turn, as did their forefathers, to consecrate and

41

share the bread of Christ, but there will be no cessation of the carrying out of the Master's words: "Do this in remembrance of me."

But how are we to picture Lucien's years at the seminary if we limit ourselves to saying that they were without incident, full of work and devotion? The directors of the seminary thoroughly appreciated Lucien's intelligence, application, good conduct, and increasing piety, but naturally their reports do not go beyond the customary terminology—one might read a good number of similar ones about other seminarians. If it had not been for the heroic destiny of Père Jacques, who would have paused over this petty business of reports? Only the retroactive light of the future tragedy brought them out of the files in which they lay dormant. But it is Père Jacques who brings them to life, and can they in turn bring to life the Père Jacques who matured little by little in this sacerdotal seedbed enclosed behind high walls? There is no record, it seems, except of consistent good work, good conduct, deep piety, almost as uniform as the colorless cassocks. All this is as dry as a chalk inscription on a blackboard. The only distinctive signs are some passages mentioning Lucien's originality, a certain gift of personal expression, a strong attachment to his own ideas, bordering on obstinacy, and something about him more serious than radiant, sad and even slightly somber that from time to time was evident in his character. "His preoccupation with his vocation must be the cause," noted the Superior with psychological acumen. And Lucien would not deny this. "Dark night since Friday," he wrote on a sheet of paper dated Easter Monday, 1922, several days after his discharge from the army.

"Dark night since Friday. Jesus, however, showed Himself a little yesterday morning in His sweet Easter kiss.

"Upon leaving the refectory, Jesus told me to remain in the chapel after the others left. And He embraced me: He asked me why I was sad. How not be sad when it is so dark and the Divine Spouse to Whom one wishes to give oneself keeps Himself hidden?

"And Jesus said to me: 'Rest in peace; above all may peace, true and profound, be yours. You are my child. You know how much I love you. Do not torment yourself; wait.'

"I spoke to Him about the Trappists, but He answered me, 'My God, your will and not mine.' "

The inner life is indescribable. St. John of the Cross, the great Carmelite mystic, pitied those souls who believed they hear the Lord speak and who, without being aware of it, formulate the questions and answers themselves. Lucien was not the dupe of this kind of illusion. He translated an inexpressible interior dialogue clumsily but with his whole soul. Beneath the words he used, one must not assume special revelations, but words constantly used which he heard each day at Mass: the lamentation of David in the *Judica me*, the call of peace that follows the *Agnus Dei* of St. John the Baptist, the intimacy of the Communion, and the great prayer of the *Pater Noster* as it came out of the mouth of Christ. In this dialogue he was reliving the Mass which he was prolonging in himself and with which his heart identified itself.

Human and divine, the word of God is divine life which penetrates human life, just as the word of a man who speaks is human life penetrating the human life of him who listens. Neither one nor the other has any magical properties; they do not instantly bring about the realization of desires, even the purest ones. Born of knowledge and action, they must return to knowledge and action. Time, trials, patience are necessary. The word of God is like the grain of wheat that falls upon the ground, dies, germinates, and grows. How many seasons are required for all the furrows of the heart to be full of these grains of wheat and ready to return full measure for one? Lucien's heart had been thrown into a profound turmoil by the confrontation with life outside the seminary and by the call of the Trappist life. It was this that disturbed him now, this that marked him with traits of enthusiasm and anxiety. But these were only moments and aspects of his life. All the rest may appear monotonous, ordinary, too much like the life of any other seminarian. But it not only occupied an immense, infinitely greater place, it was the life he had wanted to lead and which was to guide him to the priesthood.

What mattered in Lucien's life, as in the life of anyone else, was the everydayness of it. Let us not be fooled by the mental illusion that magnifies only the exceptional moments. The reality of life, its harsh materialism as well as its spiritual climate, first and foremost dwell in what seems daily, banal routine. Père Jacques did not become the Père Jacques of the concentration camps in a moment. He had been prepared for the worst of human ordeals by obscure and monotonous years, by years of inner struggle, of waiting, of inner changes and the desire to do the will of God more than his own.

This did not prevent him from chafing with impatience and anxiously counting the years he still had to spend at the seminary and in the diocese before being able to take the road to the monastery. He confessed this one day in a letter to Antoine Thouvenin, an old friend of his Montlignon days with whom he had remained intimate.

"It often happens that I yearn and aspire with all my heart after the blessed cloister where I have not yet had the happiness to spend more than a month. May the seven years that I must spend in the diocese flow by quickly, and may I at last go to lock myself up forever, alone, with God alone, in the solitude of our dear monastery. It is so good to live with God, with nothing but Him, talking with Him amicably, affectionately, as I used to with you in the evening at Fort Montlignon. It does one so much good to feel that one loves Him and, above all, that one is loved. Yes, to spend one's brief life in intimacy with God, cut off from everything that is on this earth and that perishes, and to pass lightly, at the moment God wishes, from earth to heaven to grasp God directly in an infinite embrace—how good that is, infinitely good—that is the only good on earth. What is any other happiness compared to that?

"You see, my dear Antoine, to you I open the secret part of my soul; I let escape a cry from the heart that I usually restrain. But can I not say everything to you?"

Seven more years! A long time, seven years, in the life of a man. When one later reads the story of his life it seems like nothing at all, so little time does it take to turn the pages! But in life as it passes, through the long days when one is impatiently waiting for something, days, weeks, months, years become infinitely long. And if the waiting which was a sign of absence was terrible, the desire, which to him was already a sign of presence, only became greater. In secret, but a secret nevertheless that he confided to his friend, Lucien called his room at the seminary "my silent and solitary cell." He was already living in the monastic climate by anticipation. Only he who has never loved, or never fought a battle that he has considered sacred, will not understand that this calling was something other than a careless word, an illusory fantasy. Desire colors life long before realizing itself in action. If it does not let itself be crushed or be driven to despair by the waiting, it will change what is to the colors of what will be. Lucien would never have gone into the seminary if he had not already lived the life there in thought, before actually entering. And if now he did not feel growing within him these clandestine anticipations of the monastic life, there would have been no danger that he would ever leave his native diocese.

This beautiful life had to be secret and contained, but he could not prevent it from having its moments of expansion and outward manifestation, and at such times he spoke of it. All seminarians train themselves in preaching; it is a duty that requires work. The artificial aspect of this exercise is suddenly changed if one feels that it is no longer a student who speaks, but someone who is already wholly a man of God. The youthful audience was not mistaken about this with Lucien Bunel.

"When it was his turn to speak in the refectory," according to his old friend, Père Pierre-Damien, "we would have gone without food just to listen to him. . . . On such occasions he could really preach. We always expected the best from him, but not from the others."

But everybody did not have the same reaction.

"Monsieur X had openly reprimanded him apropos a sermon which 'smelled' of la Trappe and which he had given at the Grand Séminaire," said another witness. "The Abbé had accepted these reproaches as a test, 'It is a necessary humiliation,' he said. But the students had been fired with enthusiasm by the preacher."

Perhaps this Monsieur X, a professor or director, had exaggerated
the prudent distinction between spiritual paths, or perhaps Lucien
had strained it too far. It would be pointless to argue about this now.
Like mountain guides, the great mystics laud the virtue of prudence.
One does not climb toward the top of the mountain without controlling his breath and taking account of the contours of the slopes.
It is also known that under the name of prudence and sage reason
one can camouflage all kinds of backslidings toward mediocrity. In
any case, what aroused the enthusiasm of the young listeners was
that Lucien risked his own skin.

"In the refectory," said Abbé Robert Delesque, "his only bever-
age was water and he drank only a little at each meal, hardly a
glassful, even when the weather was very hot. He deliberately ate
the coarsest and the poorest foods without ever complaining and
above all without ostentation. In the company of laymen he did the
same. He would leave the meat, eat the vegetables, and scarcely
touch the water. If wine was served, he left his glass full until the
end of the meal and drank it only to be agreeable to his hosts."

The same witness added, "I never saw him sit down and relax
against the back of a chair."

It was impossible to listen to these confidences without at the
same time hearing the irrepressible mocking laughter of the Bunel
brothers when they gathered to talk about Lucien.

"At family parties," said André, "there was always a great to-do,
an onslaught of jokes, a calling out to one another from one end of
the big table to the other. We never stopped laughing and joking.
By the end of the meal we would all be too exhausted to laugh any
more, but Lucien outlasted us all, he was such an inveterate joker.
We told all kinds of stories, true and false, and once I heard him
ask my wife, 'Is that something I can listen to?' 'Yes,' she said, 'it's
not bad!' Everybody laughed at this and so did I, because we told
many stories but nobody wanted to tell any that would be out of
bounds and displease Lucien."

"You felt you were nothing at all next to him," said Gaston,
suddenly moved with a repressed emotion.

"Vacations were a holiday when Lucien was home," his sister joined in.

They admired him, not with the admiration that suffocates, but rather the kind that liberated and brought out the best in themselves.

"He didn't want us to linger long at the table," his sister Madeleine went on, "but since he was there, we found this suggestion quite natural." The puritan affects a stiff bearing to prove his uprightness and to impose it on everybody by his unnatural attitude, fanatic and ostentatious. There was nothing of this about Lucien. He could be brusque and tense, but he was always real. He held himself straight, like the watcher who simply does not want to be surprised by sleep, at least by spiritual sleep. Later on in his career he was caught napping more than once during the day, but that is another story. He kept vigil, but if he imparted to his family something of the spiritual life of this vigil, they, in return, brought him the great breath of human joy which like a wind swept away the slightly somber and too serious air that had been noticed in him by the directors of the seminary.

"His vacations," repeated his sister, "became an enchantment for us. What wonderful evenings we spent together after dinner! He would regale us with anecdotes about his life in the school and we never tired of listening to him. . . . One had to have known him, lived with him, to know all the goodness, all the gentleness that was in him."

In one respect, Lucien's spirit was so little geared to the cloister, to silence and solitude, that he did not limit his visits home to vacations and family celebrations. Since 1915 the Bunels had been living in Maromme, and Lucien came here to see them very often.

"Every Wednesday," continued his sister, "the seminarians got a day off. Lucien never hesitated to make the five-mile trip on foot so that he could spend a few hours with the family. He would come with two or three fellow seminarians and we would serve them a little snack. They were so full of gusto and joy! They were always so happy about their hike, but we were even happier."

Passionate as he was about the silence and solitude of the contemplative life, Lucien was also just the opposite. His vacations were the most obvious indication of this. He divided them between sojourns at Maromme and retreats at the Trappist monastery. For three summers in a row, in 1922, 1923, and 1924, he set out for the Trappist monastery, Notre-Dame du Port-de-Salut, at Mayenne, where he shut himself up for a month. "He edified our community by the simplicity of his manners, his frank piety, the seriousness of his mind," wrote the Abbot to the Superior of the seminary after Lucien's first stay there. "Having come to Port-de-Salut with the aim of studying his attraction to the religious life, he made it a point not to stay in our guest house but in the community. The test has confirmed Abbé Bunel in his desire for the religious life in our Cistercian Order of the Strict Observance. . . . When the hour of Providence sounds, I shall receive him into our community without hesitation."

The rest of his time during vacations was divided between hours of morning prayer, participation in family life and in the holiday camps for poor children.

"Retiring at ten o'clock even if there was a family gathering," Madeleine related, "Lucien got up at four or five in the morning. Unless one had happened to wake up, nobody heard him come downstairs, so careful was he to avoid making any noise that would disturb the rest of us. He would then go to the church at Maromme, say his prayers, read his office, and ring the Angelus so that the sacristan could rest. Then he would hear Mass and make his act of thanksgiving. At eight o'clock he was ready to help in the vacation camp.

"Lucien was the first to establish one of these camps in town, an activity he had already begun in Barentin during his vacations from the Petit Séminaire. There were about sixty children in the Maromme camp. With the help of his mother, he often served them breakfast or a little snack, and every day he would take them for a walk in the surrounding woods. One year he managed to have them spend two days at the seashore. Another time, thanks to the financial assistance of the Dean of Maromme, Monseigneur Lesourd, and some old army comrades, he rented the Château de Goupillière during the vacation season and lodged his boys there. He was loved so much in Maromme that one day, during a great workers' demonstration, I saw a foreman who was marching at the head of a group of strikers break ranks to go up to him and shake hands. The people knew that he did not take so much trouble over their children merely out of duty, but out of sheer love."

Yet the same Lucien, upon returning from his vacation, could still write to his confidant, Antoine Thouvenin, "I have been back at the seminary now since Wednesday, September 26. You cannot imagine the happiness that I felt upon finding my silent and solitary little cell again. It's so good to restore oneself in peace and calm. Finding myself thus alone again I experience the same joy that you do when you reach the summit of one of those peaks of the Vosges Mountains. Think back on your feelings of well-being, of relaxation, of intimate and deep pleasure before the solitude and silence of the high forests of fir trees, and you will know my present happiness. For in this silence and peace I again find God with His sweet intimacy, long pauses, profound and prolonged, a way of life that recalls a little the good and dear monastic life. . . ."

A month later Lucien learned that his sister and two of his brothers were down with typhoid fever. His mother asked him not to come home for the time being for fear of contagion. But Lucien felt that there was nothing more urgent than to get permission to go home and nurse them. Permission was granted and he spent six weeks in Maromme nursing the sick members of his family and keeping up their morale, as well as everybody else's, by telling endless rounds of amusing stories. On certain nights, as he watched beside them before pretending to go to sleep—for he was constantly alert to the first signal from one of those who was ill—he wrote again to his friend Antoine:

"Take advantage of your free time to meditate on the meaning of life, on the meaning of death. In such meditations there are many strong feelings that we can draw upon to guide our activity.

One sees *all* under a different light, one appreciates *all* differently when one is penetrated by these truths: the brevity and sadness of human life from a purely natural viewpoint, the absurdity of human life if death is the total annihilation of our entire selves, or the corresponding verities, so sublime, touching, delightful to the soul and heart: the beauty and sweetness of life oriented toward God in joy and suffering, ever and everywhere. And the grandeur of death throwing us into the eternal bosom of an infinite God."

Some time later he returned to this theme in a letter to the same friend: "The emptiness of life without God becomes more and more apparent to me as I move ahead and see disappointments, difficulties, distress, and pain steadily multiply. And it is because more and more I feel and understand the futility of the world that I desire the life of the cloister more ardently than ever. There I would be able to begin to live my eternal life, since I shall be able to unite myself to God in a way ever more intimate, profound, and sweet."

But almost without a transition, he added: "Ah! yes, to live thus in oneself, with the good God everywhere, always: be it in a hotel room, in a railway coach, on the road, in the country, even in the street!"

It would be an outrageous simplification of Lucien's intimate life to see in it only a pull between the monastic and the apostolic life. Above this apparent opposition reigned the unity of God, the unity of the love of God. True charity, true sanctity do not let themselves be enclosed in one frame of life, even if it be the monastic. For the frames are but enclosures out of which life and action overflow. External action never ceases to steep itself in contemplation, and vice versa. This was to be Père Jacques's strength one day, but he approached it only little by little, in proportion to his patience in the face of what seemed to set itself as an obstacle across the path of his chosen course.

8   The Lookout on the Roof

Outside, the boys were devoured by curiosity. The window on which they were spying opened wide onto the courtyard, but the latter was too narrow, and the window too high for one to be able to see from below what was going on inside the room. There was only one way of getting a view from above: by climbing upon the roof of a small pavilion facing the room. To do this one had to escape surveillance, keep a lookout, and either climb through a skylight or up the rainspout. The young imps could not rest until they succeeded in doing just this, and, on a certain day eagerly looked down from the height of this observatory, all eyes. Nobody was there. It was too early. They knew the owner of the room by heart, they saw him a hundred times a day in their very midst, and they had even come often to this very room. But all that they knew and saw every day was not enough for them. They had a presentiment of a secret and they spied with passionate curiosity.

At Le Havre the sea is always there, mutable and immutable, shining in the sun, opening the path to the great ships that come from London, from New York, or from the ports of the southern hemisphere. Nearby are the jetties, the piers, the army of cranes lined up along the edges of Le Havre docks. The sea is always there, and the great port on the Seine estuary is shaken by furious gusts of wind and animated by a powerful stir and movement of life as before. But we could no longer see either the room or the pavilion. We could see nothing at all of what Abbé Bunel's pupils—at the time when Lucien had become a teacher at St. Joseph's school in

Le Havre—used to spy upon. The entire quarter had been destroyed by the bombings in 1944. Even the original layouts of the streets have been changed.

Nor could we find any of these young spies—who now must all be over forty—but we did find three other former pupils who had known Lucien intimately. All three immediately began to talk with such animation that their voices intermingled, but only to say the same thing.

"He was called 'petit tondu,' the little shorn one—or red-nose—petit tondu because he had his hair cropped very close around his tonsure. The first time we saw him we all laughed and said, 'He's either a monk or a convict.' He had just come from the seminary in Rouen, but he had not yet completely finished his studies and he still had a year's work to prepare for the priesthood, while beginning to perform supervisory duties at St. Joseph's. He was thin as a rail and had the face of an ascetic embellished with extraordinary steel-rimmed spectacles. Since he also wore huge hobnailed shoes, he had one of those characteristic silhouettes that one recognized at a glance."

"Didn't he become a teacher immediately?"

"No, he was a proctor. But even as a proctor, he was an unusual type. He never sat down; he concerned himself with nothing but supervising. We never saw him trying to kill time or to make use of it by reading a book, even for study purposes. He was there to supervise, so he supervised. He supervised and he prayed. He spoke very little, he was as quiet as possible except, for example, when the electricity went out suddenly during study hours—a power failure or a prank—and then he would appeal to the conscience of the pupils and such an appeal was always effective. He was a rare bird, but efficient in his way. He already had a great reputation for sanctity. He arose very early, the first one in the house, in fact, and celebrated Mass all alone, I believe. This is not the liturgical ideal, but it was necessary for him to rise early, to profit by the great silence of dawn or predawn, and to begin his day immediately with Mass."

"He never punished us," said another member of the trio. "He knew how to manage people from the inside. One day, when I had been cutting up, he made a simple sign with his finger to show me the door. I made a gesture with my hand to indicate no! and stayed where I was. I knew I could behave myself.

"He was a practical joker and very much the comedian. One day he handed me a detention slip but it was for the previous night. He was as serious as the Pope when he played one of these tricks on you. Another time, when I was kept in by a professor, he let me spend the detention period in his room. I was very often kept in after class so I began to work hard just to please Abbé Bunel. For years I cherished a note that he sent me in which he had written, 'It would please me if you would get good marks.'

"It is true that he had a great influence, especially with the stubborn and strong-minded pupils, who were the ones he preferred. Nevertheless there were days when he became bored studying with boys of our age, and besides, he could not always figure out what was going on in the back of our heads.

"The Superior esteemed him highly and recognized his merit, but he also had grave reservations. 'One Abbé Bunel at St. Joseph's is fine,' he once said laughing, 'but two would be too much.' The fact is that there was an enfant terrible side to his character. He liked to shake things up, in the beginning by temperament, later because he did not like the dustier aspects of tradition. If it had not been for his whimsical character, this would have been intolerable in a school, but one felt that he acted this way principally from love. This was his secret. There was nothing blasé about him, he was all fire and love, and he knew how to tune himself in on all wavelengths. At Le Havre he knew all kinds of people—students, parents of pupils belonging to the city's upper class (and not all Catholics), the Carmelites, the dockworkers. And with all of them he was thoroughly at home, natural, and desirous of rendering them all possible service, knowing just how to find the right word or gesture at the psychological moment. In all these relationships he did not exercise a professional or social function, not even an ecclesiastical one. He was simply a man among men. And that is why he managed people from the inside."

"But all that did not prevent him from being disagreeable!" cried another of his former pupils. "He said to me one day, 'You're a monster of pride!' "

"And he told me," echoed his friend, "you will either become a perfect religious or you will be eaten up by debauchery!' "

They broke into laughter. Both had become priests and the remembrance of faults and emotions of these adolescent years echoed in their laughter. They had felt themselves understood and loved. And in the very violence of their little Abbé they had sensed an incredible gentleness.

"After the worst dressing-down he would send you an affectionate word, during vacation. In addition he sometimes included a memento: a statuette or a violet that he had picked especially for you. It was not that he had changed his mind—at bottom he was always the same; the violence was affection and the affection was not a sentimental emotion but rather an urgent appeal. He certainly did not fit the ordinary mold. Everything that we sensed about his inner life moved us deeply, and it was this which gave an amazing value to certain outer manifestations that might have passed for excesses or unbalance that would have been intolerable in another person. His charity was not exasperating!"

"And his room? This room in which his pupils had spied on him one day?" I asked.

"He had chosen the most remote room, not even a real teacher's room. It was the old sacristy of a secularized chapel at the end of a series of corridors. Laminated partitions had been installed in this chapel to make it into a storeroom for linens and supplies. His room was very narrow; there was just about enough space to pass alongside the iron bed. It was more like a monk's cell. In addition to the bed, there was a white wooden desk, a straw-bottomed chair, and perhaps a cupboard or a shelf on which he arranged his things. Books were his only luxury. At one time Abbé Bunel had managed to acquire a fair number of books for his studies. Later we noticed that all the books had disappeared because he considered that poverty should take precedence over all else. He had a passionate, very impulsive side, so that as soon as he discovered something new he plunged right into it. But he was well aware that his spirit of obedience was a useful counterweight to this.

"Poverty was one of his passions. Sometimes it also seemed ostentatious, by which I don't mean to say that it was a form of spiritual vanity, but it sometimes happened that he deliberately sought attention and this same tendency was reflected in his room, this need for violence and spiritual provocation. He loved to give generously. One day he sold a pile of books to help some Boy Scouts recruited from among the working classes. In his zeal he had forgotten that there were some borrowed books among them. Of course we know that people often pay little attention to books. But on another occasion, after he had left Le Havre, he made a gift to someone of a portable altar which had been loaned to him a long time before, so long before that he had totally forgotten the circumstances under which it was loaned. Doubtless he had confused a loan with a gift, not deliberately, of course, since he would be the last to do so intentionally, but the lender, twice donor despite himself, was deeply chagrined. Yet at the moment of his departure, he gave one of us an alb of which he was very fond and which was really his."

His room was a veritable crossroads. The students often came to visit him there and he always took time to talk with them, to answer their questions, and to communicate all that he could of his spiritual life. But it was often necessary to wait, for he had a throng of visitors. His brother Gaston knew something about this. When he was a conscript in Le Havre at the Kléber barracks where, fortunate fellow, he served in the military band, he would often go to visit Lucien. "I used to bring my friends," he said, "and there was no need to urge them to come along. They would have fought for the chance to do so. When we arrived Lucien moved all the books and notes on his desk to one side and set cups of steaming hot chocolate and toasted bread in the cleared space. I believe he was able to manage this through a bit of connivance with the sister in

charge of the infirmary. Then he would immediately begin to talk,
putting everyone at ease, and his conversation was always stimulating.
Afterward we used to ask one another, 'Do you remember?' We
knew that we had lived through exciting hours.

"He also played host to the teachers of the establishment. When
it was their turn he would offer them a cup of mint tea on weekday
evenings and a cordial on holidays. He had found a way—I don't
know how—of establishing connections with the cooks on the transatlantic ships; when they were on leave in the port they always came
down to have a chat with him. Not all his visitors were Catholics—
far from it. So much so, it seems, that their friends twitted them,
asking, 'What's the matter with you anyway that you're always
running down to see your little curé?' "

With all these aspects of an intense and contradictory life, at
least outwardly so, Lucien also aroused a singular mixture of feelings: laughter, admiration, curiosity, and sometimes reservations.
Who was he really? Where would all this lead him? What was he
like when he was alone? This was what the spying boys wondered.
When, after a long wait, at last he came into his room, they saw
him kneel in prayer, his arms crossed over his breast. Then he rose
and, while standing, corrected papers. "He was always standing,"
said his former pupils. This was as true when he was alone as when
he was teaching. And this for the reason that he never considered
himself to be alone; in his little room he worked and prayed in the
presence of God like a monk in his cell.

For Père Jacques was constantly thinking about la Trappe, but
the years were passing and he was still at Le Havre. He had not yet
received permission to leave the diocese and his teaching duties.
After one year as a proctor, in 1925 he became the teacher of the
second form and then again a proctor for two years. In 1929 he was
assigned to teach the first form and he still had two years to go at
Le Havre. Seven years of classes in all, from the age of twenty-four
to thirty-one; seven years of repressed passion at the age of impatience, at the age when one quite rightly knows that he cannot

realize his dreams if he does not start to do so immediately. Seven years during which he never stopped working and praying with passion for the boys whom the will of God had entrusted to him.

When he became a teacher he was as individual as he had been as a proctor. He wanted his classes to be fun. They were so uproarious that, according to Gaston, "One heard nothing else when he entered. Père Jacques shot out his words so loudly and so fast that the general effect was like that of a machine gun. The teachers in the adjoining rooms had to close their windows."

"He worked steadily to carry along the whole class, constantly organizing teams and competitions," recalled one of his former pupils. "He did everything to be engaging in order to stir up and galvanize the lazy, the solitaries, and the less gifted boys. As one would expect, they simply adored him; it was impossible to resist him. I don't mean to say that certain teachers were not a bit jealous. The headmaster and the Superior were even obliged to express certain reservations. Abbé Bunel's system, or rather his lack of one, would have been catastrophic for any other teacher who might have taken it into his head to try it. Even for him there were dangers and disadvantages. He embarked on long digressions outside the program. Since everything excited him, he wanted to arouse the same enthusiasm in all the students.

"He often inveighed against the narrow spirit of classical literature. In Latin he had a horror of word-for-word translations—and it certainly is true that one kills Latin by this stillborn, pedantic servility —but when the students were not very well grounded, they along with him fell into the opposite excess. It was no longer a translation but an approximation of the original. One day during a quarterly examination, the headmaster questioned Abbé Bunel's pupils and criticized them for translating too freely. Later he registered some protests with their teacher who was invited to teach Latin in a more rigorously scholarly manner. But the headmaster got the unfortunate idea of seeking the approval of the science teacher who happened to be passing by. In a flash Lucien leaped up and without giving him a chance to open his mouth, he flung at him, in a tone that brooked no reply, 'You! You are a science teacher. This is no concern of yours!' Moreover, he did not in the least change his point of view.

"He also took many other liberties, as on the day when his best pupil was upset over a grade of 40 in natural science, which prevented him from making the honor roll, Abbé Bunel simply changed it to 100 and the inscription on the honor roll went through as smoothly as a letter in the mail, to the great bewilderment of the science teacher. It was not only a matter of Lucien's taking certain liberties; it corresponded to his own principle according to which each piece of work must not be graded mechanically and in isolation but be understood as a living part of a living whole. The result of the whole evidently being a function of the part, there should be a reciprocity so that a good over-all result should be a recommendation for raising an isolated bad mark.

"Sometimes he went even further. When one of his good students, or, from the other point of view, one of the stubborn ones whom he wished to persuade, was being kept in on a holiday because of another teacher's low marks, he would knock on the window of the room where the pupil was confined and ask to speak to the boy he wanted to fish out. The proctor naturally would not refuse permission to his colleague, but the colleague did not content himself with giving the pupil in question two or three little words of advice but would take him to serve his detention in the Abbé's own room. This was completely irregular, an obvious infraction of formal discipline, but he obtained results that discipline per se could never achieve.

"This is a kind of freedom very hard to manage if it is not to degenerate into utter permissiveness and dissipation. But when we think of the sometimes demoralizing effect of pure and strict discipline, we can say that Abbé Bunel was not altogether wrong. Moreover the tree is to be judged by its fruits. He did go rather far, however, so far that one day he took to the regatta a boy who had just been confined and who was literally sick over the idea of not being able to attend the boat races where he was to meet his brothers and cousins. The admirable thing was that the boys understood perfectly why he took such liberties, so they bore him no grudge when he reproached them violently for their lack of ardor, industriousness, and obedience. For submission was not merely a blind obedience to a soulless rule, it was a free consent, filled with eagerness. He had his tricks of the trade, those little tricks that all educators dream up, and he ceaselessly sought to invent new ones, more original and more effective. Anyone who copied them would only have made himself ridiculous. It was the overflowing generosity of Abbé Bunel's soul that let him carry them off so well. Lucien was like a torrent that sweeps everything along with it—pebbles, driftwood, old bits of paper, the debris of bones, his excesses, his extravagances—all that smells in stagnant water but is fresh and pure in a torrential spring tide.

"He longed for solitude and silence the moment he enjoyed a brief respite. Only much later did we learn that he yearned avidly for the monastic life. This dream did not put him at a distance from us, since it was for God that he wanted it to become a reality, but since God wanted to keep him within the walls of the college, he threw himself with all his heart into the life of the school to do the will of God as lovingly as if he were a Trappist. Only God knows whether he longed for that. When, having become a priest, while still a teacher at St. Joseph's, he had occasion to preach to us, he spoke to us of silence, prayer, and contemplation in a way that filled us with enthusiasm. Then, like the Superior at the seminary, the headmaster of St. Joseph protested. He went to see the Abbé after the sermon and told him that it was not well adapted to the audience—much too monastic. Of course, we came to know of this much later. One does not discover very much about people until after their departure, if not after their death. Moreover, I am not so sure that all he said 'smelled' of the Trappists. I would simply say that it was an overflow of his love of God, a love not only preached but lived. If we had not seen him living before us and for us, as he did live, probably we too would not have liked his sermon. But since he threw himself entirely into it with such passion, we understood and we felt something absolutely indefinable transpire in us: a true love of God. Abbé Bunel was not one of those who demonstrated proofs of the faith, he showed it forth.

"We believed that we knew him, but we discovered many other things after he left. He did not have the time, or perhaps the courage to say farewell to all the people he knew, so many were the friends he had, among others the parents of his pupils. As one of his oldest pupils he assigned me the task of extending his regrets and apologies to a certain number of these parents. I found Jewish and Protestant parents who were deeply moved to know that they would never see him again, that he had left to become a monk."

"Not everybody!"

"No, not everybody. Several teachers had found him odd, given to exaggeration. Then he had had those outbursts which would have been enough to place him in a very bad light unless one put oneself in his place. One day he sent a condolence card to a priest who had just been appointed vicar general and whom Lucien considered to be much too young for such an office. Another time, while coffee was being served at the teachers' table, he called out to Abbé Vignal, the Superior, and said, 'I went to see the Superior of the Grand Séminaire and I told him that he was inconveniencing us by sending us poorly trained deacons.' 'What!' exclaimed Abbé Vignal, 'you didn't say it to him just like that!' 'Of course, I did.' 'Well, my dear Abbé, you certainly have put your foot into it. You take size twelve.' The remark become proverbial.

"He did everything to instill in us his own kind of enthusiasm. At the end of his stay at St. Joseph's he had to change his room and on his window sill I still see a collection of glass jars filled with the skins of monstrous insects, small snakes, and all kinds of strange things that can be found on the docks during the unloading of freighters from faraway lands. He organized picnics for us in the outskirts of Le Havre, hikes in the Normandy forests, and excursions to the seaside. He took us everywhere to show us life and to enlarge our horizons. Sometimes it was a visit to a factory near the harbor to make us understand how hard the work was and to give us an idea of technical power. Other times he would take us even farther to the old abbeys that dot the Seine Valley downstream from Rouen; Saint Wandrille, Jumièges, Saint-Martin-de-Boscherville. With him school life never felt like something closed in and cut off; he opened all the dimensions of the world to us. He took care of us like a fond father of a family, as on that day during an outing to the city when he got the idea of buying some little sugared chicks and eggs for us. Nobody thought of making fun of him, and we all enjoyed the surprise immensely."

What his superiors, who saw him every day from a different angle, thought about Lucien was equally in agreement. One of them, Abbé Vignal, the same one who had assigned him size twelve shoes, said that this independent and indomitable Abbé Bunel had never refused to do anything that he had ever asked of him. Abbé Blanchet, who succeeded Abbé Vignal and who is today Monseigneur Blanchet, rector of the Institut Catholique at Paris, had the same impression. "Abbé Bunel," he said, "criticized his superiors face to face, and in a very lively way, for whatever shortcomings he considered were hampering the better administration of the house. But he did this without denigration. . . . He certainly was ironic and sarcastic, but an ill-natured word never passed his lips, neither animosity, nor bitterness, nor acerbity. To be sure, though, there was nothing about him of the sheep who follows. He was *himself*."

But it is of this same Abbé Bunel that Monseigneur Blanchet no less clearly certified the following: "From the beginning, he was always extremely docile. He accepted the criticism of those in authority without balking. He may have thought what he pleased, of course, but he always obeyed. When one said 'no' to him, it was 'no' and he understood that very well. He obeyed as openly as he criticized. There was no inner revolt. He accepted authority just as he knew how to use it. Thus he was capable of behaving with the same affectionate spontaneity toward a superior as with his pupils.

"I remember," Monseigneur Blanchet added, "that we had been talking one day about Père Léonce de Grandmaison who had just died. Abbé Bunel had a mortuary picture of the dead priest. How did he get it? I have no idea at all. Without being an intriguer, he was very well informed about what was going on and he had the art of making use of others—in the good sense—and of getting what he wanted in terms of things or results. He always achieved his ends. Thus he had a memento of Père de Grandmaison, containing the text of a beautiful prayer to the Blessed Virgin. He brought it to me as a gift. He did not emphasize this gesture, but without knowing why I very clearly had the feeling that he had given me this image which he prized so highly just because he *did* value it so much. He wanted to please others at his own expense.

"I loved him very much," Monseigneur Blanchet went on, "but on more than one point I found it necessary to register some objections. There was an indescribable something in him that didn't seem to come into focus for me, the sharp edges, the exaggerations, the paradoxes! Above all the paradoxes! When he himself knew that it was a paradox, it was nothing but an exciting mental game without consequence. But when it happened that this paradox was only the overflow of an idea without a counterweight, and that he believed in it! . . . In short, he was as disconcerting as he was engaging! I bore a responsibility which on occasion gave me a certain sense of uneasiness about him, but I repeat that I loved him very much. He was not only upright, but positively rectilinear! There was nothing equivocal or tortuous about him. He was incapable of any underhanded dealings: everything in him was candid and clean. . . . He went to the bottom of things. He had his spiritual infatuations, and was making religious discoveries that he could not yet master. He was an absolutist! He had an absolute for himself and for others. His cocksure judgments, his categorical imperatives got the better of his spiritual experience. . . . But all of that, which was still the fault of his youth, must not make us forget the extent, the vigor of his action. For more than one person, at this time, an encounter with Abbé Bunel must have been a decisive moment in his life."

The fact is that he was never a simple functionary, schoolman, or ecclesiastic. He was an awakener of lives.

He had all the more influence because he never refused anything, except the impossible, in the way of additional work and activity. At St. Joseph's he was the spiritual director and more and more boys chose him as confessor. In the city he was much in demand as a preacher, for he was forceful and passionate. At the beginning he was even brusque. One day he opened a sermon by exclaiming, "I, a worker, the son of a worker—I have come to speak to you of Jesus the Worker." He talked about money in such a way that his words blazoned in the church like a red flag, so said the curé who was showered with protests for having invited him to speak. Crudely, Lucien presented the Gospel truth about the question of money. On marriage, or any other question, he was always clear and passionate. At one time he was invited to speak in a parish that had just been shaken by some sort of scandal. The curé, while listening to the sermon, literally squirmed in his seat and said to himself, "This good Lucien, he's put his foot into it once more." But upon leaving the church, a woman expressed the general reaction by saying, "One listens to him and with particular attention because he seems to see right through you." Abbé Morin declared, "He said utterly simple things, just as we do, but in a tone that captivated, with a conviction that carried away his hearers."

Père Arson, the pastor of St. Francis in the port area, said: "My first recollection of dear Abbé Bunel is his sermon on the Passion which he delivered on Good Friday in my church. His fiery spirit was stirred in such a way during his description of the sufferings of Our Lord that one of my parishioners next day told me that he had never heard such preaching before in his life.

"With practice he learned how to avoid certain faults of language, but he remained a forceful speaker and he was loved because of this very forcefulness. There was no ecclesiastical purring. Lucien aroused the people in their pews as he aroused the pupils in his class. As a result he preached more and more. In the last year of his stay in Le Havre, he went beyond the call of duty, preaching Lenten sermons in three parishes at once. When he was told that this was too much, that he was overexerting himself (he had already been forced to take a complete rest during a period of physical depression), he answered, 'Why, since I have no right to rest?' "

While waiting, he multiplied his activities. He became the chaplain of a Boy Scout troop recruited from among the children of the dockworkers. In 1928, he wanted to take them to a camp in England. The boys could not pay for the trip and the Abbé was short of money. His salary as a teacher was twelve hundred francs a year which he was able to supplement only by tutoring and stipends for Masses and sermons, while during the same period he was sending three hundred francs a month to his father, who was out of work. With typical ingenuity, he managed to find a part of the sum necessary for his Scouts, but it was not enough. He sold his books to make it up.

The camp was situated near Plymouth. A great Scout jamboree was being held there, and most of the Scouts were English Protestants. Abbé Bunel loved the English language and had worked very hard in order to speak it fluently.

"I had occasion," he wrote, "to talk intimately to the head of the camp—a Protestant—who was a secondary school teacher at Plymouth, as well as with other English Protestant Scoutmasters. While talking of one thing and another, I explained to them some of the joys of being a Catholic priest, the emotion that grips us when we transform the bread of our Mass into the body of Christ, and that then we find ourselves suddenly face to face with God. These revelations affected them so much that two days later, after the campfire, the head of the camp approached me timidly, drew me into the darkness, and asked me with an intonation that I shall never forget, 'Monsieur Abbé, you may refuse what I am about to ask if you think it advisable: allow us to kneel with your Scouts around the fire in order to receive your blessing.'

"It is impossible for me to tell you what feelings swept over me at that moment, or what words I answered. But before blessing this little world of Protestant children of all denominations, I cried out to them my overflowing affection for their souls, and I put all that desire into my blessing.

"Afterward, each night before returning to their tents, everyone knelt down to receive faithfully and respectfully the blessing of a Catholic priest. Some of them—Scoutmasters ranging from thirty to forty years of age—even attended my Mass from a distance, not venturing to come too near, and during the day they came to me to confide that they were united to us with all their hearts."

II
MOUNT CARMEL
❦❦❦

1   The Shadow of the Mountain

It was about seven o'clock on a peaceful and luminous morning, the morning of May 1. We had crossed the deserted streets; the tram was not running and we mounted the steep stairs, protected by iron railings, flanking the hillside between the villas and the tall trees of formal gardens. What is called "la Côte" in Le Havre is not the shore of the sea but the green slope of Ingouville which is the northern limit of the city. After the excitement of the night before, the silence seemed limitless. The factories were silent, there were no autos on the streets, the people were still asleep in their houses. The city was bathed in the pure and profound silence of the open air. We were climbing in the direction of Carmel, as if it were really possible that a Carmelite convent could exist in a port, as if it were permitted to the daughters of the holy prophet Elias to live in the machine age only several hundred yards away from the docks and the transatlantic liners, as if the work of divine contemplation could still have some rhyme or reason in the din of industrialization and international trade. But, on this very morning of the great labor commemorations, the silence of the city looked out upon the silence of Carmel.

From the top of the hill a vast skyline comes into view: the Atlantic to the west and the Seine estuary to the south. This horizontal boundlessness, the color of rust, brick, and slate, an antheap of docks, warehouses, and factories, bristling with cranes, smokestacks and the masts of moored ships, stretches from the estuary to the foot of the hill. Closer by is the mass of districts at the city's center vibrating with the roar of business during working days.

69

In the peaceful Rue de la Crète, across the greenery, we looked for the Carmelite convent and found it behind a curtain of trees and thickets. It is a long, low house, marked by an open arcade and the spire of the chapel. This is the Carmelite convent of Le Havre. None of the ancient walls that Abbé Bunel had gazed upon are left, even the ancient site of the monastery is no more: it was originally located several hundred yards farther east, alongside the hill where the tunnel starts. After the war that killed Père Jacques and destroyed the college, the plans for the reconstruction of Le Havre included the demolition of the convent. Everything was changed and yet nothing had changed in this atmosphere of pure silence.

We entered the sanctuary of the convent through a little door in the rear of the arcade. Everything was shining bright and new. There were several bouquets of garden flowers on the white stone of the altar table and to the left were the shutters of the large black grille. It was a kingdom of silence, silence so great that, intermittently, the light footsteps of the sacristan Sister seemed startlingly loud. Silence is nothing, exactly nothing. The lightest shock suffices to break it, even the passage of unobtrusive sandaled feet. The silence of this chapel is a singular void against the gigantic roar and rumbling of the port on working days. And it was a void alongside the thunder of the armies of June, 1944, which pulverized Normandy in the clash of tanks, torpedoes, and bombing planes. It is nothing at all, nothing like the silence of Père Jacques coming lifeless out of the concentration camp. But the silence, the same silence is here once more, pure and intense, the same silence as when Lucien Bunel walked across the entire city to steep himself in it. It was so much the same silence that although we came with the intention of asking how the prewar Carmelite convent had been built, we no longer even thought about it. The silence that dominates everything was here, identical and absolute, the silence for which Lucien had always been seeking and which he finally found, pure and profound, in the Norman shadows of Mount Carmel.

Suddenly the wooden shutters behind the grille rustled, unfolding with a gentle clicking like the lovely sliding partitions of a Japanese dwelling. While Père Maurice de la Croix, who had been a pupil of Père Jacques, began the celebration of the Mass, the voices of the Carmelites rose from the other side of the grille, placed to the left of the choir, from which, off and on, in another area, I glimpsed the silent movement of silhouettes in black veils. It was the same Mass that is celebrated in any other sanctuary in the world. But if the absolute of the divine presence is always unchanging, the accent of human presences is quite otherwise, depending on the times and places. Here in the deep silence of the hill above the city the other deeper and purer silence from which was born the singing of the Carmelites became one with the limpid transparence of the silence of St. John of the Cross and of the great Teresa in the Carmelite convent of Avila. It is the same silence of the mountain as that which reigned on the summit of Mount Carmel when the prophet Elias watched for the little white cloud, the same silence as on the morning of July 12, 1927, when Lucien Bunel came for the first time to celebrate Mass in the Carmelite convent of Le Havre.

According to the calendar of this time, he had been a teacher at St. Joseph's for three years, and an ordained priest for two, having received Holy Orders exactly two years before on July 11, 1925. On the next day he had celebrated his first Mass at Maromme. The church was thronged with relatives, natives of the town, and the friends of his childhood from Barentin who rubbed elbows with Lucien's former comrades from the artillery regiment. It was the realization of a dream he had nourished from childhood and which he had sometimes believed to be hopeless. But what Lucien was discovering more and more was that this realization was but a first realization.

Relatively easy as it is to follow the exploits of Lucien Bunel in his surface life of priest and teacher, very much like those of any other man exercising the same functions, it seems impossible to grasp anything of the secret life burgeoning in him during these same years. Truth to tell, it is an unutterable secret, but in no wise incommunicable. The opposition between the interior and exterior life is entirely relative. They are as intimately and indissolubly bound together as the warp and woof of a loom, they react endlessly upon each other and each expresses itself in the other. This can be said of the intimate life of Lucien in the love of the Lord as with the life of any human being. From the outside one can explain the labor of a worker, the perils of an explorer, the words and gestures of human love. But the pain of work, the joy of beautiful workmanship, the intoxication of the explorer, the happiness of love are strictly indescribable. No explanation will ever make it possible for anyone to understand who has never worked with his hands, performed a hard job, navigated unknown waters, or experienced what human love is in his heart. The secret of saints is not to live like spiritual Robinson Crusoes, yogis who curl themselves up in the islet of an inner void. Their secret is to live in the love of Christ, as a fiancé lives in the love of his betrothed, the soldier in the fraternity of his comrades-in-arms.

Later Lucien was to say that his life at Le Havre was very far from saintly, although he had taken great pride in preaching and in forming and directing souls. What is certain is that, during this period, Lucien was like a pilgrim of sanctity. He desired nothing so much as to live ever more deeply in the presence and love of the Lord. Without doubt the pupils who had spied outside his window believed that the secret of his life was hidden like a treasure which the miser gazes upon at certain hours behind closed doors. But Abbé Bunel's prayer, on his knees and with his arms crossed over his breast and the ascetic penances that he imposed on himself were only signs of the secret, not the secret itself. One can be an ascetic out of madness, out of pride, or simply out of exaggeration. Life with Christ does not let itself be localized in any practice, even liturgical and charitable ones. One can abuse the sacraments and delude oneself with a pseudo charity. Inversely, Francis of Assisi was never a priest and Père de Foucauld deprived himself of the sacraments for many months in order to remain among his Tuareg friends. Even less can this life with Christ be localized within the space of a room, even though, like Abbé Bunel's, it became a solitary and silent cell.

The "interior" life that one might foolishly imagine could be enclosed within the four walls of a room, in the fantasies of a mind turning in a void, can be truly revealed only from a bird's-eye view, like the first peaks of a city emerging from a morning fog. But this mysterious inner city has nothing about it of the fanciful escape, the exotic; it is simply Le Havre in the open air on the shore of the sea. It is there, this inner life, in the streets of the port through which on certain days Lucien Bunel climbed toward the hill of Sainte-Adresse which extends the slope of Ingouville as far as the extreme point of the shore where La Hève lighthouse dominates the bare and steep crest of the cliff and guards the entry of the estuary. This inner life is there on this cliff from which Lucien loved to contemplate the limitless sea as the first of the hymns of praise in the first of temples. It is there in the chapel of the college where he celebrated the early morning Mass and where he returned in the evening to read the psalms and prayers of his office. It is there before the refectory table when he deprived himself of sauce and wine and sometimes, discreetly, even of food in order to feel "the sting of hunger" and "to tame the beast." It is there in the little room which he had preferred as being the least comfortable, and where he went without a fire as long as possible on winter days; or again in the classrooms where he remained standing without rest, watching and praying. It is there in these streets of Le Havre through which he walked to preach in the parishes, to see his Scouts, and to visit whoever needed him. In the mind's eye it extends from the height of Ingouville to the neighborhood of the Barentin viaduct, and also includes the house of Madame d'Auray where one day it was discovered that the holiday tutor, Abbé Bunel, had slept on the rug beside the bed; and from Maromme to the gates of Rouen, in the corner of Lucien's room where his sister Madeleine, while doing the housework, noticed one of those lashes that monks call their "discipline." But the lash that may seem barbarous to us no more sums up this secret life of Lucien than does his contemplation on the height of the cliff which one could pointlessly reduce to a poetic charm. These very material signs of Lucien's secret life could be conveniently catalogued, but there remains as much difference between them and his life as he lived it as between a stuffed animal under glass and the life of the birds in the open sky. The objects are there to signify forcefully that the inner life does not allow itself to be turned away from the world, but rather that which it brings to the world, that which it breathes into exterior life, remains an enigma which transcends the things in question. Lucien's secret lash and his laughter among his brothers, the superabundance of sentimental outpourings on the cliff or the absence of wine or even water in his glass do not contradict each other except as seen from the outside. Inwardly, they express one and the same life. Far from being paradoxical, there is nothing more human. Sufferings and joys do not let themselves be separated in love, work, or battle, and even less here where Lucien's life more and more became love, work, and struggle for God. Sometimes Lucien still became enthusiastic over the education of the children entrusted to him, sometimes over the hours of solitude when his room again became a quasi-monastic cell.

One day Gaston came to pay him a visit in the infirmary (he had typhoid at the time) and Gaston felt sorry for him when he learned that Lucien had spent the day all alone. "You must have been bored, my poor old fellow," he said to him. But Lucien replied, "Alone with God for the entire day? I have never been so happy!" The opposition is evident, but the unity that rules at the heart of this opposition is no less certain. There were not two contrary and incompatible Luciens, but a single man.

One can live for entire days in Le Havre without setting eyes on the sea, without even thinking of it, and yet the sea is there. One can live for years without ever thinking of God and yet God is there. Lucien was not one of those who "demonstrate" the existence of God, but one of those who show forth God in the measure that their own life has become translucent in the presence of the Lord. All his life became a shore battered by the sea of the infinite. The visible objects, whether they were the white wooden desk, the

"discipline," the refectory table, or even the cliff, were only the
flotsam which the last wave of this sea rolls out on the shore.

"Try to understand my deep happiness, intimate, unalterable,"
wrote Lucien, "for all the little human incidents glide over the surface without changing, without diminishing my intimacy with the
divine visitor of my soul."

Lucien was exaggerating slightly when he spoke of little happen-
ings that glide over the surface. This was only at certain moments of
grace. At other moments he would have wanted it to be true with
all his heart, but he could not achieve it. Life did not spare him the
thousand little daily vexations that annoy and irritate, any more than
it spared him the drama of opposition between the monastic life
for which he ardently yearned and the life of a teacher, which he
had not desired. He was far from bitter over it. He was the first to
say that it is natural and necessary to suffer, that without suffering
everything would really be too easy and the march of life in the
love of God would be as simple as the wave of a magic wand.

But Lucien's remark on the happiness of the presence of God
really discloses the secret of his soul to us. All his life attests to this.
The sea is there even in the black night, at the foot of the cliff of
Sainte-Adresse. And even in the worst hours of sadness and discouragement Lucien never doubted the presence of God, and this presence filled him with love. Lucien, however, had nothing about him
of those visionaries who hope to see supernatural beings on every
street corner and who out of nothing invent aberrant divine
dialogues in themselves. He knew the presence of God only by what
is expressed in the naked and blunt word "faith." When Père de
Foucauld spoke of the sea to his Tuareg friends who had never
left the world of the Sahara, the word "sea" had also seemed bare
and blunt to them. These desert folk could do no better than
imagine the Mediterranean as a watercourse marvelously filled with
ever running water. They did their best to picture all the possible
abundance seen in mirages, but even in their mind's eye they simply
could not visualize a river bed large enough and deep enough to contain a real sea of surging waters stretching as far as the eye could

see in all directions. Thus we reduce faith in God, at one time to an abstract term, at other times to a hallucinatory vision, because in our own lives we have not opened up any bay vast enough to receive even the first waves of the infinite. But in Lucien, a river bed of just this kind increasingly dug itself deeper and deeper into his life. In work, suffering, joy, desire, love, at every moment of his life, his being opened itself to the life of God.

It is not surprising that we find it hard to understand him, for he also found it hard to understand us. "What emptiness is the existence of the greater part of the people!" he wrote. "Some go to work with no other thought than to see the end of day come, to wait for this holiday or that leave, in order to enjoy this or that pleasure trip. And thus the days jostle each other aside, all of them absolutely devoid of any enduring fruit. Others are bent on acquiring wealth or a place in the public eye. And when they achieve the object of their covetousness, either they find themselves unassuaged and require still more, or they disappear from the stage of the world! Poor people!

"Yes, it does one good to live in God, to draw nourishment from Him in a continual communion with His holy will and His infinite Being!"

If God means nothing to us we can imagine Him only as a void in our inner being, haunted or not by hallucinations. But Lucien saw our lives as empty from the moment God is absent. And yet he was far from understanding everything going on within himself in this secret region which God reaches, at the summit of the soul and from where He radiates throughout the human being. St. Augustine said of God, "He is closer to me than I am to myself." For the saints no more have superhuman powers over their inner life than over their outer life. It is always difficult to understand what happens in the depths of one's own being. What we now call depth psychology is only a beginning. But God is not part of depth psychology; He operates through these depths as through all being. He is mystery as He is life, but transcendent life—ineffable, acting solely through the primordial secret of all things, as ineffable in the movements of His grace in the bosom of the soul as in the movements of stars and of animal life.

Lucien one day confided to his brother René how hard it was for him to renounce knowing human love and the joy of fatherhood, but he was incapable of explaining how a more powerful desire had grown in him. He had also confessed to René and to Madeleine that during his adolescence he had felt the demands of the flesh keenly and that it was the assistance of the Blessed Virgin that had delivered him. "Since then," he told his sister, "God has given me the grace to live like a child." Nothing is more moving than the sincerity in these humble confidences.

There were also more mysterious interventions in Lucien's life. Evidence of this was Madame Bunel's serious illness in 1926. One morning at a very early hour, René found her in such a bad state that he was afraid she was about to die. He ran to the church where Lucien was beginning to say Mass. René went right up to the altar and said to his brother, "Come quickly, maman is dying!" "She will not die," Lucien replied calmly. "I shall bring her the Last Sacrament and Communion and God will heal her."

"We prepared what was necessary," continued René (and Gaston confirmed his story). "Lucien brought the sacred Host with him. He was radiant; he ministered to maman and gave her Communion. We were all kneeling, heads bowed. At the moment when Lucien lifted the Host in his hands, a sweet fragrance such as I had never smelled before or since spread throughout the house. (It was the perfume of roses, according to Gaston.) Instinctively we raised our heads. My brother was giving the sacred Host to my mother. She then fell asleep and later she was restored to sound and continuing health. We expressed our surprise to Lucien when he came back to the house, after his prayer in the church. He replied simply, 'God can do anything.' "

If kings and presidents have the right to grant mercy, why would not God also have the same right? In any event the saints have never imagined that they had the power to work miracles; at best they have felt the necessity of intercession, the right of supplication and confidence at the court of divine love. I no longer know what scenario writer got the strange idea of baptizing the Curé d'Ars "sorcerer of heaven." St. John Vianney would have been angered by so gross a confusion. He did not attribute any "power" to himself, he was merely the interceder who came to solicit grace. Lucien was no more a sorcerer than the Curé d'Ars. Moreover one would not find more than three or four similar moments in his entire life. Miracles, if it really be a question of miracles—the guarantee of which lies beyond our competence—are but of the moment, like a star seen at random during a nocturnal awakening, whereas chastity in Lucien's life was something for always, despite the young girl workers, graceful in all their youth and beauty, who passed him in the streets of Barentin, the women passing by in Rouen and Le Havre, and despite all the summonses to love in Montlignon, in Paris, that rose everywhere in Lucien's path.

One can laugh or be moved, as one pleases, by the request of the six young girls of the parish club who asked to serve at the Bunels' family banquet in honor of Lucien's first Mass. So many Iphigenias sacrificed on the altar of what one considers to be the smothering puritanism of the Church! Yet the six did not come "to wait on table" out of duty or repressed love, any more than God had been obliged to set aside the sacrosanct laws of medicine to grant a reprieve contrary to nature to Lucien's mother. In all this there is but one master word: love.

Nowhere else, perhaps, can one better see Lucien's daily life as in a candid mirror than in the counsel that he wrote to a young girl of Le Havre: "Each time that your weakness may cause you to fall, you must not be vexed with yourself or despair, but patiently get up again and resume the struggle. A transgression is nothing if it does not bring about despair."

What makes the bad Christian is exactly the same thing that makes the unbeliever, namely the idea that God is inaccessible or nonexistent and that man can depend only on himself. As St. Paul said, "Nevertheless I live; yet not I, but Christ liveth in me." Never have the saints attributed great merits to themselves; this satisfaction they have left to the Pharisees. But neither did they ever resign themselves to going along with the stream, never did they despair of themselves, precisely because they did not depend on themselves but on Christ. But how open one's personal life to this other life? How control this kind of inner space, of infinite freedom?

"From time to time during the day you must put yourself in the presence of God. Then close your eyes for a moment, tell yourself that He is there, close to you, enveloping you with His being, waiting for a small token of affection from you, smile at Him and say a word to Him from your heart. Repeat the same thing often during the day, and soon (after several months) a great love of God will awaken in you and you will give yourself wholly to Him."

The presence of God. Not the vision of God, or an abstract thought but His presence, certain, invisible, and vivifying. The sight of the sun burns the eyes and no one looks directly at it. But one does not have to be an astronomer or even to look up at it to assure oneself that it is there in the sky from the moment the day illuminates the objects around us. Life is illuminated in the same way by the divine presence.

Lucien knew what drama accompanies this change of being. Recollections of his own experience humbly pass by in the advice that he gives to others: "Oh! come, poor child, I'm not scolding you! Not at all. I completely understand your impulses. At your age I was even more violent than you are and I would have made a worse scene than you have. But now that I can judge things better, in the light of God, I realize that I was wrong. And I ask you gently, paternally, to please recognize that you are wrong and to say you're sorry."

He was only thirty but he already had a long experience of the tortuous twistings of the human spirit.

"I have carefully noted this sentence which is a valuable confession: 'Since your first letter I have made some efforts. I asked God to send me humiliations, but at the first that He sent I bared my teeth!' A very profitable experience! Remind yourself again and again, so that this certainty will penetrate your being and stay there, that it is painful to be shaped by God, that it hurts to be a saint, that suffering is not just a word but a reality that tears the being apart."

It is necessary to quote this whole sentence to provide an exact counterweight to the one in which Lucien speaks of the unalterable happiness that dominates everything. The eyes see the light, the lungs breathe fresh air, but the feet flounder in the mud, sink into sand and bruise themselves on stones and thorns along the road; one must pause for breath, lift up his head, and not let himself be overwhelmed by the burdens of this world. Without these worldly cares, without this long, laborious march, the exaltation of the soul is but an empty and vain dream.

"It is not necessary to be one of those deluded souls who repeat over and over to God: 'I wish to be Thine,' but who flee in panic when God presents Himself with the cross. You wish to respond to the call of God. It is to suffering, to humiliation that God calls you and not to pleasure and rejoicing. But His cross, freely, lovingly accepted, will fill you with sweet and peaceful happiness, while the empty pleasures of the world will leave you, after a moment of pleasing giddiness, with only revulsion and unease."

It is happiness which has nothing to do with spiritual comfort, suffering which has nothing to do with masochism. The two are but rays of shadow and light on the mountain roads—the precipitous paths, the hardships, and then the moments of repose and contemplation on the highest plateaus of the mountain. Happiness and suffering are only ways along the path which has no other name but love.

Time is necessary, much time and perseverance, to understand in what manner God accomplishes all. Not that the human being does nothing, for he must use all his ingenuity, like the pilot of a glider, to let himself be caught up in the wind of the Holy Spirit.

"I can ascertain that God is accomplishing a real work in you. This work is being done slowly. I believe that more and more it will consist in giving you a sense of disgust with yourself, an acute feeling that in depending only on yourself you will arrive at nothing of worth, and consequently it will bring you to mistrust yourself and to confide yourself to obedience! To break oneself, to annihilate oneself, to count for nothing any more, to be nothing, and to let God guide us *where* He wills, *when* He wills, *how* He wills!

"Do not be distressed by your weaknesses, your lapses. It is only little by little that you will win control over yourself. Sudden conversions are rare. I prefer the long-drawn-out changes, realized by force of courage and tenacious struggle."

What to do? Here too Lucien's words sprang not from a book of spiritual recipes, but from his own experience. Nothing was more typical than the strategy of his advice: read the Bible, say the rosary. Read a few of Pascal's pensées slowly every day, he said, meditate upon them and come back to them several times. "What an education of the soul is familiarity with Pascal!" Neither to despise the intellect, nor despise what is not intellect. Why the rosary? "When one understands the immense profundity of devotion to the Blessed Virgin, one finds such a comfort and such a power of moral preservation therein!"

The words of love never change. They are eternally new in their eternal sameness. As they reecho from one person to another, it is the multitude which enters into harmony with the canticle of the Angel, the same portion of heaven fills our homes as it did the house in Nazareth, the perfect junction of heaven and earth, of God and man, in the destiny of the Virgin who diffuses her light in the hearts of men. Before being Scripture, the Bible is the Word. It has remained as Scripture henceforth, but nothing of His vibrant and living word has become dormant. The angelic message that opens each prayer of the rosary comes from the Bible. Live the Bible by picking up the rosary, said Lucien. Take up the Bible not as an ordinary book but "on your knees, kissing the book before and after reading," as does the priest at the altar for the reading of the Gospel, as do the monks who read the Bible in the monastery, not for useful or fanciful discussions on the commas, but to live the Bible. Scripture, to be sure, does not disclose itself at the first reading, like a novel. It is a difficult book, just as sainthood is difficult, but it too

contains within itself a mysterious assistance to one who would
understand it. "Begin with the beautiful and substantial epistles of
St. Paul. Then read Genesis, afterward Ecclesiastes and Job." In a
word: the preaching of the Apostle side by side with the creation
of the world and with human anguish. And live the Gospel as Christ
wished it to be lived. The ascetic Père Jacques knew the power and
perils of asceticism.

"Make sacrifices," he wrote to his correspondent. "It is absolutely
necessary that you put mortification in your life. When one wishes
to be master of himself, master of his body and of his sensory facul-
ties, these must be mortified. Therefore, impose on yourself the
little sufferings, the little privations which you will be able to decide
on for yourself. . . ."

But he forbade fasting. What he recommended above all was
necessary sacrifice: "Conduct your classes very conscientiously. Pray
a great deal for your pupils. Do the simple daily duties. Why be surprised at the faults of human nature? Of revolts that you note in
yourself? Of the weaknesses that constantly renew themselves? All
that is nothing. It is just poor human misery. This teaches you that
by yourself you count for very little, and that only God can gently
raise you to the life of prayer that you must reach. Be patient. Let
yourself be worked upon by the mysterious but very real action of
God. . . . Receive Communion as often as you can."

One could say that Lucien Bunel was talking about himself. His
own life is there, step by step, in its entirety while he himself,
director and directed, waited and wondered what turn his own road
was to take.

It was the morning of July 12, 1927, in the chapel of the Carmelites, when Lucien saw the little white cloud of Elias float into
view: the world of Carmelite life was becoming part of his own
life. It was a morning like the others. The factories near the harbor
were still silent and in the distance ocean liners plowed through
the vast sea.

Throughout the city people stirred in their beds, waiting the rising bell. Only an occasional early morning worker could be seen scurrying along the deserted streets. On the heights of Sainte-Adresse La Hève lighthouse had spent its last ray. On the hillside of Ingouville the Carmelites sang like an aviary of God. The voices of the Frenchwomen, singing the verses of the Israelite psalms, answered the harp of David lost in the night of time and celestial glory, while Abbé Bunel at the foot of the altar repeated the *Judica me*: "Send forth Thy light and Thy truth; they have conducted me and brought me unto Thy holy hill, and into Thy tabernacle. And I will go in to the altar of God: to God who giveth joy to my youth. To Thee, O God, my God, I will give praise upon the harp; why art Thou sad, O my soul: and why dost thou disquiet me?"

For two years Lucien had not returned to la Trappe during his vacations. He had spent a month in August, 1925, at the Trappist monastery of Notre-Dame du Port-de-Salut. Why had he not returned since then? One of his friends told us that he feared to find the Trappist Order too hard. Was it because of the great cold which he had barely been able to endure during his first stay at Soligny? Another recalled that he was annoyed to find mistakes in spelling on an escutcheon sign of the Trappist Order, and Lucien himself noted that he feared to see the Trappist life too removed from any idea of literary culture. There was a touch of the professor in Abbé Bunel and these facts certainly have a symptomatic import. But he was more than a professor. One or two bad impressions would not have held him back if the Trappists had really been in the path of his compass needle, but the magnetic field had changed. The obsessive feeling that he was not in his right place remained with him, yet the obstacle of the teaching and pastoral mission had changed into a passion. Despite his thirst for the monastic life, he was afraid to leave the apostolic life. By leaving Le Havre for the Trappists he feared that he would be working only for his own salvation and not for everybody's. His moving away from the Trappists was like the end of a childhood love; it also marked perhaps the end of a juvenile fear of the unleashed floods of life. There was an immense love of God in the call of the Trappists, but perhaps also a certain withdrawal within himself. Life at Le Havre, unwished for but accepted, had shown him that his strength had grown. Now it would be hard to renounce this role of outer expansion for it had become as indispensable to him as the role of contemplation. Far from being in opposition, they fused with and enlivened each other. Lucien's heart had opened to all the winds of Le Havre from every side.

Seeing the stir in the streets of this great port, one would not believe that amid this great roar of traffic and machines there are still tiny ancient enclosures which saints who passed by here in other days still animate. But Lucien looked for them and found them. He frequented Père Deodat, a Franciscan, Abbé Le Gentil, who brought him to the Dominicans, Père Labigne, who proposed to him that he become a diocesan missionary. Through the mouths of their disciples the voices of St. Francis of Assisi, St. Dominic, and St. John Eudes (the great seventeenth-century Norman missionary) wrangled over Lucien's soul, and Lucien waxed enthusiastic over them all.

At the same time he took as his spiritual director Abbé Arson, pastor of Saint-François, the dockworkers' parish. The abbé was an enthusiastic latter-day disciple of the Curé of Ars and St. Joseph Cottolengo (the apostle of Turin and founder of the *Piccola Casa*, which became the refuge of all the derelicts of his native country). Every two years Abbé Arson made a pilgrimage to the Holy Land where he traveled on foot from the port to Jerusalem as St. Francis, St. Ignatius, and Père de Foucauld had done. In the city Abbé Arson was looked upon as a saint. Who better than he could help the young teacher at St. Joseph's to find his path? But where was the divine will? Where would the will of God and that of His creature be joined together? Between the priest who works in a parish in the midst of the people and the monk plunged in solitude there is an infinite number of possible vocations.

Since the choice of a specific form of religious life is not decreed from on high or by papal directive, Lucien's wavering and exploring of all possible vocations are understandable. The alternatives are variable, numerous, and tangled like trees of all species in a forest.

All are born of a celestial call, but like plants in the earth they germinate from below from day to day. Lucien breathed the fragrance of each and sounded the depths of his conscience, but spiritual tastes by themselves decide nothing. They are but signs mixed with other signs and for the spiritual voyager there is no other way but to submit to the divine will, ever guiding, mysterious, hidden until at last its purpose emerges clear as the light of day.

As clear as the dawn of July 12 when Lucien awakened in the singing and silence of Carmel. The little white cloud was there on Mount Carmel, but he did not yet know it. He was still yearning for it as he had been for such a long time.

"I lead a life far from that of my dreams. Where is solitude? Where is the unknown and silent life toward which all my being aspires? Mystery of God! Why does he put such desires in us, so powerful and painful at times, and why does He not permit us to realize them?"

After Mass and the thanksgiving prayer, the portress led Lucien to breakfast in the guest room and then to the parlor where he wished to greet the Prioress, Mère Marie-Joseph de Jesus. Lucien had been familiar with the world of the Carmelites for a long time. During his years at the seminary, he had read and loved with all his heart *The Story of a Soul,* and the day of the beatification of Thérèse of Lisieux in 1924 was for him a memorable date. While he was at Montlignon, he had made a pilgrimage to the Carmelite monastery at Pointoise only because of Sister Marie-Angélique whose autobiography had filled him with admiration. His love for the Carmelite Order was of even earlier date, from the time he entered the Petit Séminaire when he had gone from Rouen to the Carmelite monastery at Bois-Guillaume for his habit.

The wooden shutters clicked gently in the peace of the beautifully waxed parlor. On the other side of the grille, the Prioress sat on a chair facing Lucien. They were forming their first ties of friendship. Mère Marie-Joseph had already heard about Abbé Bunel. "In Le Havre," she had been told, "there are two saints, Abbé Arson and he. Moreover, he dreams only of becoming a Trappist." One day,

meanwhile, on a visit to the convent, the pastor of Le Havre parish
to which the Carmelite monastery belonged had added, "Abbé
Bunel has but one dream, to enter the Trappists, but I have told
him: 'When one can preach as you do, one does not lock oneself
up in la Trappe!' " Lucien probably did not know Mère Marie-Joseph
very well, but he knew and admired Carmel as a very old Order,
yet eternally young and living. The grille before him was not an
obstacle, a privation of freedom; it was the wonder, the sweetness
of the cloister from which he was barred only by himself. The grille
was the gateway to the contemplative life.

How steeped in beauty is this grille, the threshold of the mystic
nights of St. John of the Cross, threshold of the transparent and
solar castle of the soul of the great Teresa under the sun of Spain,
austere oasis of the Sierras, threshold of divine illuminations and
nights of faith on the exalting inner road, strewn with precipices,
cut across by peaks, by shadow and light. French Trappist monasteries are deep in the countryside, but here before Lucien, several
hundred yards away from the harbor, on the very edge of streets
bursting with activity, was an enclosure for contemplation, an island
of adoration, one of the innumerable hives of prayer that dotted the
globe radiating from the Mount Carmel of old. Later Mère Marie-
Joseph confessed that on this morning of July 12 she had seen tears
fill the eyes of Abbé Bunel. He did not understand why there should
be no Carmelite monasteries for men in France. Mère Marie-Joseph
protested joyously, for the Carmelite friars had just returned from
exile. Upon coming back to France some of them had restored the
old ruins and created new houses of contemplation whose addresses
she hastened to give him: at Lille, at Fontainebleau, at Paris. Lucien
departed, completely overwhelmed. Two days later he wrote Mère
Marie-Joseph to thank her, saying: "Who knows what may result
from the conversation we two have had? Perhaps a Carmelite novitiate
and a return to Le Havre in the habit of Carmel, where it would
then be easy to find recruits!"

In these words we can recognize the old Lucien, always enthusiastic, eager for solitude and militant action. For a while it seemed that on that July 12 a seed of destiny had settled everything once for all. It was only a first sowing, however, but it was the decisive seed of his Carmelite vocation. At this moment he still dreamed of joining the Trappists, the Franciscans, the Dominicans, the Eudists, but these were only passing enthusiasms that burned out one by one, while the small flame of Carmel grew larger and set his entire life aflame.

There is only one Mount Carmel and the friars and nuns live only one spiritual life, that known by John of the Cross and Teresa of Avila. But this unity does not prevent a difference in their way of life: the Carmelite nuns never leave their cloister, and while the friars also live a cloistered life, they leave the monastery at times and under conditions fixed by the Rule in order to conduct a pastoral ministry: they are at once monks and apostles. This was the great revelation for which Lucien was waiting. He was suffocating in the world without the refuge of contemplation and the joy of a monastic Rule. At la Trappe he would have missed the active life for which he had so great a thirst. With the Carmelite life, Lucien suddenly discovered the possibility of fusing these two lives into a single one.

In the month following he returned to Carmel and told Mère Marie-Joseph: "Your prayer is answered. The Carmelite Order is my ideal of the religious life. To live in solitude with God, in intimate contact with Him, and then to leave the cloister to bring Him to souls, to let Him be known and loved—then to return to plunge back into the retreat to renew oneself with prayer: this is what draws me!"

Lucien was still to experience many unexpected reversals and about-faces. Once again he hesitated among all the varieties of the spiritual forest, and he no longer knew where to direct his steps. Again he was violently torn between the two currents of the contemplative and the active life; he no longer truly knew whether the "mixed" way of Carmel should be his. And again there came a call from the Trappists. He wrote quite frankly to Père Labigne who still wanted him to become a diocesan missionary: "I feel a need for the religious life, the life of obedience, of being crushed, annihilated, a life of obscurity that would obliterate my immense pride and subdue my terrible spirit of independence.

"But I also have an *ardent thirst* to serve God, to possess Him infinitely, to nourish myself on Him, to live in a deep and constant intimacy with Him. Hence I have always desired solitude, and since my second seminary year, the Trappists.

"However, a combination of circumstances has forced me to recognize that God has entrusted to me a facility for preaching, and I have known the good it is possible to do when one speaks from his heart, as one thinks and believes, and when one later receives in the confessional the souls who have heard him. So, for almost a year I have simply not known what to do, or where to direct my steps.

"Along with my director, I am pondering what my vocation should be—is it to be the purely contemplative life or the mixed life? Let me pray, read, and reread your meditation. I shall see my director again, and confide everything to him that I think, everything I fear, and I shall obey him blindly.

"But I am so deeply drawn to the remote cloister of the Trappists! There one is poor, one suffers lovingly for God, one finds God there, one embraces Him, one regards Him always in silence and meditation."

But these were the last signs of his interest in la Trappe. In the stir of the great port there was now a silence more powerful than all the noises of Le Havre, nearer and more intense than the silence of the Norman Trappists over the horizon. It was the silence of Carmel on the hillside of Ingouville. Lucien often walked across the entire city just to breathe an hour of silence in the chapel of the monastery, to ask questions of Mère Marie-Joseph in the parlor, or to encounter a passing friar.

In July, 1928, one year later, he went to make a retreat, this time not at the Trappist monastery but at the new convent of the Carmelite friars at Avon, the small sister community of Fontainebleau.

The Carmelite friars are few in number, about fifty in all France. At that time there was only a handful of them at the Avon convent, all elderly, survivors of exile and the war. Most of them were between seventy and ninety years old. They did not have much in the way of resources and the convent was in a dilapidated state, but none of all this bothered Lucien. On the contrary, the poverty of the convent, the precariousness of an old Order ravaged by the ordeals to which it had been subjected touched him to the bottom of his heart. "The fervor is such that this Order will flourish anew." In the pure silence of the monastery situated at the end of the park of Fontainebleau on the edge of the great forest, he found a peace that completely enchanted him. His sole anxiety was the fear that he was acting badly by deserting the souls in Le Havre whom he was piloting toward God. Did he not risk becoming a useless person by fleeing toward solitude? But the novice-master, Père Jean de Jésus-Hostie, whom he had come to consult, gave him the *Spiritual Canticle* of St. John of the Cross in which Lucien read and reread the celebrated words: "The smallest act of love has more value in the eyes of God, is more useful to the Church and more profitable to the soul itself than all other works put together."

Works are nothing without love, man can do nothing without God, whereas in the exchange of pure love between God and man everything is possible and works are animated into infinity. Lucien meditated in the silence of Avon amid the rustling of the tall trees golden with sun. Now, there was no more doubt. There could be no other path for Lucien than the ascent to Mount Carmel.

From Avon, on July 23, he wrote Mère Marie-Joseph a jubilant letter beginning with these words, "Your brother in St. Teresa and in St. John of the Cross . . ." and announced that he was going at once to see the Archbishop of Rouen to ask permission to leave the diocese and take the road of the Carmelite novitiate.

A beautiful illusion. Monseigneur de la Villerabel had no intention at all of losing him, above all so quickly, at a time when the diocese was short of priests. Lucien quivered with disappointment but bowed in submission. How patiently he had to bear it all! He was burning with desire to immerse himself in the silence of Carmel and now he had to resume teaching and preaching. For how long?

One year, at least. He submitted wholeheartedly. Heaven belongs to
the passionate, but above all to those who control their own passionate desires.

Again he faced a full year of patient and impatient waiting which
wore him out. Lucien resumed his place at St. Joseph's. But during
all this time, from that moment on, the lamp of the Carmelite convent on the Ingouville slope shone across the streets of Le Havre
like a dark lantern in the depths of the night. He climbed the hill
toward the convent as toward an oasis. He went there often to
celebrate Mass and on certain feasts (such as the feast of Our Lady
of Mount Carmel, St. Teresa of Avila, or St. John of the Cross), he
took two or three of his pupils along with him in whom he had
infused the same love. All three were to become priests, two of them
Carmelite friars like Père Jacques. In the morning they served Mass
for him in the Carmelite chapel and breakfasted with him in the
guest room. Later they went to the parlor with the Prioress and some
of the other religious. Then long conversations took place, radiant
with the poetry and mysticism of Mount Carmel.

During the winter months of rain and fog, during the final days
of the school term, Lucien champed at the bit. In the spring he
again prepared his artillery; he hoped very much that the reopening
of the term would free him and at last open the road to Carmel. In
March, 1929, he addressed a new request to Archbishop de la Villerabel. The latter now seemed less inflexible. Undoubtedly he
understood that Lucien's desire was something more than caprice,
but it was certainly not with joy in his heart that he would allow him
to leave his diocesan post. Lucien did not limit himself to a formal
request. At the suggestion of the Prior of Avon it was decided that
he would profit by a pilgrimage to Rome during the Easter vacation
to ask the Superior General of the Carmelites to intercede with the
Bishop.

"I put myself completely in the hands of Providence," wrote
Lucien in March to Mère Marie-Joseph. There was no fatalism about
this, since he also added, "I do everything I can to enter [Carmel],

but I am confident that God alone can bring this about. I leave it to Him."

Finally, in the month of June, the Archbishop granted Abbé Bunel permission to leave, but not immediately. He wanted a two-year delay, against which Lucien protested and balked, declaring that he found this unacceptable and that he wanted to leave by the end of the school year. "Monseigneur has reproached me for being stubborn. I told him that it was not stubbornness at all but obedience to my director. And on this word we took leave of each other." Lucien left, confident that the letters of the Prior of Avon and of the Carmelite Provincial would eventually obtain a favorable decision for him, and the next month he began to make preparations for departure.

"The thought of leaving so soon rejoices my heart," he wrote.

For the interim the Carmelites invited him to stay at their convent of the Petit Castelet near Tarascon. And on August 1, at 2 P.M., he wrote to the Carmelites of Le Havre: "Here I am! . . . Arriving in Paris at 8:05 P.M., I ran to the Paris-Lyon-Méditerranée line where I caught an express at 9:40. But this train had a defective engine. It seems that a rod had snapped and we stood there in the same place for hours! The fact remains that instead of arriving at Tarascon at a few minutes after eight, we did not get there until past noon. I was miserable! I had kept my fast, hoping to arrive in time to say Mass. It was too late! I asked someone to guide me to Petit Castelet. Sun! Sun! Sun! A sun beside which that of Normandy looks very pale indeed! The cicadas were deafening! An absolute silence! I pulled cautiously on the long rope of the bell; a dog barked two or three times. But nobody answered! Thinking that everybody, teachers and pupils, overcome by the heat, were taking their siesta, I did not wish to ring again. I slipped into the chapel through a half-opened door, and I stood before the Master! You can guess what I told him! But in a moment there was the sound of footsteps and a young boy appeared. I approached him. Explanation: the young novices had gone on an excursion and the house was almost empty, hence the heavy silence! The boy took me to the priest substituting for Père Eugène. A warm and brotherly welcome: I drank a cup of coffee, rested under the trees and chatted with the priest, and then I was installed in the charming, charming little cell located in the old Castelet, facing the entrance! . . . And it is from here that your little brother scribbles these words! . . . I have entered, and I won't have to leave any more. . . ."

Several days later, on August 9, he wrote again: "I pass from enchantment to enchantment. Everything pleases me, even the smallest details of Carmelite life. Everything corresponds so well to the secret desires that I have borne within me for so long and which had not found satisfaction elsewhere. I had a long talk with our Père Marie-Eugène and with Père Henri. Both are convinced that Rome will give a favorable reply. You can imagine how happy this made me! *I am counting* (what a bitter disappointment if it is not realized but *sincerely I wish only for the will of God*) on being able to enter the novitiate in September."

And on August 25 he wrote them: "I float in a tranquil happiness." But on September 1, he confessed his uneasiness. Had the Archbishop made a decision? What was it?

"I am ready for anything, to remain here, to go to Rome, to return to St. Joseph's, to hide myself elsewhere. Whatever I am told to do I shall do, with suffering, evidently, if I am snatched away from the Carmelites. But very sincerely and without any mental reservations and without a murmur, I shall go where I am told to go, even to Le Havre."

On September 8 the blow fell. It was impossible for him to be freed of his diocesan obligations, at least not before the reopening of school.

"I have accepted everything," he said. But this was said from the heights of his soul. As for the rest: "I could not sleep."

He still wanted to make a last try and he sent a petition to his archbishop. During this time Père Julien, in order to cheer him up, said to him: "Don't you believe that God is sometimes satisfied merely to put desires for the religious life in the heart without permitting their realization? This world needs priests with contemplative souls!" "I believe it," wrote Lucien, "but this is a very heavy cross that God puts on one's shoulders!"

On September 13 he lost all hope and realized that he had to go back: "The sacrifice is consummated! This morning I received the enclosed letter from Monseigneur. If he sent similar arguments to Rome, Rome could do nothing but agree with him, which she has done. Unfortunately these arguments are false! I pointed this out to him discreetly and respectfully in my reply. But that was all.

"In agreement with Père Eugène, I shall not seek to justify myself at Rome, or with my religious superiors. I believe all these events are directed by Providence and arranged step by step toward my ultimate destiny. My proud and haughty nature needs such humiliations. May God be thanked for sending them to me! My poor nature cries out and struggles. My will repeats over and over again to God, So be it! So be it!

"So here I am flung back from my dear Carmel. For how long? Only God knows. Will it be two years? Will it be more? So be it! I am taking the road back to Le Havre and entering the college again. All my being *revolts in horror* at the thought of resuming the life that I have led until now, running this way and that. . . . *It is the cross*, the heavy cross, overpowering, crushing. To have been so near Carmel, to have seen one's cell, to have savored the life of meditation, and then to be snatched away and tossed back into the midst of life. You alone, ma mère, can understand me! . . . *It is frightful.* It requires all my effort of the will to say 'yes' and to try to smile."

To conclude, he asked only for his armor: the works of St. Teresa and of St. John of the Cross, a discipline and a hair shirt.

Three days later he apologized for the weakness he had shown in his letter: "I was so overwhelmed by this blow that destroyed my most beloved dreams. For two days I struggled against feelings of sadness, of despondency and discouragement, above all of revolt.

My will tried hard to repeat a sincere 'so be it' to God, while all my sensibility and pride quivered and put evil thoughts in my mind.

"The beautiful texts of the office of the Exaltation of the Holy Cross calmed everything. Since Saturday, I suffer tranquilly without bitterness, without distress, without revolt. Over and over I kiss the hand of God who gives me this trial and I believe that I will not show too much chagrin at the school upon returning, even though I shall be broken inwardly. I do not deserve to be so proved by God. It is a great grace that He gives me and I do not know how to thank Him. At my first visit I shall ask you kindly to assemble the community so that together we may sing the *Magnificat* to help me thank God for thus wounding the heart and joining us to His sufferings."

On September 20 Lucien was still at Petit Castelet helping the monks to gather grapes under the Provence sky. On September 22 he got off the train at Rouen where he went to greet Monseigneur de la Villerabel and ask for his blessing. At Le Havre station his pupil and disciple, J. Lefevre, had come to meet him so that he would not be alone on this day of his return. But there were long silences as they walked through the city. The young man saw clearly that never had a pupil had such a horror of returning to school as this teacher had.

Again classes and rain, winter, Le Havre, the cycle of the same life taken up as before, after the moment in Provence, the moment of monastic life. Lucien felt the mocking gaze of those who thought to themselves: Here's another who indulged in illusions! He dreamed only of Carmel and here he is back again like everybody else. Was all this fuss necessary?

However, Lucien was far from being crushed. He was still the master who inflamed the ardor of the students, the preacher much sought after in the parishes. And he himself a hundred times took the path to the little Carmelite convent on the flank of the slope, an oasis where he kept vigil. During the vacation at the beginning of 1930, he made a retreat at the convent in Lille. He returned there in July, immediately after the distribution of the scholastic awards.

Lucien was patient, but this patience was first turned against himself: "I find it hard to believe that I can really do some good. I am so lamentably worthless in the eyes of God, and I feel with such intensity my unfathomable moral misery."

What misery? Those who knew him intimately were well aware to what an extent he was far from leading a life of self-indulgence and dissipation. It was not a problem of morality; it was the intimate and primordial misery: before God, man is as poor and naked as a worm.

"I am very sorry about what the Fathers in Lille have written you. I suffer because of the illusions they indulge in on my account as you yourself did once for that matter. They will be very disappointed when they finally get their bird. . . . I have much, so much pride. And what a lack of charity!"

Then again it was July vacation, and the waiting for the reopening of the school. Dead calm—there was no sign of change. In October he again had to take up the yoke. But in the course of these months the visits to the Carmel convent of Le Havre, the retreats at Lille which for a long time now had replaced those at the Trappist monastery, marked the intervals of the school rhythm. In January, 1931, Lucien wrote from Lille: "I had come to hide myself in the monastery to find at least a few hours of peaceful freedom. What tranquillity one experiences in the cloister! One feels himself bathed in an atmosphere of eternity! Everything takes place there calmly, slowly. One understands that one has come into a land where time does not count, where one lives as if already in heaven. And what can I say to you of the Offices, the hours of prayer? One kneels and one goes off into a joyful contemplation of God. And one feels that He is there, one lives under His gaze, almost touching Him, one remains for hours under the sweet caress of His being in which one is wrapped! What a difference from the burning restlessness, feverishness, and emptiness of the world!"

He had one more year to go at Le Havre. The months were endless. When would he get out of this system which went round in circles, indefinitely, but where he nevertheless worked with ardor, even passion, as if he desired to do nothing else?

At last, July, 1931! The two years fixed by the Archbishop had expired. Monseigneur had not granted him a reduction in his waiting period, but now that the time was up, he kept his word and granted Abbé Bunel his freedom.

The road to Mount Carmel was wide open.

2   "You Cannot Imagine"

The Holy Land was devastated by drought. Elias the prophet climbed to the summit of Mount Carmel and cast himself on the ground to pray. Then he called his servant and ordered him to go up the promontory from which the entire horizon of the sea was visible. The servant went up to the promontory and returned saying, "There is nothing!" "Return seven times!" ordered the prophet. Seven times the servant made the climb and when he returned the seventh time he announced, "Behold, a little cloud no larger than a man's foot arose out of the sea." This was the sign for which the prophet had been waiting. Several months later the clouds broke in a cloudburst and the rain came to quench the thirst of the earth.

Not seven times, but more than a thousand times, evening after evening at Le Havre Lucien had turned to the Lord in his constant waiting for the day of joy when he would become in his turn a servant on Mount Carmel to know at last the harshness of the rock, the wild flowers, the burning sun, the tempests, and the dark nights. But for him everything was sweet in advance, like the rain after a torrid and interminable season.

On August 28, 1931, Lucien plunged into the province of the collieries and the miners. Everything happened as if, above the somber streets besmirched by factory smoke, out of sight, a minute, invisible, and mysterious white cloud floated at the zenith, unnoticed, a small cloud white as snow, all bathed in the immaculate summer light. But for Lucien alone it was the storm cloud of the prophet over Mount Carmel.

The convent lay like a mysterious island in the dead center of

Lille, on the Rue des Stations. The noise of the city, the factory whistles, the upsurge of human voices, the roar of motors, all the excitement of a great city in an industrial era beat against the doors of the convent like the waves of the sea against the promontory of Carmel.

But once the door is closed behind one the city disappears at one stroke. The interior of the monastery is steeped in the peaceful silence of eternity. This time Lucien was no longer a visitor, a friend passing by, a guest for the day, or even a retreatant. Nothing else held him back, nothing else could force him to leave except the unforeseeable. He had come there to be, definitively, the brother of the other Carmelites. In a single stroke he had been thrown into the high sea of his dream which had become an immediate and total reality. But at this same moment his heart was torn by an opposite torment: "I entered the cloister, upset by extremely painful struggles, my heart in shreds. And the devil continually let images of the apostolate parade before my eyes. What days and what hours! I went to get my habit with something approximating disgust or at least with a very lively apprehension. I clung fast to God with all my will, and I said to my rebellious nature, 'You may talk and act up till you're blue, you are here and here you are going to stay.' And to God, 'My God, even though I shall never again see those whom I have left, and Thou knowest how much I love them, even though I should remain in the throes of this frightful struggle throughout my novitiate, I accept all.' "

Little by little peace returned and the joy of Carmel invaded his entire being: "I float in divine joy. I have the beneficent impression of having regained possession of myself, of having begun my life all over again from the start, of having placed it in its true direction. A page of darkness will remain between my departure from the Grand Séminaire and my entry into the cloister. What is it worth? What have I done? I have run about a great deal, talked, confessed, I have tried to bring God to souls, but I put so much pride in all these things that I have no idea what value these years have had in the eyes of God. Nor do I even seek to know. I ask God's pardon and that's all. Now, forward!"

On September 14 he took the habit of Carmel. He exchanged his black cassock for the brown woolen frock and long scapular. At the same time he received his monastic name, Frère Jacques de Jésus. He had finally crossed the threshold of the cloister, he was a Carmelite novice. From now on he had nothing more to do but serve his apprenticeship in the monastic life.

"I have found at Carmel all I have been waiting for, and of which I had a deep need," he wrote to one of his former Scouts. "I experienced the joy of receiving the habit on the evening of September 14, a ceremony which almost overwhelmed me, so much did it move me by showing me as clear as day what an immolation the religious life is and how fruitful for the good of souls. I have been a monk for twelve days now—at least in dress. My life is entirely cloaked in silence and is passed almost completely in the choir in an affectionate encounter with God, or in my cell where I again meet God, as everywhere else for that matter. If you knew how good it is to feel oneself denuded of everything, reduced to nothing, more insignificant than a poor little infant, and all this out of love of God with Whom one never ceases to converse."

Here in the Lille monastery Lucien's cell was a true monk's cell, a cell which he had succeeded only in glimpsing like an annunciatory image in the small rooms of the seminary and the college, a real cell on which neither alien obligations nor the opaque obscurity of the future encroached, a cell in which the Rule of Carmel reigned supreme, a real cell received as a heritage of heaven and of poverty, among all the cells bound together throughout the world like bunches of grapes, like the beehives of Mount Carmel. The cell for which he had so greatly yearned was there, transfixed in space, as he himself was transfixed in prayer and meditation. The fever of the future no longer came to obsess him, it was the present, here and now, that utterly absorbed him.

Carmelite friars spend long hours in their cells and gather at the canonical hours for the Divine Office, for meals and the material tasks of the convent. But, whether they are praying alone in their silent cells, chanting together the hymns of the office, or attending to an intellectual or material duty, they have only one aim:

to live continually the life of prayer. There is no religious Order that does not orient its entire life toward God, but some show a particular concern with missionary action, others with religious study or with liturgical celebration. What differentiates the Orders is not the effect of an absolute division of work, which would be unthinkable in the domain of the spirit, but the emphasis put on one or the other tendency. Thus with Carmel the life of prayer is the magnet of all life.

"One enters Carmel, above all else, to find God and to have the personal and living contact with Him that is achieved by the most intense prayer. The whole efficacy of the Carmelite life rises from this deep source: the invisible action of the Carmelite nun as well as the ministry of the Carmelite friar among souls," writes Père François de Sainte-Marie in *"La Règle du Carmel et son esprit"* (Ed. du Seuil, p. 63).

"The aim of all religious and the perfection of his heart," wrote the blessed Jean Soreth, general of the Order in the fifteenth century, "are to tend toward a continual, uninterrupted, persevering prayer insofar as human weakness permits" (*Ibid.*, p. 65).

If you think that a Teresa of Avila or a John of the Cross remains inaccessible or even incomprehensible, then listen to the voice of one who was the cook in the Carmelite convent on Rue de Vaugirard, under Louis XIV, Frère Laurent de la Résurrection: "The time of action," he said, "is no different from that of prayer. I possess God just as tranquilly in the confusion of my kitchen, where sometimes several persons ask me for different things at the same time, as if I were on my knees before the Blessed Sacrament. My faith itself sometimes becomes so enlightened that I believe it to have disappeared;[1] it seems to me that the veil of obscurity has been lifted, that the endless light of the other life begins to appear.

"And it is not necessary to have great things to do so," he added. "I turn my little omelette in the pan for the love of God. When it is done, if I have nothing else to do, I cast myself on the floor and

---

[1] He means that it went beyond to the point of living no longer in faith but in the evidence of God. (*L'Expérience de la présence de Dieu*, pp. 77–78.)

adore my God from whom the grace to do so has come, after which I rise more content than a King.

"One searches for methods in order to love God; one seeks to arrive at it by I don't know how many different methods. One takes great pains in order to remain in the presence of God by any number of means. Is it not simpler and more straightforward to do everything for the love of God, to make use of all the works of one's station to mark and retain His presence in us by this commerce of our heart with Him? Here no finesse at all is required, all that is necessary is to go about it simply and plainly."

This is very much what the new Frère Jacques de Jésus wanted. He was thirty years old, he was a priest, and had several years of teaching and pastoral ministry behind him. And now he had to conduct himself like a newcomer among twenty-year-old novices.

He, who was always moving about, bestirring himself in class, walking the streets of Le Havre and its environs, became almost immobile, the willing captive of this great white-walled abode with its bare cells, and its long corridors paved with yellow and red tiles. Life could be of intolerable monotony without faith, without the vocation and the grace of God in this house which almost unchangingly enclosed the lives of twenty men all caught in the net of a Rule which holds for each hour of life, every day of the year, and where prayer impregnates everything.

Lucien spent hours in his cell, alone and silent. When he left it, it was only to find himself inside another sacred circle, that of the cloister. He was not a madman, he knew himself to be enclosed, he was a willing captive. But he would have inevitably become mad if the presence of God were merely imaginary, if his personal ascent toward God were based on a false illusion. The only activity permitted the novices was their weekly promenades in the outskirts of Lille in the late afternoon. This was just enough for them to stretch their legs.

One day René Bunel came to Lille for a retreat during Père Jacques's novitiate. He was soon bored to death. "I could never hold out!" he said. He went to see his brother, who looked at him re-

provingly and cried, "Silence! Silence!" Completely at sea, René
then went to visit the porter, wishing to smoke a pipe in his company just to kill time. But it was impossible to continue this way.
In the end René could stand it no longer and decided to leave.
Père Jacques accompanied him to the station, René boarded the
train, and they exchanged farewells. Suddenly, a moment later, Père
Jacques reappeared and ran up to the door of the railway carriage in
which René was still standing and threw him a bundle of tabloids,
Cricri, *L'Epatant* and so on, and, laughing, cried out, "Here! This
is all you're capable of reading!"

Lucien always loved to laugh and he continued to do so as if he
were twenty, and it was all the easier since he was now a novice.
There were seven of them that year under the direction of Père
Louis de la Trinité, a former naval officer become novice-master.
Another younger religious, Père André de la Croix, was the "good
angel," that is to say Père Jacques's personal monitor whose task it
was to initiate him to the ways and customs of the novitiate. Now
a simple trainee, the former director of souls submitted with good
grace to the Carmelite initiation. He delighted in it and drew from
it an agreeable lightness of spirit. At other moments he could not
avoid feeling a tinge of bitterness.

The Rule is monotonous, but life within the Rule is far from
being so simply because it is life, not an inert and set contemplation,
but an itinerary of a human being with his struggles, humors, and
even his light clashes with others. Lucien was a Carmelite, he became
as much a Carmelite as he could, but he remained Lucien and the
waves of a life open up a way for themselves even in a monastery. A
monastery is not necessarily a pious, inaccessible fortress. The noises
from the outside infiltrated terribly at certain times: from one side,
while the novice meditated in his cell, he heard the throbbings of
motors in the garage near by, or the sound of tennis balls being
bounced against the wall. On the other side there were the smoke
fumes from the laundry which made it necessary to keep all windows
closed, and the shouts of the children in the Jeanne d'Arc school.
The silence was shattered in pieces. But Frère Jacques was taking

lessons from Frère Laurent. Instead of being annoyed at this interference with the holy perfection of silence, he delighted in it. It was the voices of the children, however, which were the most redoubtable.

One day, during a visit at the convent, Lucien and René were walking around the little garden. The joyful shouts of the children rose up endlessly from the other side of the wall. René knew his brother well, "How can you stay here, listening to these gay cries from the other side?"

Père Jacques stopped for a second, closing his eyes.

"Yes, I suffered atrociously; I suffer still, my little René. In my cell I sometimes fall on my knees and stop my ears so as not to hear these children's voices. I believe I suffer a hundredfold the suffering you feel upon losing one of your little pupils. I was wrong to attach myself so firmly to the children. It was necessary that I be broken, even as Jesus, who loved us so, accepted being nailed to the cross. Yes, I loved my children but I love them even more now since it is my entire life that I consecrate to them in prayer."

At the same time Père Jacques was the novice who with a concealed foot tipped the scales of the convent in order to introduce a bit of the unexpected into the apothecary weights of the Father Master. In the refectory he quietly ignored whole pages in the books he found too boring to read aloud, or else he introduced some strange variations. Thus while reading from a monumental history of the clergy which described a "perverted clergy" at a troublesome time of decadence, Lucien had added, "above all in Alsace-Lorraine," a remark directed especially at a novice from that region.

Père Jacques was also a difficult novice who somewhat disconcerted Père André who was charged with taking him in hand.

"This role," recounted Père André, "did not create a special link of intimacy between us. Later, I learned that he was disappointed over my welcome. I had heard him murmur, not without bitterness, 'So I've got to become a little seminarian once more.' But in view of his severe mask and his rather cold bearing, I could hardly suspect that he would have liked to carry on a prolonged conversation. In fact, these first days of the novitiate were very hard on him and his stiffness was the result of a will tensed toward its aim. I appreciated this courage; it seemed to me that Abbé Bunel was strong enough to endure silence and solitude. I was not mistaken; he made his profession. . . .

"During the novitate I saw a strict religious of an ascetic type, hard on himself, whose deep piety expressed itself in outpourings too sentimental for my taste. I felt him vibrating with enthusiasm or very bruised by what he judged—sometimes a bit hastily—to be pettiness. He remained strongly oriented toward the care of souls and I suffered to see him constrained to hide and perhaps mutilate a magnificent apostolic temperament. For me Père Jacques will always remain just that, an apostle! All the grievances that one could harbor against him disappeared once one glimpsed the intensity and the purity of his zeal for souls.

"His difficulties were his constant teasing which could become cutting, a stubbornness that sometimes distorted the true terms of an argument, a will power that rather rudely pushed aside obstacles, even if they happened to be his brothers. On the other hand, what true charity, what a good companion, always ready to lend a hand, to give of himself! His outbursts earned him some calls to order, they remain one of the fresh memories of the novitiate. He was very well liked. . . ."

One day, alarmed to find Père Jacques in a bad state of health which might have hampered his later work, Père André expressed his worry and distress.

"He answered me with a sincerity that I felt to be complete. 'It's of no importance at all. If God wishes it, I would willingly remain a sorry specimen all my life.' That day I entirely understood Père Jacques's deep prayer and his impulses that had slightly annoyed me. They were true, and from then on I was less sensitive to the romantic cut in which they were clothed."

Outside of the little episodes that ruffled the calm order of his days, one could find Lucien about to read a pile of pious works ranging from Psichari to Pierre Termier, Ozanam or Thureau-Dangin to improve his mind. It goes without saying that he gave more time and attention to the reading of St. Bernard, Suso, St. Catherine of Siena, and of course the Bible, St. Thomas, and the Carmelite saints. From this reading he drew a series of little notes for his personal use and the citations were copied on the backs of envelopes received by the Carmelites at Lille.

Manual labor took up much of his time—dishwashing, serving at table, cleaning the stairs and corridors, and so on. He also had a voluminous correspondence, unusual for a novice, for though Lucien had left Le Havre and Normandy, he had not put a wall of silence between himself and those who had confided in him and who continued to ask for support and spiritual counsel. In principle, according to the Rule, a novice must cut off all correspondence save now and then in exceptional cases. But Père Jacques, as the ex-Abbé Bunel, had charge of souls at a distance and he was constantly obliged to ask for permission to read this mail and to reply, a permission that was not refused. The Rule is made for man and not man for the Rule.

Lucien Bunel had not yet come to the point reached by Friar Laurent who felt close to God, even while making his omelette, while others concerned themselves with occupations apparently more elevated. It sometimes happened as Père Jacques, in his cell, watched the flies buzz about, he sighed—not without laughing, at himself— "Aren't they happy, these little beasts, they have their freedom!"

He was still far from the summit, in these mountainous regions where, though far from the point of departure, one is nevertheless still clambering up the side of the mountain and no longer sees the top, hidden by intermediate areas. But patiently, obstinately, he sought the road, following the great Carmelite masters who have left so many marks of their passage on the precipitous path.

"The more I study the life and works of our saints, the more I love them with greater attachment, like parents or older brothers and sisters," he wrote to the Carmelites at Le Havre, "and I appeal to them with complete assurance that my prayers will be answered. What trusting tenderness I have for our most beloved father, St. Joseph, for our father, St. Elias! I do not speak of St. John of the Cross, of the sweet and strong and good John of the Cross but I melt with affection for him the more intimate I become with him. He is my very particular friend whose counsels I carefully collect. It is he who is training me and who is instilling in me the true spirit of Carmel. I visit him every day and I listen, and little by little he reveals the Carmelite ideal to me. And it is splendid!

"I request the same service from our mother St. Teresa. Each of her works is read slowly and I take hold of them, drink them in, take notes, and I float in a great spiritual happiness. It is a revelation that is making itself clear and completing itself and which, I feel, will never stop growing until the end of my life. Such springs of sanctity and love of God gush forth with enough force and abundance so that they may remain inexhaustible here on earth. My John of the Cross! I ask his pardon for not having known him earlier, and for having been his neighbor for so many years without listening to him with more attention. . . ."

At night in the convent, when it is time to retire, the religious of the Carmelite Order go up to their floors and each one kneels in front of the door of his cell. Then the Prior comes to give them his benediction. The Friar bell ringer who accompanies the Prior announces him by three light blows of *tablettes*, or wooden clappers, repeated three times, and in a loud voice amid the peaceful silence of the convent he pronounces a poetic couplet of prayer which he has prepared as a vigil light for the night. The Carmelites of Lille have preserved several of the couplets composed by Père Jacques for these occasions:

"The bird who takes God's bounty where he may,
    Like us, trusts God, and lives from day to day."
On another occasion, he sang out:
    "It's nothing worth to say, 'God, I love Thee!'
    True love is to proclaim, 'God, I give me.'"
And, without doubt, the most exquisite of these evening calls:
    "Brother,
    A leaf that falls, a little bird that sings,
    What need you more to touch the heart of things?"
For it is not paradise that is missing on the earth, it is man who can no longer see it or live it. Heaven is here, intact and virginal, in the

beauty of flowers and leaves, in the song of birds and in the rainbow of the colors of the universe. But it is man who has lost the sense of heaven when he has broken his bond with God; it is he who now reduces nature to a by-product of chance and again exalts it to the point of confusing creation with the Creator. For Père Jacques as for all Carmelites, as for Francis of Assisi singing the canticle of the sun, creatures, flowers, leaves, and birds, all these are neither God nor the negation of God but joy and praise of God, the pure passage of beauty between man's first paradise and the future paradise.

At the end of his first year at Carmel Père Jacques was allowed to make his profession. The ceremony took place on September 15, in the chapel of the monastery.

"There is no name for the happiness that was mine during those days! I did not savor a like joy—calm, profound, overflowing—when I became a subdeacon or even when I entered the priesthood. I felt myself enveloped by tenderness, the tenderness of God, the tenderness of so many souls who wanted so much to unite themselves to my poor soul on this occasion. For two days my heart was happy to the point of tears at feeling itself too small to contain this immensity of happiness," he wrote to Le Havre. He confessed a single momentary shadow over this joy: "Before certain evocations of a past which was and remains dear to me—this was during the Prior's sermon—it was only with difficulty that I overcame my emotion. I understood so well and felt so deeply that it was farewell to that very dear and delicate work of guiding children's souls."

But joy was the stronger emotion and on the day after this moving ceremony, he wrote to Jacques Lefèvre: "You can't imagine to what a point one is overwhelmed with happiness and peace on such a day! . . . One is rewarded a hundredfold for the sacrifices one has made to enter into the religious life. The cloister may perhaps be frightening seen from the outside. But when one lives there it is entirely bathed in light, peace, and joy. In living the best possible life in accordance with our vows, what a splendid harvest, although invisible, is gathered in the poor world of sinners. It is enough just to see the radiance emanating from our little Norman St. Thérèse.

The day Lucien made his profession, he was far from solitary. The chapel was thronged with people and after the ceremony Frère Jacques came into the parlor.

"How wonderful! All my brothers and sisters, except the youngest, had come despite the tiring journey it involved for them. Although they left Rouen at a very early hour, they could not get back there until nearly midnight, then going on to Saint-Etienne [du Rouvray], Elbeuf, or Maromme. . . . People came from the town where I had been a soldier ten years ago, with the curé at their head. Young people from a parish club I had organized in Maromme when I was at the Grand Séminaire arrived. A Boy Scout troop and many others came from Le Havre. . . ."

All of them spent the day at the monastery where the Father Prior invited them to luncheon and dinner. He even offered to put up for the night those who desired to stay longer, so that on the following morning there were still about twenty friends to attend the first Mass of Père Jacques, now a professed Carmelite.

Auguste Roy, who had once played with Lucien at Pavilly and who had met him again in the army at Montlignon, was at this celebration. Since they had remained close friends, Roy could not restrain himself from drawing Père Jacques aside for a moment to ask him, "Well, are you happy now?" "I feel myself unworthy of this life," was all that Père Jacques replied, his face radiant with happiness. A little later the Prior whispered into Roy's ear, "Père Jacques? His holiness overflows the monastery."

In this enclosure, which lay like a mysterious garden of the soul in the heart of Lille, Lucien approached the shores of infinity.

"If you knew how quickly the days go by in the monastery. . . . When one places himself before God, when one touches Him, when one embraces Him in the mystery of the spiritual life, the hours flow by with amazing rapidity. What is an hour passed thus in silent adoration of the very Being of God, forever living, there, close to us? One has the presentiment of His gaze, one feels it rest on us with all its weight so sweet with love. . . . My life is there. . . . It is the unending contemplation of God in the calm of my poor little cell, or beside my stall in the choir. . . . If men only knew how to discover

His invisible, ceaseless Presence, and if only they knew how to live with Him in a peaceful intercourse of friendship, what unutterable happiness they would savor, a happiness so calm and beneficent. What is suffering when it is enveloped in this infinity of love?"

On the day after Christmas, he wrote to the Carmelite monastery at Le Havre: "What exquisite happiness the soul derives from the celebration and contemplation of the mystery of Christmas! God spoiled me! He gave me the privilege of serving Mass after Lauds at a time when the chapel was empty or nearly so. It was wonderful for the soul! And what to say of the three Masses celebrated slowly, while savoring the theological richness of the sacred texts, weighted with divine infinity. It was at such moments that I implored grace and more grace for your Reverence and for your dear community. You cannot know how much gratitude I owe you for having led me to Carmel. Since my profession I never cease to exult with happiness at being a monk, at being totally consecrated to, wholly given to God. To be the 'servant' of God! I cannot tell you everything my poor soul sees and reflects upon in this word! They are the splendors of eternity! At every prayer I engulf myself in an adoration of my Master, not knowing how to cry out my happiness to Him, my over-flowing happiness and my appreciation.

"God allows me to know my wretched misery better and better that I may increasingly understand from what a dangerous life of over-flowing action He snatched me away, and this does me immense good! Yes, it is quite true that with my *insane pride* and my aptitude for apostolic action I would have surely lost myself in the world. . . . How the little cell is transformed when one fills it with Him and His love. How quickly the hours and days flow by, almost too quickly! What is an hour of Holy Scripture when one passes it with Him! . . . May I confide to one of my sisters that sometimes I linger over a single word or a single verse through several lessons of Holy Scrip-ture!"

But the solitude of contemplation is also a secret multitude because it is not only filled with the presence of God, it overflows with human presences. It was not only in a little memento hidden on his person that Père Jacques kept the names of all those he had known and loved, he also always kept them in his mind.

"Carmel must be a kind of reflection of heaven, because I never forget a person, and I even noted that my friendships were fortified and at the same time spiritualized. It is truly necessary that it be God who speaks and asks, so that the heart definitively breaks off such sweet relations and renounces these noble friendships in order to live spiritually only in God."

The past often returned to the surface, inundating his heart, and again it would become necessary to learn how to deprive himself of everything and to renew all in the unique love of the Lord. "How not to suffer atrociously when one leaves behind the souls whom one loved more than oneself! . . . But the acts of submission that are most costly are also the most powerful over the heart of God. Only those who have already known, before entering here, the inexpressible and very delicate joy of caring for souls, or preaching, guiding, and following the invading action of God in hearts will be able to understand the painful struggles one experiences upon suddenly feeling the frightful void of apparent uselessness. . . ."

It was a strange reversal of perspectives. Formerly Lucien suffered from lack of contemplation because he had been deeply involved in all-encroaching activity. Now his suffering was reversed. It would have been a simple absurdity, and the act of an unstable disposition, had this swing occurred on the same motionless base. But Lucien was not motionless. Just as he had left Le Havre for Lille, he was now also on a long inner journey and his perspectives necessarily changed as they do during actual journeys. Keeping in mind his harsh criticism of his own activity before entering Carmel, what he would have liked now was a new activity, but one purified by the fire of contemplation. When one climbs mountains the first summits that seem to dominate everything are summits, to be sure, but in reality they are only spurs above the plain and they seem to be hardly anything more than hills alongside the increasingly higher peaks that are revealed in the immensity of a chain of mountaintops. Everything that was behind Lucien was really sacrificed and he now had but one desire: to plunge

further and further into the new defiles toward the final summits of
Carmel.

Then a single summit seemed to dominate all the rest, the summit
of death, but not out of romanticism or despair. For Lucien, death
was not the final slumber, the abyss of the tomb, but the ultimate
pinnacle of contemplation, the moment in which the secret presence
of God in the soul becomes evidence.

"I don't like that ugly word 'death' when it is really the true birth,
the birth to true life, to splendid eternity . . . the infinite satisfaction
of the soul in the indescribable embrace of the very being of God, in
union with all our rediscovered loved ones."

3   The Trees of Fontainebleau

One could not imagine a more enchanting solitude, a dwelling more bathed in peace, surrounded by a thousand forest fragrances and in the branches a thousand voices of birds as beautiful as the song of paradise. Only thirty-seven miles from Paris, this corner of the Ile de France on the Dijon line is as peaceful as a verdant wilderness. Built at the time of Anne of Austria, the old main section of the building lies below the church of Avon at the end of the village which serves as a tranquil neighbor to nearby and equally tranquil Fontainebleau encircled by its nearly forty thousand acres of forest. As soon as one arrives one is immersed in the fragrance of lined trees, almost a hundred years old, which stand before the entry to the convent on the Rue de la Charité. On the other side of the buildings one enters a vast garden bordered with yew trees, containing a vegetable patch planted in a pumped-out reservoir, small groves, and an ornamental lake shaded by a weeping willow tree as in old prints. Farther, still within the enclosure of the monastery, is "la solitude," a cottage used for retreats. Beyond this rise the tops of innumerable green trees, the legendary lane of elms that borders the entire length of the great canal; here one is very close to Porte Rouge at the end of the park of Fontainebleau opposite the celebrated palace haunted by kings and water nymphs.

The old convent had known long years of neglect after the laws of expulsion at the beginning of the century—not to speak of its misfortunes of other times. It was at various times a priory, a hospice, and even a seminary. It had emerged from all these vicissitudes in a rather dilapidated condition. At the end of World War I the

Carmelite nuns of Fontainebleau had purchased the property to present it as a gift to the Carmelite friars. Thus new years of life began for the ancient dwelling, but a life of silence and pure contemplation, with the arrival of a handful of old monks returning from exile.

Suddenly the peace and quiet were destroyed by a great din and uproar. Throughout the year 1934 the grounds reverberated to the noise of picks and shovels, the grating of wagons loaded with dirt, quivering pulleys lifting quarry stones, bricks, beams, girders, scaffoldings, and to the hammerings of roofers and glaziers. Then came the painters, constantly whistling as they worked, followed by trucks that halted in the lane and unloaded their cargoes of dishware, linen, tables, desks, and iron beds. Workers swarmed endlessly around all sides of the old convent which dumbly protested for a modicum of silence. At the same pace a new building was being constructed as an extension of the old structure next to the garden. Then one day in autumn, although the construction work was far from finished, about thirty young boys arrived, one after another, alone or in small groups. Carrying suitcases, they entered through the little door on the Rue de la Charité and began to take up positions under the giant trees. The youngsters were still daydreaming about their vacations, still green in their memories, yet already tremendously distant, ended. They walked around in a state of anxiety, boredom, and curiosity.

They did not have long to wait. Nobody ever waited long for him. He was already there with his quick voice, strong and authoritative, and his ardent eyes sunk deep in his ascetic face. He was the headmaster of this junior school of Avon, Père Jacques, recently come from Lille and hardly less surprised than his pupils to find himself present at this opening of a term.

Was it not only yesterday that he was still at the Lille convent, totally immersed in the meditations of the novitiate? No, there had been six months of this already, six months during which the stillness and the enclosure of the novitiate had been swept by a hurricane of goings and comings in connection with the preparations for setting up the junior school. Père Louis de la Trinité, the former novice-master at Lille, had become the Provincial of Paris and the Order had decided to establish a *juvenat*[1] close by the Avon convent.

The Carmelite friars have no teaching role. In principle a *juvenat* could be only a kind of petit séminaire receiving young boys desirous of becoming Carmelite friars, just as Lucien Bunel had formerly entered the Petit Séminaire through an inner call more powerful than all the obstacles in his path. However, the Order in no way wanted to establish an institution that would have resembled a kind of novitiate in miniature. "My wish," said the Provincial, "is that the boys in no sense play at being Carmelite friars, either in the refectory, or in their functions, or in their dress." No junior monks! Nor was it a question of putting pressure on the pupils to recruit them into the Order. The Order wanted only to open a center of education with a spiritual atmosphere, as when it arranged for sermons, retreats, or cultural projects. In a word, it was seeking to root itself once again in France after years of exile and to resume, under diverse forms, the active tasks suitable to the Order.

On March 14, 1934, Père Jacques was chosen headmaster of this junior school, dedicated to St. Thérèse of Lisieux. Père Jacques was stupefied by this complete reversal of his ordered way of life.

"You see," he wrote a friend, "I am just one more example of those who flee the world in order to find peace in silent contemplation, and whom God puts back in their former occupation to make supple their will and to mortify their too natural taste for complete solitude. Now I must wait for heaven to enjoy God, as I had dreamed of doing in the shadow of the cloister."

Here Père Jacques was simplifying things somewhat. His situation at the junior school of Avon in fact marked an exceptional change: save for a brief meeting every two weeks with the community of the monastery, he no longer participated in the routine of monastic life. He lived within the same walls as the other religious, but the Avon institution was as if cut in two. On the one hand was the cloister where the community pursued its traditional life, on the other the

[1] A church school where students preparing for a teaching career serve a kind of apprenticeship while reviewing a program of classical studies.

junior school where Père Jacques gave all his time to his task as educator, as he had in Le Havre. But this time it was as primary inspiration for young boys and Carmelite monk at the same time.

Although he was separated from the community, absorbed by innumerable occupations of a scholastic order, nothing of all he had discovered and lived during his novitiate years could be erased. There might be all the barriers, all the divisions of labor that one might imagine in the organization of life at Avon, but there was no impassable barrier in Père Jacques's soul. The junior school, dedicated to St. Thérèse of the child Jesus, is nestled in a small valley of Mount Carmel and it was as a passionate pilgrim of Carmel that Père Jacques was also the headmaster of the school.

There is no spring so royally pure, so delicious in its freshness and tang of the native soil that can be summed up in the formula H_2O. There is no freshness of soul or ardor of heart that lets itself be labeled by the term "headmaster." The way the day-to-day life of Père Jacques differed from that of any ordinary school principal or proctor can be translated only by the emotion, unique of its kind, of those who lived with him day after day. Some signs remain, however.

The sign which perhaps would suffice to make us understand everything is the love of beauty. Père Jacques defined his ideal by saying that the first thing he wanted in the school was a feeling of joy, because joy is that power of life that opens hearts, whereas sadness closes them. Joy must be fulfilled with beauty or it is stifled from the start. Père Jacques wanted the school to have nothing about it that would risk making the word "jail" rise to a boy's lips—no big dreary rooms where the child would feel alone, no walls with dull colors to daub out of boredom, no tasteless food, repetitious and monotonous, unappealing to the appetite. The monkish Père Jacques understood what *bon vivants* do not understand. He wanted "everything to laugh and sing, from the basement to the attic, that everything be studied—even to the last nail—so that it too could contribute its own original note of gaiety and proclaim throughout the day that the soul dwelling between these walls is a familial soul filled with trust and love."

He wrote this as a directive and carried it out. Why should it be necessary for scholastic ugliness to serve here as a foil in such close proximity to the palace and the forest? Pupils, proctors, and teachers all ate in the same refectory, but this old, hackneyed, disabused name truly underwent a change. Père Jacques insisted on having small tables and tablecloths in the dining hall of the college, tablecloths whose gay colors he selected himself, just as he had selected the colors of the sweaters worn by the soccer teams, just as he took some pupils to a Matisse or a Picasso exhibit, or to see Claudel's play *L'Annonce faite à Marie*, just as he revealed the delights and marvels of the forests to them on Thursdays and Sundays.

"In Balloy, we went out rowing," recounted Claude F. "Père Jacques showed me at nightfall a water lily dropping off to sleep, the branch of a reed bent in slumber and grazing the surface of the water. He taught me to enjoy the sun setting on the countryside weighed down and heavy with the labors of man, the prayer that rises with the night like a song of hope. He showed me God in a small blade of grass that bends under the weight of a ladybird, in the flowering of my strength in the freshness of a morning bath. He showed me God through Bach and Beethoven, and I enjoyed with him the song of love of painters and poets, the freshness of a symphony, the hymn of beauty of the countryside. Père Jacques taught me to sing, to chant my prayers, the expressions of my life, of my love, of my work. I enjoyed the shimmering of colors, the harmony of sounds, the purity of lines. I also learned the part that must be assigned to them in life, the way of loving them, of making them a reward for effort, an incentive to intelligence. It is to Père Jacques that I owe my power to stop in the midst of work to look upon a landscape, a flower, a painting."

Where the devil (for it's a good time to talk about the devil) did one get the idea that religion is the enemy of Creation? Or that the love of Francis of Assisi for flowers, stars, and birds represents an exquisite exception, bordering on heresy? There is no mystic of Carmel who does not lovingly enjoy what God created with love. There is nothing pantheistic or epicurean in this appreciation of nature, nothing easy or facile in this love. Love, beauty, yes, but

Père Jacques wanted them to be loved with a virile heart. In order to enjoy the marvels of the heights from the top of the mountain, there must be no fear of its hardships or precipitous paths. Entering his school was a trial of a disconcerting kind.

"It was in the summer of 1934 that I got to know Père Jacques," confided Louis M. "For a child of nine and a half a visit to a school is an impressive thing. To be introduced to the headmaster affects him even more, and this introduction involved the dark look and the severe face of Père Jacques; it was solemn and terrifying. My terror was so evident that Père Jacques compassionately took me with him to visit the house and to feed bread crumbs to the fish. He was so full of kindness that the word 'headmaster' lost all its solemnity for me and my greatest desire was to come to this school which only a few days before I had emphatically hoped never to see again."

"I enrolled at Avon in the third grade," declared André H., "in the second year after the opening of the junior school. One of the things that struck me immediately was Père Jacques's look; I confess that he frightened me very much. But this first impression disappeared very quickly when I got to know him a little better. And it was in his office, when we were summoned there, that we learned what Père Jacques was really like. His eyes peered into our innermost depths so well that nobody could hide anything from him."

"My first contact was in 1934," said Jacques A. "On one side a young boarding school boy, egotistical, unresponsive, mistrustful of and almost hateful toward adults, and on the other side Père Jacques. The contact was a shock for me. I was curious to see a religious because I had never been so close to one. I had a romantic conception of a monk. And even though Père Jacques did not have the big white beard and the sunken eyes I expected, I was not disappointed. His eyes were like two flames, his face ascetic. Despite the austerity of the setting, of his dress, when his look enveloped me, I did not feel the chill run down my back that I had counted on. On the contrary it seemed that a warm wave of sympathy went through me. Père Jacques was so constituted that for him a child

was a new and wonderful being—he had to get around him immediately and make him feel that he wanted only to be his friend. I
understood instantly that this man would be my confidant and
guide. I was reassured, less reticent. He satisfied my curiosity by
taking me on a tour of the grounds. He showed me the school not
as the place where he worked, but as my home, so that it would
not be *a* school but *my* school. He explained the use of each room,
described his projects, and asked my opinion. It made me feel important. For the first time in my student life, I was ready to give
my trust. Later I realized that this was not a reaction peculiar to
me, but that there were many others who came to him, reticent at
first, who came back trustful, not because he had dominated them
but because he had made them aware of themselves."

This first free and friendly contact, before or during vacations,
was one of Père Jacques's great powers, so that the beginning of the
school year was not like all the others, a launching into a cold and
unknown world, but rather the hope of finding the same warm welcome in a world already loved. Moreover, this opening day did not
have the formality traditionally required by regulations.

"Were we going to go through these dreary recreation periods, real
tortures for the pupils and the proctors?" Jacques A. went on. "No,
we knew at once that here our life would be free, open, and happy.
We were all brothers together in a game of 'hawk and bird,'[2] giving
confidence to us all. This hawk and bird game is the very image of
the school. Père Jacques did all that he did to train us in an exciting
game, that of life itself, in which he knew how to make us par-
ticipate by loving us to the best of his ability. And the game extended
beyond the limits of the school, it shattered our egocentricity."

"No, Père Jacques never fostered melancholy and his great ambi-
tion was to remain young, psychologically young, until death," said
J. Chegaray. "He was a good companion who told funny stories,

---

[2] A game in which there are two sides with the "hawk" in the middle. At a
signal the two sides try to change places and the hawk tries to catch as many as
he can. Those caught join him as hawks and the game goes on until everyone is
captured.

loved games, laughter, tomfoolery. During walks in the forest with his pupils his greatest delight was to trip them up, and to tease them by gently hitting them on the legs with his rope. In winter snowball fights were his passion. He had a horror of soccer because he played it so poorly, but like a child, he passionately loved the 'snatch the handkerchief' game, jubilant if his team won and very unhappy if it lost. Returning from such walks with his boys, he delighted in asking the most unexpected questions. 'What is the first thing you will do on arriving in heaven?' And when his pupils answered in a serious or reflective way, Père Jacques would say, 'When I get to heaven I'm going to run to shake hands with the good poets I love: Rostand, Baudelaire, Verlaine. . . .' "

Classwork became a game, an ardent sporting competition designed to inflame the desire to learn and win.

"In his classes," declared Dominique P., "he knew how to communicate the enthusiasm he had felt himself in reading the poets from François Villon to Claudel."

"He loved to read us selections from his favorite authors, readings during which he very often paused to digress," added André d'H. "We listened spellbound, and it was often only the bell that recalled us to the reality of things as Père Jacques left the classroom."

"A Latin word or a poem of Villon might be the taking-off point to discuss any problem from love to controversial social questions," said Jean M. "Sometimes Père Jacques would relate his past experiences to us and let his thoughts run along in a meditation full of charm. Other times it would be a discussion, often passionate, particularly on two favorite subjects, social problems and modern art. These digressions were our delight; we thought at the time that they were involuntary because Père Jacques simply could not avoid straying from the subject, but now I think just the opposite. He prepared them carefully in advance and gave great weight to them, and he was not mistaken. I am convinced that it was here that he carried out his essential groundwork."

The most beautiful roses have thorns but if they are true roses, no one gets angry at having been pricked. Louis M. never forgot this: "For me recitation in the religious instruction class was always a period of anxiety, terror, almost agony. I never studied my lessons and Père Jacques knew how to inspire fear in lazy pupils. No inertia, and mine was great, could resist such domination. Père Jacques, in fact, had a marvelous power to hit home, severely and spontaneously, with the two or three biting words necessary to dominate a situation. He 'took possession of us' without recourse to punishment or bad marks or any of the usual methods used on young people to give them a taste for obedience. . . . While my first year had been a torture, my second year became an exciting reward. He had the knack of dominating the imagination immediately by some introductory words, just as the public is drawn by a poster, a roll of drums. Then he would take us along on a magnificent verbal promenade so marvelously chosen that it made us regret the ringing of the bell at the end of the lecture."

The digressions, the passion for culture, the organization of teams in the classes were the least of Père Jacques's pedagogical secrets, for any imitator can pick them up. Père Jacques put all his ardor in all his contacts with his pupils, as when he brought oranges, books, or eau de Cologne every day to little Jean C. during the forty days he was in the Fontainebleau hospital with scarlet fever.

There was not one of his charges who was not a person for him. Did he demand perfection? Not at all. But Père Jacques did presuppose perfection as a principle, since he himself from time to time asked the pupils and their parents for criticism, inviting them to express their opinions frankly.

It is true that Père Jacques preferred to be extreme rather than slack. It is quite possible that at times his zeal made him go too far. But how often this violence allowed him to awaken the slumbering, to infuse strength into the weak! Even an expelled pupil remained ardently convinced of this: "I have a very vivid memory of the junior school, and of all of you," he wrote. "Père Jacques? I remember especially his look which radiated goodness, sweetness, joy, nobility, and the consuming ardor of an apostle. A marvelous look which, even though I was a child, astonished me and which I liked.

"But I was a youngster then and I could not understand the meaning of the education they were trying to give me there. I kicked over the traces. If I had remained at the school, I would certainly have been damned. Père Jacques understood this, and he had me expelled for my own good. He did it as only he could do it, and for me it is an unforgettable memory. After making his decision he summoned me to his office and talked to me like a father to his son. He blessed me and gave me a holy image which I still have and which I hope to keep forever.

"I have made my way in the world since then. And I have gone along the right lines. The seeds that Père Jacques planted in me against my will developed and the demon inside me is dead or nearly so. Hence I owe Père Jacques a debt of gratitude."

It is enough to leaf through the testimony of his former pupils, gathered by Père Philippe, to get an idea of Père Jacques's magnetic power. An indelible imprint? But an indelible imprint is revolting, because in its origin there is something about it of the branding iron, a shameless violation of love. This is what one never feels in this bundle of tender and enthusiastic confessions. One revolts against coercion because it is not a healthy and happy transformation of being, but love is never violation, and nothing breathes so much love as these reports of the former pupils of Père Jacques.

One day in the garden of the school of Avon, while all kinds of recollections were being discussed, teachers who had known Père Jacques began to talk about him:

M. Gonbaud: "Père Jacques had a great hold on his pupils. Right from the start the pupil knew that he was not an individual in the mass, but himself, and in Père Jacques he did not see a functionary of authority, but the man himself. After the event it is always hard to make others understand why a man exercised a profound influence through his own peculiar magnetism. All that one can say now is that Père Jacques was not a typical functionary who punctiliously carried out his role and then hastened to think about something else as soon as he had a free moment. Père Jacques thought about his role day and night, he lived only for that, and the boys felt it more than anyone else. This is why he succeeded where anybody else, even the most able and astute, would have failed. He loved with all his soul and there was an incomparable power, unique of its kind, in this love.

"Père Jacques," M. Gonbaud went on, "was very much inclined to play the dictator with parents in order to have a free hand. One day when an officer, the father of one of his pupils, imperiously asked him for a favor on behalf of his son, Père Jacques answered quite clearly that he didn't ask favors for the officer's soldiers and that he counted on reciprocal courtesy to the school. On the other hand, Père Jacques did not concern himself only with his pupils. There were about twelve lay teachers at the time of the school's greatest expansion when it had about ninety students, and Père Jacques did not consider that his job was over once he had paid his teachers. He showed a friendly concern in their personal difficulties and came to their aid more than once during the German occupation.

"Père Jacques," continued M. Gonbaud, "was quite a practical joker. He adored such jesting."

M. Tranchant was in complete agreement with all this, which did not prevent him from adding that Père Jacques, very much the Carmelite despite the whirl of his school activities, gave the impression of living in a continual state of inspired prayer, or in more simple language, in a constant and intense consciousness of the presence of God. On this point there was a great stir of diverse and vividly contrasting views.

"Père Jacques," said M. Trouillard, "was an ardent polemicist. He could be very caustic and sometimes provocative, as when he cited Gide with praise. Why? Primarily to stir people up. Naturally, he would have been the first to protest against an admirer of Gide, but he wanted to make people think. He did not admire mediocrity any more than evil. He was a trainer, sometimes with a good dose of naïveté and utopianism. But in the end everything contributed to making a peerless teacher out of him."

"He aroused passion in all discussion," confirmed M. Le Franc, "because he had a strong propensity always to take the opposite view of what was being said. On the other hand, he was very clever in his administrative affairs. He had a very mystical side to him but another that was most practical and prudent. Sometimes he had his disappointments with the pupils. Some of them, particularly some of the older ones, did not like his invitations to confidences: it's 'bunk,' they said, phony and sentimental. Sometimes also, when he had put a pupil on dry bread as the result of a serious misdemeanor, he would discover that the cook had put some nice little dishes aside to console and nourish the culprit. The pleasing thing about this was that Père Jacques never got angry. He let it be felt that a principle was a principle, but that gentleness also had its role. To him such rare exceptions had an excellent effect. They merely confirmed the rule. He participated spiritedly in the games with the boys, but as soon as the bell rang each of the children returned to his proper place."

"He stayed up very late because in addition to his double job as headmaster and teacher, he corresponded with a great many people whom he loved and guided from afar; he was a glutton for work," said M. Gonbaud, who knew something about this because he was often charged with the task of mailing Père Jacques's letters.

"Yet in the morning he showed up fresh and fit and smiling," declared M. Tranchant.

"Even though he sometimes fell asleep during the day," interjected M. Trouillard, "it seems that this happened only once in class, but more than once at teachers' meetings or on the evenings when there were outside lecturers he himself had invited. But he always woke up at the right moment, that is, at the last minute, just in time to thank the lecturer."

To trip a pupil during a game or to make a quick sally at a teacher passing by in the corridor was only casual child's play. But it often happened that Père Jacques wove real plots. On a certain night, April 1, 1937, he picked up the inside telephone and alerted a priest in the monastery that he had just seen two prowlers in the school courtyard. He pretended to be very disturbed. Then in a most sincere and anxious tone, he announced that the danger was drawing nearer and nearer, and that something had to be done. While the person who had been called hesitated at the other end of the wire, an accomplice standing at Père Jacques's side struck a violent blow on a drum, finishing by smashing an old window all prepared in advance, while Père Jacques gurgled into the mouthpiece with an imperturbable trailing off of his voice. Then he hung up the receiver, and in a delighted tone declared, "That's it! It went over. I heard him say, 'Père Jacques has been assassinated!'" An instant later the entire establishment was agog with excitement, and even the monastery bell chimed in. Père Jacques had taken care to cut off communication with the outside so that nobody would call the police.

"One must not forget that a child loves laughter," he wrote in a serious vein. "He is just beginning his life, he has not yet experienced any of the wickedness of existence. He has trust in everything and everybody. Everything in him knows the joyous thrust of life. The normal child is not sad because everything in him sings."

Père Jacques would have not understood this so well if he himself had not also remained a child. Yet he could be very demanding when the occasion required: "Watch the details carefully, my little ones," he would often say in his Saturday night instructions. "There is nothing that is of no importance. I want the beds lined up straight in the dormitory, tidy cabinets in the lavatories. Watch out in the refectory: no elbows on the tables, no noise with the chairs, keep your tablecloths clean, don't waste the bread. Bread is a sacred thing! I don't want a single nail, a single drawing pin in the walls, not a single scrawl on the tables. Anyone who puts his initials on the desk will become its owner. He can take it home with him if he wishes, and I'll have it replaced at his expense."

Men act much more by what they are than by what they say, and even by what they do or seem to do. Viewed one by one there was nothing unusual about Père Jacques's remarks and exploits: sometimes he was the chief of the establishment who was a stickler for discipline, sometimes he showed himself to be easygoing and compassionate and even prankish, and the whole might seem like the results of an unstable disposition. If this sufficed to summarize it the alumni of Avon would not have preserved such a vivid memory of Père Jacques. The value of his sharper remarks depended on the fact that the pupils knew of his affection for them, and reciprocally the value of his clemencies depended on the fact they knew him to be capable of severity. The manifestations alternated, but the essence did not. He was at one and the same time both one and the other, for Père Jacques was all of one piece.

If he had a method, it could not be summarized in a few more or less important principles; it was his complete absence of method that showed him to be first of all humane. For his primary aims, to awaken souls and to form characters, cannot be expressed in pre-fabricated formulas; it is an adventure that must be acted out.

"True education," he wrote, "the only one that gives complete and definite results, consists in *teaching children to make use of their freedom.*

"I believe this is the most important point. One must realize that the child is born to be free, that he is very conscious of and avid for his freedom, and that he does not allow anyone to meddle with this precious right. . . . The child must feel in his teacher a true and deep respect for his liberty. Sometimes the teacher should even insist that the child become more clearly conscious of this freedom. . . .

"Too many educators and parents believe that education consists above all in imposing their personal views on the child by means of unquestioned authority. Too often adults wish young people to live an outmoded form of life!

"You must know your profession. And the profession makes this fundamental requirement: respect the person of the child, his life impulse, his freedom. Your role will be not to break the lively spontaneity of your children, but to teach them, by following step by step in a climate of trust and confidence, always to use better their freedom as men."

This was his aim and his means of achieving it. He led his students toward it by all kinds of experiments. One day, for example, he left them alone, without supervision, to write a composition. Before vanishing he made it amply clear to them that the lack of supervision was not an oversight, but a test of their characters, hence much more important than the composition.

"I shall leave you alone," he concluded. "You will not copy from one another. Now if any of you feel that you cannot resist temptation you may leave the room with me or go and sit in another classroom so that you will feel entirely relaxed."

In short, he drove his pupils into a corner. They had to take the initiative, make a choice: either the courage of self-discipline or the courage of sincerity.

Said Augustin de C.: "We were able to confirm that with very rare exceptions the compositions were written without incident. I believe that I can also say that we were much more concerned to be beyond reproach once we were left on our own rather than when we were under surveillance."

But Père Jacques had not brought off such experiments success-fully at first. On a certain night, during the school's first year, he had left the dormitory unsupervised as a test. Passing through the corridor, the assistant headmaster, Père Philippe, heard the sound of muffled laughter and then suddenly a small mocking voice, "It's going to be hilarious, he still wants to trust us!"

In view of Père Jacques's orders, Père Philippe did not intervene, but went to find the headmaster and blurted out: "Not worth much, your system!"

"Yes, yes, but you will see. This is only the beginning. It must go gradually. You have no faith. . . ."

Père Jacques had faith, he held out, and patiently began all over again. He even organized whole days without supervision, prepared long in advance. To be sure, this was not done every day and Père Jacques's incredible influence was necessary for the success of such days; they were islands of freedom which illuminated the entire life of the school.

"Let us frankly confess," said Père Jacques, "that every time we have wanted to inspire respect in children through external compulsion and by using threats, we have failed. For it is a failure when discipline is obtained only by the fear of punishment, whereas nearly always an appreciable result is obtained, even from undisciplined children, when one uses gentleness. How many times during days when the children's restlessness rubbed off on the teacher have we gently requested complete silence and then asked their good will in a low tone with a few words springing from the heart, spoken slowly one by one? The effect was always the same: one had the impression that in this charged atmosphere where a word of reproach would have produced an even greater tension, the words chosen for their gentle and strong simplicity relaxed nerves, lightened the atmosphere, and discharged the accumulated tension."

"There are no bad pupils," he repeated hundreds of times, "but only bad educators!" To which the teachers replied, "There are no bad teachers, there are only bad headmasters!"

Père Jacques could not prevent himself from smiling at this repartee, but he was not disarmed and retorted vigorously.

"We must will it!" he said to Père Philippe.

"But," objected Père Philippe, "will is not always powerful enough."

"Yes! When one wills, one can. But one must will!"

Père Jacques and Père Philippe were each scarcely more than thirty years old. They liked each other cordially, teased each other frequently, and their discussions got pretty lively at times. Père Jacques was always about to come up with something new and to upset regulations without consulting his colleague.

"The junior school," it was said, "is a meteor of which Père Jacques is the accelerator and Père Philippe the brake."

"From time to time I got the impression that I was running in all directions," confessed Père Philippe, "of being out of breath, of not being able to take it any more. In short, I had had enough. No ascent halted him, no descent scared him. At times I felt out of patience and fagged out. I longed for a calm and less hectic life."

Since he knew of Père Jacques's passion for Pascal and saw him perpetually running around in all directions, he shot this arrow at him with a smile, "You are a mass of contradictions!"

"I never said that!" was one of those phrases that recurred in Père Jacques's speech like a refrain: he was not afraid of contradicting himself because he had no system. For him there were only particular cases, not pupils whom one limits oneself to counting like samples of the same material, but souls, each of whom had its own color and its moments which sometimes called for reprimand and sometimes for clemency. There are people who educate by systems, just as there are people who think they can write poetry by versification. But true educators are like true poets: they need neither rhyme nor systems, they create poetry, they educate, just as easily as they breathe. Thus, Père Jacques was very fond of this saying of Don Bosco who was an extraordinary awakener of souls: "There is no method of education, there are educators."

To rear a child is to show him how to become the master of his freedom. This does not boil down to a system of restrictions or rewards: this gift of mastery and freedom is not learned like grammar or the multiplication table; it is communicated from soul to soul in the stream of life as it is lived.

One day a housewife was caught stealing wood and coal from the monastery grounds. What did Père Jacques do? He talked with her and discovered the poverty which had driven her to do this. Then he authorized her to take home as much wood and coal as she needed to keep warm during the winter.

His ascendancy over persons, his contradictions, have no other secret except the love such as Christ teaches at length in the parables.

"We all noticed how well he knew how to adapt himself to the character of each of us. We all loved these little affectionate words that he would whisper in our ear during the morning study hour or in the evening in the dormitory. He knew immediately if something was not going right, and calling us into his office he would restore our courage and bring joy to our hearts with a few affectionate and fatherly words," said Pierre M.

"One could go see him any time one wished," said Jean F. "And in his office one was with a real friend, not the headmaster of a school."

"I liked to talk with Père Jacques," said André d'H., "and I remember a conversation that lasted more than two hours. I was seventeen then. From that day on I would have followed Père Jacques anywhere, so great was my trust in him."

"All the religious training of the school would have been most wearisome, indeed even impossible," declared Louis P., "had it not been for the radiant holiness of Père Jacques. His burning love of Christ showed through all his works. . . . It was enough just to see him pray for prayers to come immediately to our own lips."

"His prayers," added Claude F., "revealed to me throughout my stay at Avon just how artificial and conventional was my faith. Then I began to pray in his sense and it was a revelation which it would be vain for me to try to describe."

"I was always particularly struck by Père Jacques's aspect of joyous holiness, above all at the moment of the elevation during his Mass," recalled Xavier de V. "At such a moment it seemed to me that he was talking with God as to a person close at hand."

Père Jacques took great care to see that this intimate life of faith sprang up in freedom in each pupil. Mass was not obligatory during the week and he never imposed an obligatory day of Communion on his pupils, not even on Sunday.

"Above all do not forget, my boys," he said to them, "that you are not obliged to receive Communion. Each must follow his own conscience."

Once he roundly reprimanded a pupil who came to see him with a pious air and who announced that he had received Communion to please Père Jacques. He had a horror of Jansenism and he would not have prevented the boys from taking Communion frequently. But he had no less a horror of imposing love, even by sentimental stratagems. On the other hand, what he did practice very much was the "little evening chat" in imitation of Don Bosco.

These chats were not sermons as much as they were a kind of recapitulation and blending of all that he had said, or listened to from each one of them during the preceding days. They were not simple passwords to prayer or study, but frank talks on the life of Christ, the lives of saints and heroes, the problems of love, social questions, all evoked in the light of the future and of love.

"He spoke slowly, very gently, so gently it was like a prayer. From the first words we were all captivated. The atmosphere of this room was truly extraordinary, for each one felt himself directly touched and moved—not because Père Jacques was a very good orator but because of the conviction that he put into his words. And if the comparison is possible, the words of the disciples at Emmaus could very well be applied to us, 'Was not our heart burning within us, whilst he spoke? . . .' "

4   "Only Love Has Worth"

Late at night, while everybody slept, within the inner court of the junior school the light burned in the headmaster's window. He watched, prayed, and disposed of the pile of correspondence from all those who from afar had begged him for a letter of affection and support. Day and night, in the soul of Père Jacques, the lamp of Mount Carmel kept vigil.

In 1935, a year after his arrival at the school, he took his perpetual vows. It was not just a rite, it was the essence of his life that was at stake, the bond that forged a unity of all his occupations.

"In the midst of all this I try to preserve my peaceful contemplation," Père Jacques wrote to the Carmelites of Le Havre. "From time to time I escape into a grove and there, forgetting the worry of my office, I immerse myself in God as best I can and I am appeased in Him."

If he had contented himself with meditation in the groves of Avon, one would have never known what was going on inside him. But when he left to preach retreats in the Carmelite convents—at Le Havre, Chaville, Verdun, Pontoise, or in Lisieux—what he said at these places disclosed the secrets of his soul. At such times the living waters of contemplation, subterranean, hidden under the sand dunes of the scholastic life, flowed in great waves. As he talked the Carmelite nuns on the opposite side of the grille copied down what he said, assembling his words that they might read and meditate upon them later. Now that Père Jacques is no longer with us, what remains is the thick bundle of these notes. They do not represent

everything that Père Jacques said, but they are the testimony, intact
and living, of everything that the Carmelites heard from him that
they preserved.

"Prayer," he said at Chaville, "is the heart of man in the heart
of God, it is the eyes of a poor being loving in the eyes of God;
it is the silent soul, wordless before God, bent eagerly toward God,
melting with love before God, wearying of its God, weeping with
weariness of God, frightfully tormented by a terrible hunger for
God and seeking in the flight of its outpouring to seize God, to embrace Him, to embrace Him without end. . . .

"The soul savors the exquisite joy of loving God, it savors above
all the love that God pours into it. It savors the contact with God
because the soul touches God in prayer. And at the same time it
suffers because here below the soul can gather up only crumbs, and
the soul has an absolute, infinite hunger for all of God.

"And what is called prayer, the hour of prayer, is an intensification
of this intercourse of friendship, it is a repose of the body that permits the soul to go to God completely, to plunge itself into God,
to surfeit itself fully of God.

"There is no need for a prelude, for a preparation, for a complicated system. The body sinks to its knees when it has time, leisure,
when its exigencies permit, and suddenly *the soul loses itself in
God, in the living God,* in God touched there, in Himself, in God
who envelops the soul, in God whom the soul sees obscurely, darkly,
in God whom one contemplates without sound, without words, with
whom the heart nourishes itself without knowing how.

"But this prayer, which is thus so intense at certain moments,
continues always, everywhere—this prayer always continues in the
depths of the soul, as one who walks in flat open country notices
fields in the immediate foreground without raising his eyes to the
horizon, but is aware of it even though he is not looking at it. For
the soul throughout the day there is a supernatural and divine
horizon which encompasses all the actions and works which it
undertakes."

One could not make a more candid, a clearer confidence. It is most clear that he who speaks in this way is something other than a pious commentator on John of the Cross or Teresa of Avila. In each word, one glimpses again the little boy of Barentin who already had the taste for contemplative prayer, and Père Jacques, while directing his school at Avon, felt this supernatural horizon all around him, this mysterious horizon of life that everywhere adds a dimension of heaven to the three dimensions of space.

"Silence," he told them further, "is not an empty word. Silence is not nothingness. Silence is not an absence of thought. Silence is a richness, it is a thought too rich and too personal to share with others. . . .

"Mary prayed in silence. And it was in the silence of this silent, withdrawn prayer that Mary heard the voice of the Angel. She would not have heard it had she not been silent. All the silence of prayer is necessary to hear and recognize the voice of God, the call of God, the desire of God in a soul.

"And every soul of silence tests the same divine communication. God takes possession of a soul, a mysterious embrace, a profound, living, and personal embrace in which one feels that a mysterious being is present who envelops us, who takes us, who holds us captive, who preserves us forever. When God takes possession of a soul in this way and draws it to the most profound depths of itself, this soul becomes silence.

"The saints walked soundlessly, looking for quiet corners, suffering at being compelled to mix with the crowd or to appear in public. The great movement of souls gripped by God is typified by hermits fleeing to the desert. . . . Our first Fathers were hermits, souls eager for solitude and silence, souls greedy for silence, who hid themselves in the mountains for days, weeks, and months to listen to the *divine depth of silence.* . . .

"Our soul, if it wishes to realize its destiny profoundly, if it wishes to find God, must shed itself of itself, without keeping a thing for itself in order to let God take possession of everything in it. *Now silence, more than anything else, detaches the soul from itself, renders a soul virginal, silence gives it God.* . . .

"We must therefore hold to silence according to the possibilities of the duties of our state of life, we must establish and respect the various degrees of silence: material silence, as long as it is not necessary to break it; silence of the lips; silence of the imagination which one does not allow to roam in moments when one should be meditating; silence of the heart that does not permit itself useless tenderness; silence of the spirit that mortifies its natural curiosities to reserve itself solely to the questions which are of God, in the greatest measure possible.

"A total, virginal silence. But a silence which above all is a silence of the depths, as in the ocean. The ocean deeps are troubled by nothing while the surface is furrowed by boats that come and go. If the surface of our life is ruffled by different problems, by multiple cares, it is necessary that the depths of the soul be steeped in silence —there where God is found, there where God is recognized, there where one loves God.

"For this blessed silence, this silence charged with God, is made up of deep prayer, but it does not prevent and should not hamper the duty of one's state. If one must animate all our enterprises and houses with joy, our games and activities, it must be done without harming this profound silence, for underneath the surface of a restless person, the soul ever remains in the presence of God."

Another day, after Mass, at the Carmelite convent of Pontoise, he told the religious the story of Zacchaeus who, being short of stature, climbed up into a tree so that he could see Christ above the heads of the crowd. Jesus saw him, spoke to him, and Zacchaeus sold all his possessions for the poor.

"The fact is that one cannot see Christ and remain what one is; one cannot exchange a glance with Christ and not be overcome to the point of total conversion. If we are lukewarm, still attached to our comforts, if we do not profoundly fulfill the requirements of our monastic vows, it is because we have not exchanged a glance with Christ, because we have not really 'seen' Christ. And that is what I would like to help you to do: to lead you up to Christ so that in the silence of your retreat you could exchange a glance with Him, a true glance, a living glance, in a real contact and not something that is the fruit of the imagination, but the reality of things as they are. Christ is a living being, who is there, who is in His own home here, but in order to see Him one must do as did Zacchaeus, one must make oneself poor, otherwise the weight of the world's possessions drives Him away. When one is rich one is burdened down; one must be short, that is to say not be rich in worldly goods; to be rich is to have earthly desires, to be held back by something of this world.

"What is sanctity?" he asked one day while addressing the Community of Le Havre. "In the world one is easily mistaken about saintliness. As a consequence of the deformation of the true idea of sanctity, as the consequence of a whole baneful literature that one finds among many of those who have written lives of saints, above all in the nineteenth century, many think there is no saintliness without a parade of penance and frightening torments, numerous, very numerous vocal prayers, vigils, exhausting fasts, and so on. All that is explained, emphasized in the lives of saints, and almost exclusively so.

"Among religious souls it is easy to confuse saintliness, with its special tastes and favors, with all that flowers around sanctity as weeds sprout up around a rosebush. This is not the essential thing, neither are the visions nor the ecstasies. . . . Saintliness is no more in penances that crush the body than it is in the ecstasy that transports the soul far from the senses. . . .

"Only *love* has value. What God seeks in us is not a quantity of material works, it is a hymn of love that rises from the bottom of the heart, composed of strophes of contemplation or action, it matters little which, provided that it is a melody of love. The saints have never attached importance to what their hands do, they did what they had to do but they did it for love. . . .

"Love of *sanctity* and not love of *sensibility*. Certain souls believe themselves near saintliness because charity comes easily to them; tender sentiments toward God, good actions toward others, and so on. The *love of sanctity fuses with total abandonment*. When the soul has understood that *only* love counts and that God is Providence and directs *all*, then this soul abandons itself fully. A single concern: to know the will of God. For the rest, disagreeable or agreeable tasks or duties, joys or pains, rest or work, and so on—everything is a gift of God for the soul. *A saint is one who perpetually says yes to God.* This is the 'so be it' of the Virgin. Our angels bring us little annunciations from God at every moment. . . ."

"But," a Carmelite nun in Le Havre asked him, "how does God act toward souls removed from Him?"

"God concerns Himself with them much more than with others," he answered. "God is the Father. In a family do not the parents show more solicitude and affection for the sick and unfortunate children than they do for the others?"

Another Carmelite nun told him that she was tormented by anxieties and doubts about the faith.

"If death surprises me in this state, how will God receive me?"

"But God will receive you as he received Our Lord at His death. . . . Our Lord wanted to know by experience all our sufferings, and He wanted to experience this apparent abandonment by God. . . .

"We must love so much," he said further to the Carmelites of Le Havre, "that our love, by throwing itself against this veil that hides God from us here below, spreads the meshes apart so that the rays of a pure divine light, freely darting at our soul, consume it with love."

And when the Prioress expressed amazement to hear him preach on death on Easter Day, he exclaimed, "Just think, ma Mère, *to see God, to see God!*"

5   Five Hundred Signatures

The years passed and while Père Jacques seemed more and more absorbed by his duties as a teacher and headmaster, he remained a true Carmelite, ardent in contemplation. He demonstrated admirably that contemplation is not opposed to action but to blinkers. It is the achievement of not losing sight, from a distance, of the spiritual horizon which without our knowledge never ceases to accompany life, but which is not alien to the contemplative. Contemplation is not opposed to action as is heaven to the earth, dream to reality. On the contrary it is the refusal to make a separation between divine and human life, between heaven and earth.

There were not two Pères Jacques, one lost in dreams and ecstasies, the other regretfully forgetting his status as a monk in order to teach Greek or to count the sacks of potatoes in the school storeroom. There was but a single Père Jacques for whom work and contemplation were one: there was now no longer in him that inner opposition that had made the years so difficult for him at Le Havre. In the crucible of the novitiate he prepared himself to forge action and contemplation into a single life, for there are not two religious lives but only one, just as there is but a single divine life, a single love.

The years passed and when Père Jacques was called up for the war in 1939, he lived for his comrades with all his strength, just as he had lived for his pupils. There was no reopening of the school in the autumn of 1939. The junior school was turned into an auxiliary hospital of the Red Cross, and Père Jacques became the sergeant-major of the 21st Artillery Battery in the east, in Bazailles at first, then in Remenoncourt where he spent the whole winter.

Billeted at Madame Comon's farmhouse, Père Jacques lived in an enormous room cluttered with discarded furniture, and he was glad to have an old cot equipped with a spring carefully battered by the years. He celebrated Mass every morning in the opposite corner, after placing a white cloth on a chest and hanging a white curtain against the wall.

Once again he had his "little cell, silent and solitary." Did he himself not call it his "Duruelo" in memory of the first foundation of St. John of the Cross? But before long this quasi-monastic cell was filled with visitors, like his room at Le Havre.

"Père Jacques," recounted Madame Comon, "had a stove put in his 'Duruelo.' He lit it every morning before Mass for the intention of the faithful, and in the evening when his comrades gathered in his room. The stove remained empty for the rest of the time even though it was very cold, freezing! When he came to see us to give François—the little boy of the house—his evening lesson the temptation to offer him a cup of piping hot tea was strong, but I was always afraid that he would answer with a gentle smile of stubborn refusal. Nothing led Père Jacques to go where he did not want to go. Nevertheless, one time when he was coughing pitifully François' aunt just could not restrain herself from putting a cup of tea in his hands with a determined air of authority. 'Oh! Oh! mademoiselle, you have a natural aptitude for command!' he declared, surprised and amused, while submitting with good grace."

In the evening he organized gatherings. It was the period of the "phony war" and the worst enemy then was idleness, the father of boredom and demoralization. Thus Père Jacques did not dream of locking himself up in contemplation like a hermit. His "Duruelo" was an assembly point for free hours, a crossroads of encounter, study, and action. He organized friendly talks and discussions on all kinds of social and religious questions. Once again he acted as an educator and a trainer of souls. And always with the same success.

But not to everybody's taste. Keenly patriotic and respectful of military discipline, he was all the more outraged when he saw officers gorge themselves while their soldiers were poorly lodged and fed, and no less so at the sight of noncoms who took pleasure in ordering the heads of their soldiers shaved by way of punishment. Père Jacques did not think much of such practices; he did not exactly place them in the category of necessary sacrifices, and he said so. In short, he was looked upon with disfavor by some of the officers in his unit, and cast aside in a kind of semidisgrace, of which, however, he took advantage in order to increase his pastoral work among the men.

When he could do nothing, he left the barracks and would walk for hours in the snow-covered Lorraine countryside.

"I love a hard life for the body and muscles, but all bathed in contemplation. Here, I sate myself with poetry. Everything seems beautiful to me. Often I roam alone through the countryside—the Lorraine countryside with immense wind-swept horizons—and I look, I look. . . . Everything always seems new to me! In the heart of winter when it was well below zero I would take off through the snow, whipped by a north wind, for miles and miles. I never could tire of discovering the infinite variety of colors and songs that are found everywhere here."

In February, 1940, it was learned that he would be transferred and assigned to the chaplaincy of the division. Suddenly there was a great stir of excitement in the battery and the following petition was circulated:

"February 24, 1940: The noncommissioned officers and the gunners of the 21st Battery have been deeply affected by the decision taken by Sergeant-Major Bunel to leave. Without disregarding the value of the reasons which he cites in requesting a new assignment, they urge him to take into consideration the affection and attachment that everybody feels for him. Accustomed to seeing him among us, they have undoubtedly not made felt the appreciation which animates their feelings with regard to him. But today they beseech him to reconsider his decision and to continue to perform beside them his everyday duties which have ever been a source of great joy."

Five hundred names were affixed to the petition. But it was too late. In the face of the animosity of some in the unit, Père Jacques preferred to leave.

Taken prisoner in June, 1940, he began to play the same role among his fellow captives. Although he had not yet been named a divisional chaplain, he was liberated as such in November, 1940.

It was a stroke of luck. But it was to cost him his life.

6   "Priests Are Needed in the Prisons"

In a certain way the three years that followed the return of Père Jacques to Avon were only a continuation of the years prior to the "phony war." Once again he became headmaster and teacher. But to the horizon of divine contemplation was added another, that of a time of oppression. The German occupation made its mark deeply felt. The reopening of the junior school did not take place until January, 1941, with only about fifteen pupils. Père Louis de la Trinité, the Provincial and a former naval officer, had returned to the sea and become the admiral of Argenlieu in the service of Free France. The new Provincial, Père Philippe, used his "leisure" to establish contacts with the first general staff of the Resistance, notably Jean Moulin and Pierre Brossolette.

Events, however, became constantly more somber and horrible. On January 22, 1942, Cardinal Suhard transmitted an official protest to the Vichy government in the name of the cardinals and archbishops of the occupied zone:

"Deeply moved by the reports brought to our attention of the mass arrests of Jews carried out last week, and of the harsh treatment that has been inflicted on them, notably in the Vélodrome d'Hiver, we cannot suppress the cry of our conscience. It is in the name of humanity and of Christian principles that our voice is raised in a protestation on behalf of the inviolable rights of the human person. It is also an anguished appeal of compassion for these immeasurable sufferings, above all for those that afflict so many mothers and children."

The year 1943 saw the establishment of the Service du Travail

141

Obligatoire (Obligatory Work Service), that is, the mass shipment of young workers to Germany. A new protest on the part of Cardinals Suhard, Liénart, and Gerlier condemned this abuse of power and legitimized in advance all disobedience. Each time the cardinals protested a propaganda campaign was launched in the "collaboration" press accusing the cardinals and bishops of being Judaized, Stalinists, or anarchists.

Père Jacques, in agreement with Père Philippe, made the junior school into a relief center for the victims of Nazism. There he offered refuge for months to five seminarians of Saint-Sulpice threatened with shipment to Germany, Maurice, a young manservant of Jewish origin, M. Lucien Weill, a teacher at the Lycée Carnot, and many other transients in flight. With the beginning of the 1942-1943 school year, Père Jacques enrolled three young Jewish boys as students under the assumed names of Jean Bonnet, Maurice Sabatier, and Jacques Dupré.

In October, 1943, Père Jacques was warned that denunciations were feared in connection with the three unfortunate boys. He tried to hide them elsewhere but this was impossible since he could find nobody to take them in. So he kept them at the school.

"Sometimes I am criticized for my imprudence," he declared one day to Colonel de Larminat, a member of the resistance committee of Fontainebleau. I am told that since I am in charge of and responsible for the children of the junior school, I have no right to expose myself to being arrested some day by the Germans. But don't you think that if that happened, and if by chance I were shot, I would thus be leaving my pupils an example that would be worth more to them than all the instructions I could give them?"

He sensed the danger to be more and more imminent, and on January 13, 1944, he wrote his brother René, "It is very possible that before long something will happen to me. *If I am shot, rejoice, for I shall have realized my ideal: to give up my life for those who suffer.*"

He foresaw everything so well that he gave one of his teachers, the father of six children, a check representing a year's salary.

Suddenly on January 15, 1944, at a quarter past ten in the morning, while Père Jacques was giving a French lesson to the first-year pupils, the thud of boots was heard in the front courtyard under the linden trees. It was the Gestapo. Led by a man named Korff, the Nazi police burst into the room. Père Jacques was snatched away from his class, isolated, and taken to a room where he was kept under constant armed guard. At the same time and in the same way the Gestapo seized the three Jewish pupils and a seminarian escaping the Obligatory Work Service, who were herded together in another room. Only the little Jewish servant, Maurice, miraculously escaped. He had curled up in a closet of the infirmary and some student accomplices had piled up a load of firewood in front of it. When the Gestapo searched the establishment, a policeman glanced at the woodpile, kicked lightly at a log, and then went off without looking more closely. Moreover, the search was poorly organized; they inspected only the storeroom and the classrooms, but not the rooms of the teachers who hastily got rid of their compromising papers. Korff doggedly conducted a personal search of Père Jacques's quarters and found it hard to admit to himself that Père Jacques did not have a room of his own, aside from his headmaster's office, and nothing more than a monitor's bed in the older boys' dormitory. Evidently this did not correspond with his conception of power. Korff recouped his losses, however, in the office, where he unearthed a letter of a political prisoner, the ration card of André Lavavasseur, the former servant of the school, who had been shot the year before at Vesoul (as a member of the F.F.I. of the Guy Moquet resistance group), and a letter addressed to M. Gaud and Melun, an evader of the work law.

At eleven-thirty, everybody—the pupils, the teachers, and the staff—was ordered to assemble in the main courtyard under the linden trees.

"Are there still Jews among you?" shouted Korff.

"No," answered the boys.

"They're our comrades like the others!" cried one of the students, Germaine de M.

"You cannot be comrades with a Negro, you cannot be comrades with a Jew!" shouted back the Nazi.

Another Nazi came out with the ration cards seized in the storeroom and the roll call began in the freezing cold courtyard.

Meanwhile the three Jewish children had been led away, but not without having been subjected to rough treatment and vicious kicks. Then it was Père Jacques's turn. A few minutes before, while two of the teachers helped him pack his meager baggage, he had been as white as a sheet and trembling. But now he came out, his suitcase in his hand, his brown beret on his head. He appeared very calm. Suddenly he stopped in his tracks, looked at the mass of unmoving children and joyously cried out to them: "Au revoir, boys, see you soon!"

"Au revoir, Père Jacques!" shouted back the boys and teachers, and all of them, seized by an irresistible impulse, applauded frantically.

"Shut up!" Korff howled. "Shut up! Silence!"

Escorted by two bodyguards, one of whom carried his blankets, Père Jacques crossed the courtyard, climbed the little stairway to the Rue de la Charité and from there waved a great gesture of farewell. Never again was he to see the junior school.

In the courtyard the Gestapo gave their last orders.

"The school has hidden Jews and lawbreakers. The guilty one, your headmaster, has been arrested. In addition, the school must be completely vacated by three o'clock. You have the right to take your personal belongings with you. By three o'clock there is to be nobody left in the school."

By chance the Gestapo did not inspect the monastery. There they would have found young Carmelite friars who were also evading the work draft.

Pére Jacques was imprisoned at Fontainebleau, on the Rue Damesme. The administration was still lenient. He was given numerous books, he could have errands run for him by Frenchmen who were visiting other prisoners there, and he took advantage of this to request that the school pay its debts to several of its creditors. During this time Père Philippe vainly tried to obtain Père Jacques's release and to plead his case with Korff. In vain he told him it was he who had given Père Jacques the order to shelter the Jewish boys, that in any case it was not legally a crime, a fact acknowledged by Korff. But the Gestapo did not trust Père Jacques and it did not want to let him go now that he was in their hands. They suspected him also of having hidden those who evaded the work laws.

Later, through persons employed at Police Headquarters, it was learned what went on during the interrogations to which Père Jacques was subjected:

"What do you think of the laws of Vichy?" asked Korff one day.

"You will have occasion to talk to me again about them in a year or two," replied his prisoner.

"And the laws of the Reich?"

"I do not know them; I know only one law, that of the Gospel and of charity. Shoot me, if you wish. I am not afraid of dying, quite the contrary! It would be the greatest joy for me. Rather than killing fathers of families, and making widows and orphans, take me and shoot me! You do not frighten me and death was not created to frighten me."

Korff was the wretched individual who several months later, in July, killed five religious of the Oblates of Mary Immaculate at the scholasticate of La Brosse-Montceaux. After torturing them, he had seventy others deported. Strangely enough, he did not flare up at Père Jacques and subjected him to no violence. In front of his prisoner and in the presence of Père Philippe he even confessed: "What a man! He has only one fault, that of not being a Nazi!"

But he did not release him nor did he have him shot. Père Jacques had been reserved for an even worse fate. While waiting to know what was going to happen to him he was kept in a narrow cell on the ground floor of the prison; it was too narrow for him to be able to move about for exercise and too dark to be able to read, except when the lights were on. Unexpectedly, two days after his arrest, Père Jacques saw a new prisoner being ushered into his cell. It was M. Guémard, a Fontainebleau electrician, who had been denounced as a Communist.

"The first thing that struck me on seeing this religious," said M.

Guémard, "was his candid and peaceful look. Absolutely nothing in
his face would make one guess the kind of a place in which we
found ourselves. Instinctively we shook hands as though we had
arranged to meet. That very evening we had become something
more than friends, real brothers. I have never known anyone who
knew how to find such comforting words, spoken so naturally, in
such a difficult situation. By that very evening I had stopped worry-
ing, my morale had been restored, and I even remember that I slept
as well as in my own house despite the cold and the planks that
served for beds. The next day anyone seeing us would have assumed
that we had known each other for at least a year."

The two of them played checkers interminably. In between games
Père Jacques told thrilling stories about prison escapes that he had
heard about when he himself had been a prisoner of war in Luné-
ville: stories about prisoners who vanished in a watering cart, or of
a prisoner who talked to himself while marching behind the guard
in order to give his comrade time to escape before the warning
signal could be sounded. Guémard, for his part, showed off his
repertory of songs and his talents as an acrobat. They made plans
for the future. Père Jacques asked Guémard to help him set up a
small tool and lathe shop after the war so that his pupils, future
industrialists and engineers, would know something about manual
labor. Père Jacques's great regret was that he was never in a position
to offer scholarships to his school to the sons of workers.

They were not without news and support from the outside world.
Mère Marie, Superior of the Sisters of St. Joseph de Cluny who ran
a clinic nearby, sent four or five baskets of food to the prison every
day. She was assisted by Père Marie-Léon, the clinic chaplain, who
spoke German fluently and who served as intermediary with the
jailers. They could get nothing out of them if they were members
of the Gestapo, but those of the Wehrmacht permitted many things
when cigars or cigarettes were slipped into their hands. Moreover
one of them, Willi, an Austrian Catholic, did not require this kind
of bribery to do anything in his power on behalf of the prisoners.
M. Guémard testified to the "kindness of two German guards,

Willi and Hartmann, both of whom made our life as prisoners tolerable—as well as the sergeant who often closed his eyes to what was going on." Madame Guémard also took advantage of this complaisance to pass on provisions to her husband.

"Père Jacques," said M. Guémard, "gave me about two-thirds of the gifts that were sent to him, and to please me he would take a little bit of what my wife sent me, but only to please me, and finally I really got annoyed."

On two occasions Père Jacques was able to celebrate Mass in the cell while Guémard stood guard before the spy hole. For a few minutes each day they were let out in the little courtyard for a breath of fresh air. Here they found other prisoners with whom they immediately became friends, particularly Charles Meyer, who was very moved to see Père Jacques in the same prison with him, for he had already met him at Thonery, near Avon, where Père Jacques had preached at a retreat that had greatly stirred his hearers.

One day Korff came into the cell unexpectedly. Guémard, who had not yet seen him in the prison, was stupefied to recognize him as a man whom he had seen in June, 1940, and with whom he had had a lively altercation because he had quite rightly suspected him of belonging to the fifth column.

On the following day, after Père Jacques had been subjected to a new interrogation, he was transferred to a different cell. He and Guémard embraced fraternally before taking leave of each other, then he was conducted to a large cell, furnished with two skylights and a stove, which already contained M. Binet, Abbé Talard, and M. Meyer. It was the latter who had intrigued with the guard Willi to have Père Jacques assigned to their cell when the order for his transfer was issued.

During this time of imprisonment Père Jacques had established a rule of life in this new kind of silent and monastic cell. "He immediately laid out a timetable for himself," testified M. Meyer, "but in a manner so as not to disturb his fellow inmates in any way. He asked us for permission to say prayers, and it was only on our request that prayers were said at the table or together in the evening. How

moving was the evening prayer by candlelight! In no circumstance
did Père Jacques ever seek any advantage or preference whatsoever.
'Always after the others, if anything is left' was his refrain. Thus
every day he asked how much of the food that we received from the
outside could be set aside for the more unfortunate prisoners. Père
Jacques would have performed the detail of sweeping out the cell
every day, and I had to quarrel with him many times to stop him
from emptying the bucket. 'Let me do it, Charles,' he said to me;
'the comrades must not say, "Who is this priest who doesn't want to
do anything?"'

"His influence, his heart, his gaiety, and his humor, always the
same, were for me the greatest benefit of my detention period. He
understood people and things so well!

"His greatest joy," added Charles Meyer, "was the day he saw
carried into the cell a small portable altar, which he had procured
with Willi's complicity. Always that kind Willi, whose son had
just been killed in the war. Père Jacques was very moved and he
decided to celebrate the first Mass in our cell for Willi's son. Willi
had gone out of his way to be good to us, but we were quite shocked
by this—after all he was our guard and all we had to look forward
to was a dreadful fate. But Père Jacques insisted and he was right.
There were five or six of us there during the Mass. Willi was also
there with his ring of jingling keys and he wept openly."

On February 25 Père Jacques managed to have a postal card
mailed secretly to one of his pupils: "Here I am completely accustomed to my new novitiate. The cloister is extremely narrow, at
least for the novices, but I am pleased to be able to send you these
few words. A curious novitiate, marked by ordeals of all kinds! I am
still undecided about my profession. Shall I take vows for a year?
for six months? I hesitate. Will my superiors even send me abroad?
It's their secret. At any rate I am smilingly optimistic about my
novitiate and my prospects. And I pray so much for my little ones
who are so dear to me. Don't answer this card, and for good reason.
J. Lermite [The Hermit]."

This remarkable humor did not conceal a deep truth. Père Jacques had not only made a personal oratory of the prison cell, he had also made it a center of charity, of true brotherhood. With an incredible tranquillity of spirit, he organized study centers even in the small triangular courtyard when the prisoners took their day's walk. Just as if he were still at the Avon school, at Le Havre, at Montlignon, or at Remenoncourt, he gave talks on morality, dogma, the mysteries of the faith, on all subjects touching on the Christian life.

This need for initiative, for linking spiritual reflection with charity and prayer and this gift of warmth and sympathy were unvarying traits of Père Jacques's character. During these brief moments of enclosed freedom, despite expectations of the worst atrocities, he was as cordial and as enterprising in the milieu of the prisoners as he had formerly been among students and conscripts. It was the same life but at the level of heroism.

"He unveiled his true spiritual countenance among his persecuted brothers," declared M. Junguenet, a fellow inmate. If he had experienced a great happiness in doing good in the deep glow of his monastic dedication, he was really born to the apostolate in prison. His road to Damascus, that is to say his new orientation on the road of evangelization, was the Rue Damesme. There he meditated, totally forgetting his personal situation over which he felt only joy and threw himself with passion *on the new path which, quite obviously, according to him, God had marked out for him.*

Père Jacques was transforming himself in great haste into what a prison had disclosed him to be, more solid and more devoted than anyone might have imagined him to be before.

"He lifted us above our human miseries," added the same witness, "and he made us enjoy the beauty of our faith."

At the beginning of March Willi informed his prisoner that he was soon to form part of a convoy to be dispatched to an unknown destination. Then, with the complicity of several guards, plans were made for a monastic reunion. On the morning of March 5, Père Jacques was suddenly pulled out of his cell and conducted to the guardroom, while the "brass" were on an outing somewhere. A veritable parade of persons stood facing him: Père Marie-Léon, Père

André, Père Philippe, and even a pupil, François-Xavier de Siéyès. While Père Marie-Léon talked steadily to the guards to keep them occupied, Père Philippe surreptitiously slipped some money to Père Jacques which would be useful for all purposes. They talked a long time.

"I felt Père Jacques's look, laden with intense affection," recounted the pupil who had come to the prison to see his former headmaster. "In me he saw the junior school for which he had sacrificed his rest, his health, the best of himself. Père Jacques had changed physically during the two months of his imprisonment. We were all affected by seeing him look so thin and in particular by the sight of his gaunt, emaciated face and his hollow eyes. And God knows fat was not his strong point at the junior school where he so overexerted himself. He had suffered from enteritis from which he had recovered thanks to the medicine that it had been possible to slip to him in the last few days. But he bore himself with nobility and assurance. He was wearing his homespun habit, he was freshly shaven and, at his request, that day Willi had even given him a monastic tonsure. Willi had asked Père Jacques for a photograph of himself and had said of the priest, 'He's a man; I'm proud of him.'

"One can expect certain human gestures from the guards, above all when they are alone, not being watched by a comrade, Père Jacques told me. But those who belong to the Gestapo, those present at the interrogations, are nothing but brutes. They are the ones, Père Jacques explained, who prescribe the torture, the most commonly employed being the 'bath,' leather whips, hanging by the wrists with the prisoner's hand tied behind his back, shoes lined with nails (a sort of vise in which the feet are broken), and others.

"Père Jacques had not been tortured but he described the condition of those whom he saw return from the cursed torture chamber every day. M. X. was forced to stay several nights in a basement cell with water up to his knees, and unable to sit down anywhere. The sinister Korff had said to him, 'You're too proud, I know how to humble you.'

"Père Philippe demanded insistently that Père Jacques leave the jail if he were liberated. But Père Jacques replied, 'No, really, I can't leave the prison without M. Mathery and without M. Canus, my companions in misery.' 'But M. Dumoncel (the mayor of Avon) is taking the necessary steps through his deputies,' answered Père Philippe. 'The result might be that everybody cannot be released at the same time, but you must leave as soon as it is possible to do so.' Père Jacques entreated them not to make an effort to obtain his freedom. 'Priests are needed in the prisons—if you only knew. . . .' "

Before the end of the conversation, Père Jacques knelt to make his confession to Père André.

That evening there was a new group of visitors, this time in the prison office. Père Marie-Léon had taken along Père Ernest, the Prior of Avon, M. Dulac, M. Tranchant, and M. Chegaray, all three teachers at the school and old friends of Père Jacques. Again Père Jacques insisted: he absolutely refused to be released unless M. Mathery and M. Canus were released along with him. He went so far as to return the ten thousand francs that Père Philippe had slipped into his hands that morning. He entrusted his fate entirely to the Lord.

On the next day, March 6, he was yanked out of his cell and herded together with about thirty other inmates, among whom were Meyer and Junguenet. They were locked up in a tarpaulin-covered truck, chained to each other two by two.

The truck roared out of Fontainebleau, escorted by two smaller vehicles, one in front and one in the rear, equipped with machine guns.

III
THE HELL ON THE
BANKS OF THE DANUBE

❖ ❖ ❖

1   "My Place Is Among My Comrades"

When the tarpaulin was raised the truck had stopped inside a camp. Still chained to one another the prisoners got off. Père Jacques was wearing his homespun Carmelite habit. Some SS men noticed this and immediately began to make fun of the new arrival. Charles Meyer, who knew German, did not miss a word of the refined SS pleasantries. Père Jacques not only did not try to guess, he insisted on knowing exactly what they said, and as if he were in class he asked Charles Meyer for an exact translation. The latter tried to avoid answering. The SS noticed this scene and one of them found it a good pretext to administer a vicious kick to Meyer in the seat of his pants. The "novitiate" had begun well.

The camp was located on the edge of a forest of the Ile de France, about two miles from a château almost as famous as that of Fontainebleau. Louis XVI met Marie-Antoinette there, and Napoleon Marie-Louise. Joan of Arc had been a prisoner in the nearby village, and the armistice of 1918 had been signed in a railroad car under the trees of the forest.

This was the camp of Compiègne, and it was situated exactly on the spot called Royallieu. In the way of a château the inmates had only barracks filled with pallets stacked on top of each other. When they came to Block 7, Père Jacques and Charles Meyer found their friend Paul Mathery, one of the faithful who had been at Père Jacques's Mass in the Fontainebleau prison. They spent their first night in this room.

Despite the welcoming kick, after months in a prison cell the camp régime seemed relatively liberal. The inmates were enclosed behind barbed wire, housed in barracks, and constantly in the menacing glare of searchlights. But they had nothing to do with the Nazis except twice a day, for the morning and evening roll calls. During the day, there were kitchen and cleaning details, and during the rest of the time the inmates were free to sleep, to walk around the barracks, and to talk among themselves. They could even play ball, read books, and listen to literary or scientific lectures given by the other inmates. In one of the barracks there was a chapel and a chaplain.

In short the treatment was similar to that of a prisoner-of-war camp. Captivity weighed heavily but after the isolation and confinement of a cell, one had the consolation of being together with many others and of being in the open air. Idleness is also a heavy burden, but it is less burdensome when borne along with others than alone within four cramped walls. Undoubtedly the thing most to be feared was anxiety about the morrow. For Compiègne was only a way station.

Newcomers arrived every morning, but every Monday morning fifty men were called out, set apart from the rest, and taken to an unknown destination. Nothing was known about their fate: one could expect the worst. It was not even certain whether death was the worst that could happen. Every Monday morning each one anxiously asked himself whether he would be called too.

About twenty-five hundred inmates were waiting for their fate inside these barracks. Most were French, except for some Italians and Spaniards. They were of all kinds, Communists and non-Communists, members of the resistance, black-market operators, and persons who were simply picked up during police raids. Nor were the professions less mixed up: workers and artisans rubbed elbows with teachers, priests, tradesmen, career officers. The two groups that stood out most strongly were the Communists and the priests. The former were the more numerous—about four hundred at the time of Père Jacques's arrival there; they formed a solid bloc, closely united, used to leading a communal life, to organizing material solidarity and clandestine political conferences. There were only seven or eight priests in the camp at that time; they had found a relative asylum in the chaplain's section where they lived apart for eating and sleeping. Every morning they celebrated Mass in the barracks that was used as a chapel.

The moment Père Jacques arrived he was offered a place in the chaplain's section as a matter of course. His reaction was immediate: "What, be set apart? Ah, no, my place is with my comrades."

It was a long time since he had known the old contradiction between the small enclosed community and the multitude. Now that he was on the route leading from one prison to another, the contradiction became all the sharper, but it was not one to shrink from. As soon as he arrived he found a way of getting a note through to the Prioress of Carmelite convent of Compiègne whom he knew very well.

"My dear Mother," he wrote her. "Here I am but a few steps away from you. This time I did not come to preach at a retreat or to hear confessions, but as a prisoner. I left Fontainebleau handcuffed, and this will remain one of the best and proudest memories of my life."

It was his joy. Christ too had been shackled before He was led to His torture. The apostles had known the same fate; they too were chained and led to their death. Père Jacques was overjoyed to be handcuffed for having hidden three little boys who belonged to the same race as Christ.

Then, as if to reassure the Prioress, he wrote: "I am glad to be among my comrades. The little caravan from Avon is still all together and gets along marvelously. All goes well. The food is decent. I can say my Mass every day. One can bring a five-kilo food package to the gate addressed to me."

There was a slight contradiction between the last sentences. The Carmelites were not confused by this, and they were quick to understand that Père Jacques depended on them to send food parcels. He continued: "Will you be good enough to pass my letter on to the Fathers at Avon so that they may know how happy I am to carry out this particular apostolate. What good comradeship here! What first-rate men one finds!"

He did not speak about the waiting, the disquietude over the immediate future. What dominated everything was the apostolate, the joy of fulfilling his mission as a priest in the prisons, the joy of meeting men of a kind whom he would have never seen in the peaceful school of Fontainebleau. And he concluded his letter with words especially addressed to the religious of his Carmelite Order: "We are eight priests in all, one of whom is a Jesuit. How great is my affection for my brothers at Avon, for the entire Order, for my dear family and the children of the school. Let us pray. Frère Jacques de Jésus."

After this brief plunge into memories, Père Jacques again moved forward. He did not want to set himself apart, no matter how slightly, any more than he wanted to be absorbed by the crowd. To live with the mass in order to be a friend and a director of souls, this was the only role that he wanted to fill. He had but one thirst: to give himself to the camp the way he had given himself to the school.

"Where are you off to now, Père Jacques?" said Charles Meyer to him one day. Meyer served Mass for him every morning, and every morning he watched him tirelessly take off for other barracks to meet unknown inmates.

"You fellows don't need me," replied Père Jacques with a smile that admitted of no reply. He had found his close friends of Fontainebleau again in Compiègne, he had established contacts with other Catholics, showing them affection and helping them. But he had no more intention of letting himself be confined among Catholics than he had wished to take up separate quarters with the priest-prisoners. He went out to look for the others, the isolated and the forsaken, for those who were not sustained by the solidarity of a group and who ruminated over their anxiety in total isolation from others.

"From morning to night he was at the service of others," said M. Godlewsky. "I never saw him alone, I never saw him idle, and I don't believe he went looking for support from others. On the contrary it seemed to me that his constant concern, his sole preoccupation was to bring spiritual aid to his brothers."

"He had quickly ferreted out the most unfortunate inmates in the camp," added Charles Meyer. "When he received a Red Cross package, he went out at once to distribute it. It was very often necessary to intervene to prevent him from going too far, and to make him at least keep what was strictly necessary for himself so that he would not die of hunger. Invariably his reply to my remonstrances was, 'Providence will take care of that.' One day a large parcel received from the Carmelites of Compiègne, containing food and linen, was completely distributed in the space of twenty minutes.

"We admired him for this, but we were not surprised. What was surprising was the eagerness with which he had gone to meet the Communists, the assiduousness with which he visited them. The Communists were the first persons he wanted to get to know in the camp.

"Why do you go to see them?" he was asked.

Yes, why? Since it was the most homogeneous and solid bloc, it was not there that one would find the lonely and forsaken. And furthermore it was a group which, in the matter of religion, professed ideas that were the most irreducibly opposed to those of Père Jacques.

"They don't think the way we do at all," others insisted. And Père Jacques replied, "But it is precisely for this reason that I wish to see them."

The first reason, obvious and moving, was the community of sacrifice and the horror of barriers that the prisoners themselves could raise between themselves. But there was still another reason. Père Jacques had been born in a worker's family and he did not need anyone to tell him about the old rupture that had separated the worker masses from the faith of Christ. He had always known this suffering and now, by an amazing dialectic of destiny, it was the barbed wire erected by the Nazis that reunited him in the same community with a band of these militant workers. How could he stand aside and not "find himself" among them despite the serious and irreducible character of their opposition. He would not have been Père Jacques had he seen in this encounter mere chance or an opportune occasion for dialogue. The will of God had permitted that he be thrown into prison; it had permitted him to rejoin his original brothers. He could do nothing but listen to this call with all his being. A light, says the Gospel, was not made to be placed under a bushel, sheltered from drafts.

He paid calls on the Communists and at first they looked at him with surprise. They were not used to people coming around to see them that way, especially a monk in rough homespun robes. What did this man who looked as if he had just stepped out of the Middle Ages want from them? But the frankness of his approach, the simplicity of his friendship, his energy, his devotion, all these old words that mean nothing to the blasé, that seem futile when one reads them, are bathed in human warmth and light when one sees somebody who lives them. Without any false concessions on either side, without deceptive cleverness, Père Jacques became the friend of these Communists of Compiègne.

"Among these men," testified Michel de Bouard, now Dean of the Faculty of Letters in Caen, "several far surpassed the others in loftiness of thought: Auguste Havez, permanent secretary of the Communist group in the House of Deputies before 1939, and Maurice Lampe. Later Père Jacques became the friend of another Communist, a railway man from the Somme named André Debailly. They were to meet again in Güsen I at the Steyr factory, and both died there shortly after the liberation of the camp: I am convinced that Debailly (who was my interregional chief before his arrest) was led back to faith in God by Père Jacques without, however, renouncing his Communist convictions."

Père Jacques helped other prisoners to find their faith again. M. Junguenet was witness to this, but there is no other example known among Communists. On the level of "propaganda" it would be nothing more than a drop in the sea, but it is important precisely because it was not a question of propaganda.

There was something here that was quite different in character from those "dialogues" that satisfy superficial minds, the contact was profound. Père Jacques did not conceal his admiration for the energy and the strong solidarity of the Communists put to the test, to which his Catholic friends still testify today. His Communist friends have also testified to what they felt on seeing him among them: "Père Jacques was a true believer, he had an absolute faith," said Julien Jacques to me.

This sentiment was repeated by Emile Valley, "Père Jacques was a believer, a Christian, as Christ wanted one to be."

They were Communists, they still are to this day, but they have not forgotten what they went through in the concentration camp years ago when they met Père Jacques.

One may not understand, may find strange these friendships, these intimate communications between man and man within the very framework of opposition. If so then one will not understand any better what Père de Foucauld and Moussa Ag Amastane understood and lived: the intimate friendship between a Catholic priest and a fervent Moslem. It had nothing to do with syncretism or confusion of minds. Charles de Foucauld had formerly lost his faith while pondering—from afar—the diversity of religions, but he began to find his faith again on the day he saw the Moslems of Morocco prostrate themselves on the ground to adore the Lord.

Words are always powerless to capture time flown by. Père Jacques's secret (but a secret the effects of which were felt by all his companions) was that he really did what charity inspires, true charity, not that which gives alms as a leftover of its surplus, but that charity of which St. Paul speaks: the charity of him who gives himself entirely to what he does for his brothers. Père Jacques did not cease his efforts along this path, and now that he was entering the world of the concentration camps he pushed this true charity to the point of heroism. He not only shared his food parcels, he also gave all his time.

"Père Jacques was known by everybody, he was asked for advice, questions were posed to him, he was never left alone," said Charles Meyer. And Michel de Bouard added, "He was always active but it was an overflowing activity of the spiritual life."

Propaganda and activism are human deformations as understandable as they are useless. The monk—and at bottom Père Jacques was just this—could not adopt these methods and turn away from the essential thing, which is union with the divine will. "Let us pray" had been the last words he had written at the end of his letter to the Prioress of the Carmelite convent of Compiègne. They were, in fact, his master words.

At the time Père Jacques arrived at the camp there was a chapel, a chaplain, and seven or eight priest-prisoners. They celebrated

Mass every morning and during the day Catholics could come there to pray. What could the presence of Père Jacques contribute? An additional unit?

But when such a man has a sacred flame at the depths of his heart, when he is determined to face things, not to withdraw into himself but to be the light that illumines, one such man is enough to change the whole climate.

"Before Père Jacques's arrival," declared Michel de Bouard, "the religious life in camp was lethargic. When a priest celebrated Mass there were hardly more than three or four persons present."

Père Jacques arrived. He too celebrated Mass every morning. How many assistants did he have? Charles Meyer, who served him at Mass, and the small handful of Catholics come with him from Fontaine-bleau.

Several days later there were two hundred prisoners at Père Jacques's Mass, according to M. Devémy, who added, "And about a hundred received Communion."

The chapel, however, had not changed. It was only a barrack among other barracks. No carpet, no altar steps, no prie-dieu. No organ and no bouquets of flowers. Nothing spectacular whatsoever. The divine mystery of the Mass remains unchanged. The other priests who came to celebrate Mass in the same room also paid their heavy share of suffering and heroism. Who would dare claim that their faith was less deeply felt? But the fact is that the faith of Père Jacques radiated like no other.

"I saw this priest celebrate Mass," said M. Zamansky. "He created an impression of peace, power, and joy. These first feelings were certainly accurate because at a distance of more than two years I felt them again and just as strongly and clearly at their mere evocation."

"I still see Père Jacques kneeling on the floor of this wretched barracks, without a prie-dieu, without any support, his whole soul concentrated and united with God," resumed M. Devémy. "Nothing comforted me so much as this sight of Père Jacques. I still see his eyes fixed on the altar, his eyes in which burned a gentle flame like that in the sanctuary lamp."

MY PLACE IS AMONG MY COMRADES

In all the movements of Père Jacques celebrating Mass one saw something quite different from a repetition of ancient rites, one felt the presence of Christ through the movements of His priest. Père Jacques had stirred up such a revival of faith among Catholics that every evening, at five o'clock, about a hundred prisoners gathered in the chapel with him to recite the rosary. But this was not enough for him. He was not a man to separate the practice of faith from the knowledge of faith. As if he had eternity before him, in this camp of transit between the first prison and the unknown which hovered menacingly each Monday morning, he got the idea of organizing catechism courses.

The catechism! There is no more hackneyed, more used word. Yet one morning, Lorin who was the representative of the young Christian resistance fighters on the National Committee of the Resistance came to see Michel de Bouard and told him, still amazed and delighted, what Père Jacques had just said to him: "Spread the word around that I am going to give catechism lessons. (He had received authorization from the chaplain.) But to everybody, including non-Catholics. I am not interested in meeting only Christians. It's the others that I wish to meet."

On the first day there were five or six listeners, the second day twice as many, and on the third the chapel was full. On the following days people outside pressed against the big open windows to listen.

For lack of a pulpit Père Jacques perched upon a piano stool. What he was giving was certainly catechetical instruction, but the old words took on a new life because he lived them. He spoke of the education of children, of marriage, of chastity, then of the highest law: the love of God and one's neighbor. One might find the first subjects he touched on a bit surprising and ask oneself if Lucien still imagined himself to be at the junior school among adolescents. But the fact is that in this prison he was thinking about the future. He wanted to help these men refashion their lives against the time when they would once again have found freedom! Père Jacques thought boldly about the future, he saw higher and further than the immediate tragedy. But, at the same time, he faced one of the most burning problems of prison life when he insisted on the sixth commandment of God, "A lustful condition must not exist; the body must not consent." How many men were there present who once might have laughed at this. But in the terrible test of prison they discovered the other aspect of chastity, not simply its negative side, but its positive affirmation of self-mastery.

"He formulated almost a system of education, training, resistance, and morality appropriate to our anxieties, our needs, and our hopes," said M. Godlewsky.

"One day," said M. Zamansky, "he touched on the problem of purity among young people. You can guess just how far we had been carried away. The problem of love, respect for the body, the meaning of the family and children, the role of the State, the problem of teaching—everything was discussed. The great majority of the listeners approved of what Père Jacques said when in response to a small group, and basing himself on scientific testimony and studies, he proved that chastity until marriage was possible and desirable. All the others, half of whom were Communists, warmly applauded his assertion that it was necessary to respect man as a whole. And what significance this affirmation assumed knowing only a few days remained before deportation to Germany, the mark of which was the debasement of men by every means."

The days went by and every Monday they watched a new contingent of fifty men leave. Michel de Bouard and others disappeared this way. Père Jacques could not bear the suffering of this separation.

"I would like to leave with one of these transports!" he exclaimed one day before Charles Meyer.

"What! Not me!" retorted the latter, as any other man would have done in his place.

"Yes, because it is there that men have even greater need of help."

Gratification of this wish was not delayed for long. A week later, perched on his stool, Père Jacques was giving his talk in the chapel at eleven o'clock in the morning, as on other days. There was a sudden scuffle and the noise of hobnailed boots. The SS had burst into the barracks. A sergeant shouted at the priest and began to pull him by his scapular.

"What right does he have to speak? Who the hell is he to give these lectures?"

"I am teaching catechism," protested Père Jacques. "I have been given permission."

"That! That's catechism!"

One hour later Père Jacques came back from the Kommandatura. He had not been beaten, but violently reprimanded. Thenceforth, lectures, rosaries, and Masses were suppressed. And on March 27 Père Jacques was designated for the departing convoy. Immediately when the news was known in camp, a crowd of prisoners gathered to say good-by to Père Jacques. It was a procession. Everybody wanted to say a word to him and shake his hand. Some knelt to ask his blessing.

For a moment, despite his courage, Père Jacques's features contorted with fear at the idea that he was leaving for an unknown destination. Charles Meyer watched him go with a broken heart. They were never to see each other again.

2   The "Circus" of Neue-Breme

Handcuffed, chained together, the fifty deportees were taken away in a truck and driven toward Paris on the next day, March 28. They got out at the Gare de l'Est where with kicks from hobnailed boots, rifle blows, and floggings they were piled into cell-like coaches. They were so closely packed, testified Jean Berthelot, that they could no longer move their bruised bodies and the coaches were suffocatingly hot. The compartments were bolted and one could hear the guards constantly move up and down the corridors, armed with submachine guns.

Departing at 9:30 P.M. the train rolled along rapidly. At 5:00 A.M. the next morning it arrived in Saarbrücken. They were in Germany.

After a suffocating night the jailers threw themselves at the prisoners and pushed them off the train, raining curses and blows on them. There was no question of water, food, or rest. Then came a march on foot for about a mile. The blows and kicks began again and continued all along the march, after which the fifty prisoners were piled into two trucks partitioned into cells made to hold six inmates.

The trucks came to a halt inside a camp. This was Neue-Breme. A new descent, a new shower of blows. The deportees were led into a courtyard facing the offices of the Gestapo. They were still carrying their packs under their arms. They were ordered to pile them on the ground, and then they were assembled about two yards behind the pile and ordered to remain at attention.

It was still very early in the morning. The minutes passed. They waited. For what? Nobody knew.

166

Hours passed. Slowly, interminably, the sun rose.

The guards were changed.

Only the fifty deportees, one of whom still wore his Carmelite habit, remained still. Anyone who tried to move was immediately whipped or hit with clubs. Anyone who dared reach for the last provisions hidden in his meager pack was threatened with death.

From time to time one saw poor wretches in convict uniforms slip by. Living skeletons. If the guards turned away for a second, one of these "veterans" of Neue-Breme, with the ruses of an Indian, silently darted to the heap of parcels, at the risk of his life.

The luncheon signal blew. Again the guards were changed. The bloc of fifty did not budge. They stood at attention, without food or drink, until 5:00 o'clock. They had had all the time in the world to meditate on what was awaiting them. At 5:00 o'clock, finally, they were led into the offices of the Gestapo. Their names were registered, and their packages, watches, jewelry—if they still had any—were snatched from them. To the accompaniment of another series of kicks and blows they were taken to the "barber," a brute who pulled out their hair rather than cut it. And to wind things up they were locked in a revoltingly filthy barrack full of vermin.

A heavy silence fell.

Then—"For an introduction, it's not too bad!" declared Père Jacques.

Everyone was at the end of his rope. They slept as best they could, huddled close to one another like sheep because it was bitterly cold. But the day was not over yet.

"At 11:00 P.M.," recounted M. Berthelot, "a guard came into the barracks: it was the call to stand at attention, which lasted an hour. He left at last and we resumed our places. We were left in peace until four in the morning. Then we were up again for roll call. We went in and out of the barracks I don't know how many times, then we stood at attention for about two hours. There were seven inches of snow, and we were half frozen.

"At the end of the roll call we were ordered in and out of the barracks at least twenty more times. Then there was breakfast which consisted of a quart of hot water, a tiptop dinner for us who had not eaten for forty-eight hours. When this was over they made us run around and around a stake without letup. We were completely exhausted. Some of our comrades fell, but we were forbidden to help them get up. The guards clubbed these poor fellows with all their might, shouting, 'Get up, you dirty Frenchmen!' Those who could not get up were hit again and again until they died.

"A kind of bugle call announced that it was noon. Then we were served a big meal which consisted of a pint of hot water with a spoonful of dehydrated vegetables. Mealtime lasted about twenty minutes and then we were again ordered to run around the pole: we were constantly ordered to stand up, lie down, start running again."

This was the normal routine in Neue-Breme. It was to be repeated every day. The only foreseeable changes were to be an increase in the refinements of the cruelty.

There were no more than six hundred deportees in the barracks at Neue-Breme. Lieutenant Schmoll was the camp commander. The chief of the guards was a sergeant nicknamed "the Panther." Especially conspicuous among the noncoms was a certain Hornetz, celebrated for his crimes in the camp, and "Shorty," a man of sixty-two, who had formerly been a pork butcher in Saarbrücken. The guards were also assisted by a group of "young Russian pervert prisoners." There is no need to explain their role.

No work was done at Neue-Breme except for routine details. These sometimes took on the character of sheer fantasy as on the day the prisoners were yoked to a plow to till a neighboring field under the whiplashes of two guards.

The Neue-Breme camp had no other reason for being except to inflict sadistic torture. The deportees were housed in groups of one hundred in barracks about eighteen feet long and twelve feet wide. The cots were two feet wide and crawled with vermin. The deportees were locked in from 9 P.M. to 4 A.M. except for late roll calls. Thus the morning roll call took place at 4 A.M. as Père Jacques and his companions had already experienced it. Whether it rained, whether it snowed, or whether the wind blew with hurricane force, the roll call was always made outdoors, the bareheaded prisoners standing at attention, while the well fed and warmly dressed guards walked around them looking for somebody to club. The roll call lasted two or three hours. Even the sick had to be present, motionless and at attention like the others. Even the dead had to be present: their cadavers were laid out in a straight line.

After the "meal," such as M. Berthelot described, came the "circus."

It had been a week or two since Michel de Bouard had left Père Jacques at Compiègne, and since then he had been an inmate in Neue-Breme. Suddenly, with an inexpressible mixture of joy and horror, he recognized Père Jacques's rough homespun habit, and watched the goings-on.

"The newcomers were being made to march in ranks around a reservoir in the center of the courtyard. The veteran inmates were called as usual to perform the same drill. It was not long before the jeers fell particularly on Père Jacques whose robe attracted the attention of the SD (the cadre of this small camp was composed of SD men, not SS). He did not seem to be affected in any way by their jeering. Among the oldest of the inmates (who had arrived two or three months before) there were some who had already lost all their strength, and who could barely walk. They formed a group apart, a lamentable contingent which walked around the reservoir at a slower pace. In mockery the master-Führer of the camp ordered Père Jacques to walk at the head of this group. Père Jacques obeyed, and he immediately took care to adjust his pace to that of these poor wretches. From time to time he would turn around to see if they were following him and this look of goodness in this inferno of brutalities heartened them. At this moment the courtyard was under surveillance by the SD man, Hornetz. I myself was working in an annex of the kitchen overlooking the courtyard, washing the big jugs into which the soup was poured. I often looked up to watch what was going on in the courtyard."

Suddenly something incredible happened in this place where the executioners thought of nothing else except to dishonor themselves more and more with each passing day, something materially insignificant but which nevertheless sufficed to stupefy the onlookers.

"All at once," continued Michel de Bouard, "I felt that Hornetz had been subjugated by the dignity of Père Jacques: this could be seen in his look. How I understood him! Never, I believe, did Père Jacques seem greater to me than on that day."

But the foul machine never stopped. The "circus" began all over again every day. The simplest exercises, the marching in step, the run on the double, the playing of leapfrog seemed harmless, but the refinement consisted in forcing the prisoners already exhausted by hunger to perform such exercises for hours on end.

Each time, moreover, it was necessary to give a new twist to the sport to "amuse" the guards. Père Jacques had to walk for hours on the little walls separating the pools, while carrying an 18-foot beam on his shoulders, said Abbé Barbier, and he often had to perform this feat stark naked.

For years Père Jacques had read and reread the Gospel, he had meditated on the passion of Christ, he knew each one of the features of this Passion which in turn the Apostles had countersigned with their own blood: Christ burdened with the beam of the Cross, Christ falling under the weight of the Cross, Christ stripped naked by the executioners in front of the mob in order to be nailed to the Cross. Père Jacques could not but think that in his own flesh he was reliving the very suffering of Christ on Calvary.

If the guards stopped these exercises something even worse had to be expected. They hanged a prisoner whom they caught trying to escape. Or they would arbitrarily pick a man out of the ranks and throw him into one of the pools. And if he tried to swim in order to get out of it, the executioners would hit him on the head with long poles and drown him forcibly.

A great spectacle was put on on April 15, 1944, during Père Jacques's stay in Neue-Breme. Lieutenant Schmoll was on hand with his wife, his ten-year-old daughter, his fourteen-year-old son and the noncommissioned officers. All of them laughed and the men smoked cigars while two prisoners were delivered to four savage watchdogs to be killed.

If the deportees at Neue-Breme were not directly assassinated, they were condemned to die of exhaustion in the shortest possible time. Out of the fifty inmates of the convoy of which Père Jacques was a member, there were only seven survivors after a three-week stay in camp, from March 29 to April 21.

But national socialism had provided for everything. There was an infirmary, the "resuscitator" in the Neue-Breme camp. It was part of the barracks which included about fifteen two-tiered bunks. The "doctor" was a German, a common criminal and a sadistic brute. Moreover, he had no medications at all, except for those that it had been possible to steal from the packages of newcomers.

The sick, most of whom suffered from dysentery, lay on a pile of straw, dirty, verminous, and dung-ridden. Exhaustion and suffering quickly drove them mad. Some ate the lighted matches which the Nazis threw at them; others, in wild laughter sent the "soup"—for which they had been waiting for hours with a mad impatience—sprawling to the floor. At each arrival of the convoy, some of the sick were yanked out of the so-called infirmary and thrown into a pool to serve as a warning to them. No hope here, ever. The infirmary itself had not been set up to nurse the sick, but to finish them off.

Here there were no such things as a chapel, the Mass, lectures, or recitations of the rosary. The junior school was infinitely far in space and time. Instead of clear windows and a lovely garden under the hundred-year-old trees of the big park, it was a world of barracks. Instead of contemplation and study, a circus of death. The three great theological virtues, faith, hope, and charity, were banned from here. At Fontainebleau, as everywhere in the world, it had not been all perfection. The sun has its spots and the sky its clouds, but here the rule rested only on despair and hate. Compared to Neue-Breme the camp in Compiègne was almost a paradise.

Here in all its ignominy was the hell of the concentration camps. What could the greatest of saints do in an infernal pit? Yet it was there that Père Jacques had wished to be. At the time he had been a prisoner in Fontainebleau he had protested against all plans for his release proposed by Père Philippe, a protest he repeated to Charles Meyer in the truck that took them to Compiègne, and again when in this same camp he told Charles Meyer that he wished to accompany those who were leaving for an unknown destination. Now he was there. But to what purpose? Was he not compelled like the others to take part in this indefinite series of senseless roll calls and sadistic drills which offered no respite, was he not as exhausted as the others—the survivors—when he drank hot water and stretched out on the vermin-infested straw pallets?

In a single glance, he could see around him those who were holding out—Christians, Communists, persons of unknown creeds and political persuasions. There were still some whom the vileness of the executioners could not succeed in subduing. But what more could be done beyond this furtive call of the watcher over his fellows? There was always a guard somewhere, it was obligatory to run always, even to the latrines, this undoubtedly being part of the exercise in hygiene. It was always forbidden to talk, except in the evening in the barracks when night fell on the exhausted inmates.

But faith in life stubbornly persisted. Very often when a prisoner passed near Père Jacques, if only for a second, this prisoner would throw him a word of supplication or encouragement. And Père Jacques would repeat it to his friend Bouard as if it were the most precious thing in the world.

"One day," said Bouard, "someone in the corridor called out, 'I have faith in the Blessed Virgin,' and another day, a stranger passing by him, murmured, 'Laudetur Jesus-Christus.'" Père Jacques was deeply touched by these testimonies of faith.

Faith and love! May Christ be praised! This muffled cry, heard for a second among these gloomy barracks, in this domain of vermin, executions, and torture was the most sublime of challenges to hatred and suffering. Nothing is more extraordinary if one thinks of all the men who lose their faith because of the "problem" of evil; but hurled alive into an abyss of suffering, men also succeed in finding faith or feeling it more strongly than ever.

But it must not be said that Père Jacques did not dare all to do something in a material way, even in Neue-Breme. And for whom would this be first of all, if not for the sick? He longed to transform the sinister infirmary in which they lay. Was there any sense in caring for men who were systematically subjected to hunger and exhaustion so that they would die? Père Jacques did not doubt it for a second. The sick had to be cared for and comforted as far as possible and unconditionally.

At the risk of his own life, he dared take the initiative to ask if he might take care of the sick. In response he received only insults and blows. Suddenly one day, after a "circus" session, Hornetz approached Père Jacques and asked him if he wanted to take charge of the infirmary. He accepted, of course, and started on his duties that very evening. He began by scouring the building from top to bottom. Every morning he started afresh by scrubbing the floor, and then he bathed the sick one by one. He washed sheets and shirts and made bandages. Since there were no medications, he protested. He was answered with a beating. Then at the risk of being condemned to torture, he went to steal some from the pharmacy of the Nazi personnel.

One of his great joys was that he was not alone, for he had so much to do that one man was not enough. Another deportee, Nicolot, a Communist, had also succeeded in infiltrating the infirmary. Very active and devoted, Nicolot admirably seconded Père Jacques.

"Very often," said Captain Petrou, "Père Jacques gave his food ration to a sick person. It was heroic folly, a mere drop of water in the ocean. There too Père Jacques wished to be as effective as possible. He had not failed to notice the mysterious ascendancy he exercised on Hornetz, and he managed to bring about the extraordinary feat of having Hornetz himself accompany him to the kitchen to ask for leftovers on behalf of the sick. These leftovers were from the bottoms of the soup jugs, the debris of potatoes that came from the billets of the SD. Every day Père Jacques began all over again. He was cursed, he was hit, but he persisted and still showed up in the kitchen. In the end he managed to get these leftovers on behalf of the sick as a matter of course. Michel de Bouard was a witness to this when he worked as a dishwasher.

Michel also carried to the infirmary the jugs of soup that formed the ordinary ration of the sick. And each time he took advantage of his errand to exchange some words with Père Jacques on the sly.

"Père Jacques told me one day," declared Michel, "that in this place where the fall from grace was the rule he had heard an appeal to God rise from this suffering band. The fact is that for us his own beautiful face, transfigured by an inner life more intense than usual, was like a magnetic pole of attraction. . . .

"On the vigil of Easter," he added, "Père Jacques made bold to ask Hornetz for authorization to celebrate Mass next day in the infirmary. Hornetz could not take such a decision by himself. He said that he would refer the request to the camp commander, Lieutenant Schmoll. Did he do this? I do not know. For a little while we hoped, until evening. Then the answer came. No."

Several days later Michel de Bouard left with other deportees for a new unknown destination. Next it was Père Jacques turn to be put on the departure list. There then took place an unheard-of scene which Michel de Bouard learned about a little later. Père Jacques asked something of Lieutenant Schmoll. This was in itself an act of madness. And what he desired went beyond all that one could imagine—he asked to remain at Neue-Breme.

"To remain at Neue-Breme would have meant death in four months at the most," said Michel de Bouard. "To get out of Neue-Breme was everyone's hope. One did not imagine that one could encounter anything worse elsewhere. I saw men, at the end of their strength, hardly able to stand up, who literally ran when their name was called out to join the group of departing prisoners."

Père Jacques wanted to stay behind so as not to leave his sick.

The camp commander replied that he did not have the power to change a list drawn up by the Gestapo in Paris. So Père Jacques left Neue-Breme on April 20.

3   In the Silence of Mauthausen

In the south the snow glistened on the mountains as the spring sun rose in the sky. On both side of the train endless forests on the slopes streaked by, green valleys with wildly roaring torrents, viaducts spanning awe-inspiring rocky abysses, romantic landscapes dotted with small exquisite baroque châteaux.

Where were the deportees going? They did not know. The train rolled steadily eastward, always farther and farther from France. Nevertheless the deportees were "filled with happiness," said one of them, Captain Petrou. The Neue-Breme camp was so abominable that it was not possible to find a worse one.

After Saarbrücken the train crossed the Rhine, passing through Stuttgart, Ulm with the famous spire of its Gothic cathedral, Augsburg, Munich with the art treasures of its Pinacoteca. The train rolled on day and night. From time to time there were interminable halts. It had already traversed all of Bavaria. Where would it stop?

At departure time each deportee had received a one-kilo bread ration and a quarter pound of margarine. April 20, 21, 22, and the train kept on rolling. The windows were blocked. Everywhere—in the train corridors, on the station platforms—bayonets and sub-machine guns glittered in the hands of the guards.

For three days the prisoners were given no chance to stretch their legs, or to procure supplementary provisions for themselves. The convoy crossed the former Austrian frontier. It skirted the foot of the mountains of the Tyrol, in and out of verdant and snowy landscapes. It arrived at Salzburg, city of beauty in Mozart's delicious little fatherland, the city of thirty-three churches. But the train kept on rolling toward the east. Now the railroad track ran along the beautiful blue Danube in the direction of Linz.

In Linz, on clear days, when one walks down from the railway station toward the river along the Landstrasse, brilliant with a thousand windows, everywhere one can see the bright green bell towers of baroque churches rising in the sky. St. Ignatius and St. Ursula are close by, and the church of the Minorite Brothers of St. Francis of Assisi and that of the seminary a bit off to one side. A little church is hidden in one of the folds of the banks of the Danube, the oldest church in Austria. Built on Roman foundations, it goes back to the eighth century and it is dedicated to the famous Danubian officer who became the great evangelizer of the Gallo-Roman countrysides, St. Martin. On this side the streets of Linz almost immediately lose themselves in the labyrinth of parks and country roads. The tramways ride gaily by along the Landstrasse in Linz, some toward the wooded hill of Pöstlingberg, others along the banks of the Danube, and still others in the opposite direction toward St. Florian, the oldest Augustinian monastery in Austria.

At ten o'clock on the evening of April 22 the train came to a halt at last and the deportees got out at the Linz railroad station. They were immediately piled into trucks and the convoy rolled along a road following the Danube for a long time, and always in an easterly direction. Then the road turned left and the trucks climbed the hairpin bends of a hill. Suddenly at the top of a still higher hill light flooded the black night. In the implacable glare of the searchlights, rose a Chinese wall with a great entry portal flanked by two squat lookout towers. Above the main gate, a Nazi eagle spread out two wings the color of mourning.

This was Mauthausen, the enormous concentration camp which overlooked the Danube, fifteen miles downstream from Linz.

Mauthausen is now deserted. Everything is calm, still, empty. One arrives there by going along a road which follows the Danube. The countryside is green and still, enlivened only by peasants working in the fields. Everything is Virgilian, bucolic, as restful and reassuring a scene as one could wish. After the marvels of art of the ancient cities, the marvels of nature in the Tyrol, the landscape here is more rural; it is as peaceful as the fields, as rich and as fertile as all the Danubian earth.

When one arrives here in peacetime on a clear day and stands on the top of the hill, the eye is enchanted by the dells that line the great river on the west and south, and in the distance, at times veiled in mist, by the last spurs of the Tyrolean mountains. But if one then simply turns around he will see the entrance to the Mauthausen camp nearby. Now serving no purpose, the walls simply seem ugly and low.

Inside, after going through a small gate, one comes upon the dark avenue, smooth and straight, flanked by sidewalks. It is about nine hundred feet long. Not a tree, not a flower. The avenue is lined only by rows of huts. Those on the right are of concrete material. Those on the left are wooden. All of them have only a ground floor. No upper stories, but there are basements in the concrete structures.

Today everything is calm and silent, but the whole remains flat, repulsive, and monotonous. After the many splendid regions that one has passed through, here one enters the world of ugliness. One would call it a military camp of the lowest class. That's all. In reality one has seen nothing yet. Time has conjured everything away.

Even the crosses in the cemetery, even the listing of the thousands of dead on placards now on the barracks and on the monuments to the dead erected at the entrance to the camp do not suffice to give an idea of what went on here. There is something too "natural" in death, too peaceful in cemeteries which enclose only the mortal remains of a being whom one has personally loved. There are too many vast cemeteries in the world, near big cities or in the vicinity of former battlefields.

One grasps nothing about Mauthausen as long as one believes he hears nothing but the silence, as long as he does not lend an ear to the immense clamor of the thousands of young men who were piled into these barracks, filthy at that time, as long as one grasps nothing of the delirium of the furious madmen armed with cudgels and submachine guns who never stopped their savage attacks on the captives. And all of this would never have been known if the staggering number of captives and the lightning-like rapidity of the liberation had not made it possible for the *survivors* to get out.

Even the deportees who came here from Neue-Breme with Père Jacques indulged in illusions as they rolled along in the railway in the direction of Linz. They could not imagine anything worse than Neue-Breme. But they could not have supposed that Mauthausen, in variable forms, could be the indefinite continuation of the same system of atrocities. They suspected without great distress that they were en route to forced labor. This is a frightening prospect to a man living peacefully at home. But it reassures a man condemned to death. On leaving Neue-Breme the prospect of forced labor evoked the possibility of being occupied, of being fed at least enough to hold out until the hour of liberation.

In the spring of 1944 it was already a year since Hitler's Germany had lost the decisive battle of Stalingrad; the Allies had recaptured North Africa, occupied Sicily, and were readying the offensive in Italy. Aerial bombings over Germany increased, and everybody was waiting only for the new Russian offensive and the landing of the Allies on the Western Front. For a deportee to hold out for a few months, only for a few weeks, meant perhaps to save his life. But if there was forced labor in Mauthausen, in contrast to Compiègne and Neue-Breme, it was no less closely associated with the same will to degradation and extermination that prevailed in Neue-Breme. Here and there this system was somewhat curbed by the necessities of work, but it was constantly started up again by the new columns of deportees who poured into the main gate of Mauthausen. Some dreamers have imagined that formerly slavery guaranteed a certain security to the slaves because the masters had an interest in feeding them and nursing them when they were ill. But when the "slave mart" is gorged with merchandise the life of the slave counts for almost nothing. And economic interest does not prevail over unleashed sadism.

Massed along the inner avenue which served as an assembly area between the barracks, Père Jacques and his comrades could not see well what was hidden in the new camp, all lit up at night, against the glare of searchlights placed outside the walls. The latter were relatively low but one could see long lines of barbed and electrified wire stretched along the top of the wall. In the same terrible light one could see the sentries who walked around with their submachine guns, and hear the howls of packs of savage police dogs.

To the right of the main entrance, on top of one of the concrete buildings, a thick, squat chimney poured out torrents of smoke mixed with tall flames. It burned day and night. At night one saw this light everywhere from the surrounding countryside. Day and night its insatiable furnace sent forth an abominable stench into the air, the odor of the flesh of bodies being burned there. This was the chimney of the crematorium oven.

Landru reigned here.

The deportees had already lost all their illusions about what was awaiting them. They might have been saved from Neue-Breme, but here everything was geared to making any further escape elsewhere impossible. As soon as they got down from the truck, they were marched to the first concrete building immediately to the right of the camp entrance. They went down a flight of stairs to the base-ment, and entered a vast low room, a shower room, with white tile walls. It served them as a dormitory that night. Exhausted by fatigue and hunger, the new arrivals stretched out on the ground, even on the cold white tile squares. Some fell asleep immediately; others, seized by the terrible insomnia of anxiety, endlessly asked themselves what the morrow would bring.

Next morning the deportees undressed. Their clothes, which they were not to see again, were taken away, and everything that had escaped the thieving guards during other searches in other camps was taken away from them here, including their wedding rings. They stood naked as worms waiting to go under the showers. Other deportees, veterans of the camp, far from considering them as brothers in misery, treated them with an ultimate contempt. It was a Babel of languages of all kinds and nothing was ever done without abusive insults and blows. The newcomers were quickly shaved all over their bodies, and then they were swabbed with kerosene. Hygiene first of all! Then they were thrown some drawers, shirts and wooden clogs, most of which were unpaired. There were too few convicts' uniforms to go around so they were given the bits and pieces of castoff clothing snatched from the bodies of the multitudes of captives who had already succumbed.

The prisoners were lined up in columns in the assembly area in front of the main entrance through which they had come the night before. They were counted and re-counted. Then with blows of cudgels they were marched to the inside of the camp. In the full light of day they saw other endless rows of barracks behind the first row of wooden barracks near the gate. Some of them were also enclosed behind barbed wire reserved for categories of deportees who were set apart from the others. The new arrivals were kept in quarantine, while awaiting their transfer to a labor detail.

Locked up in Block 16, Père Jacques found himself with Bonsergent and Captain Petrou who had come from Neue-Breme with him. The room was already thronged with men, but it continued to fill up with more and more of them. By evening there must have been several hundred men piled upon each other in this single room. Moreover there was no furniture at all, not even those miserable tiers of bunks that one found in the other barracks. There were only piles of meager straw pallets which at night were spread on the floor.

When the SS retired for the night, one would think that the captives would be able to relax a bit at least. A useless illusion. They were handed over to the power of the "kapos," a kind of commissioned slave who enjoyed the confidence of the SS and who ceded nothing to them in the way of baseness and cruelty.

But still, even in this hell, there were men who held out. At the moment the newcomers arrived from Neue-Breme, men on the ration detail were distributing "breakfast": it was a kind of a *pâté* which masqueraded as cheese and a pat of margarine of the worst quality. One of these men approached two of these new arrivals and offered a ration of "white cheese." After the treatment at Neue-Breme this was a windfall and all those who arrived threw themselves on the rations. But the two men refused, they wanted to leave their ration in order to supplement the food of the weaker ones. The man on the ration detail insisted. Despite their reiterated refusals, he was obstinate and managed to make the two newcomers take their ration. They ate it and confessed that they found the "cheese" excellent. One of these was Père Jacques, the other Captain de Bonneval, one of his companions of Neue-Breme. Both were unrecognizable under their prisoners' garb. "They must be starving!" thought the man on the ration detail, "It's impossible to eat this so-called cheese without its turning your stomach." This new friend was M. Augé, a Parisian architect.

Nothing was more precious than these gestures of kindness. Courtesy is a matter of course, or at least it should be, in ordinary life, but in the world of the concentration camp it bordered on the miraculous.

The last row of barracks in Mauthausen, now empty, well swept, silent, can explain nothing of what went on in this sinister world. A casual glance discloses only a gloomy and military air about them. As for the records, let us not talk about them—it is easy not to open them at all or to believe that they are exaggerated, if not propaganda. But M. Augé, ten years later, spoke with a calm and measured voice. He did not evoke such and such a horrible scene, or such and such an outburst of criminal insanity on the part of the camp executioners, but simply, if one dares say so, the day-to-day life in the quarantine block as he had lived it with Père Jacques and his friends.

"The quarantine in Mauthausen was horrible. They piled three hundred or three hundred and fifty men in barracks built for fifty.

"You had to remain lying down for hours without moving, waiting for the morning roll call and the evening roll call. We lay head to foot alongside each other on the floor, because there were no bunks as in the other barracks, but only thin straw pallets on the floor. The room was so crowded that it was impossible to hold everybody unless they were literally packed like sardines, with one's neighbor's feet in front of one's head. One couldn't even sleep because our nourishment was so liquid that it led to continual incontinence so that people were always getting up to go to the latrines. And since there was no room for any passage to the door, those who had to go out could do nothing but walk over the bodies on the floor. All night long it was a concert of curses, complaints, furious protests, and blows struck wildly at anything and anybody. All that I could do was to huddle up in a corner sometimes, curled up against a partition so as not to be walked over, and get a little sleep.

"Obligatory reveille woke us all up at 4 A.M. This was pure madness for people who had nothing else to do but fatigue duty. We first had to line up our pallets, filthy, full of dust and vermin. After taking a shower, you slept with the same vermin that night in the straw. This lining up of the pallets raised great clouds of dust, after which we were ordered outside in total darkness, in the rain, the cold or snow, no matter what the weather. Outside of the roll calls and the fatigue duty we had absolutely nothing to do except to remain locked up near the barracks in an alley about thirteen feet wide and one hundred ninety-five feet in length. Most of the prisoners huddled up close to each other against the wall of a barracks in an attempt to shelter themselves from the wind, or to struggle against the snow that piled up on them. Sometimes, to keep warm, we paced up and down briskly like guards and I often did this with Père Jacques and Captain de Bonneval.

"During one of those glacial nights while we were talking together, I could no longer control myself and I said, 'After all, Père Jacques, it is not possible to continue to suffer like this, Christ should certainly be here to help us.' 'Never doubt it,' he said in a tone of absolute certainty: 'Christ is here in the midst of us just as truly as we three are here, as He was on His cross, and you can behold Him.'

"I am sure that Père Jacques beheld Him."

In the block or in the sinister small courtyard, day and night, without letup, the same torments began all over again: insomnia on verminous pallets, bodies herded together and stepped on, curses and blows, the endless waiting outdoors on the cold nights, the roll calls, the abominable delousing inspections, blows again, and the interminable hours of idleness awaiting the worst.

The single visible aid was to see a friendly face from time to time. The most moving experience was to come upon some friend whom one had formerly left in another camp and who suddenly reappeared. Nothing more than the sight of such a one was a joy for friendship and a message of hope; it meant that both had held out. One of Père Jacques's great joys in the quarantine block was certainly to meet again one of his Communist friends from Compiègne, Emile Valley.

"Père Jacques was admirable throughout this period of quarantine," said M. Augé. "Often I saw him pass his bowl of soup to a comrade despite all my protests."

"Never once did Père Jacques complain," added Emile Valley. "I often heard him comfort comrades discouraged by all the moral and physical sufferings to which we had to submit."

4   The Society of Crime

Around the quarantine block in which Père Jacques and his companions were confined the whole huge camp groaned in misery together. Mauthausen was a monstrous marshaling yard for slaves. New arrivals were thrown into it constantly. Despite the inner activities of the camp (fatigue duty and the maintenance shops), despite the granite quarry that employed one thousand five hundred inmates, despite the accelerated mortality rate produced by hunger, exhaustion, and on-the-spot assassinations, Mauthausen by itself could not absorb the endless flood of deportees from all regions of Europe. They were grouped in "kommandos," that is to say in labor companies, and assigned to the smaller camps that ringed Mauthausen like satellites. There were thirty-four of them which stretched out from Linz and Ebensee to the outskirts of Vienna. The worst one, perhaps, was the château of Hartheim, a center for so-called scientific experiments. The less bad ones in general were those that involved assignment to a factory, but even these were horror camps.

As in Dante's Inferno there were circles and degrees of descent in the concentration camp world, but it was always hell. Everywhere the system was the same. The survivors were unanimous in asserting this, whatever their backgrounds or nationalities. The living conditions were hideous. The clothing was not even the usual convict's garb but old worn rags stripped from countless cadavers. The lodging was a wooden barracks (a block), boiling in the summer, freezing in winter. The prisoners were piled in on top of each other from one end of the year to the other. When the men did not sleep on the ground, squeezed together like sardines, they slept on triple-

184

tiered bunks where two, three, and even more slept in the same
bunk. And everywhere the straw mattresses crawled with filthy
vermin.

The food, so called, was below any life-sustaining minimum. In
the morning they were given a cup of unsugared "tea," at noon
about three cups of hot water in which floated some traces of turnips,
beet greens, or some vague dehydrated vegetables, and in the evening a little more than an ounce of sausage. The bread ration varied
according to the kommando and the times. In the best moments
it oscillated between fourteen and twenty-one ounces, dropping to
five ounces during the final days. Of course it was an ersatz bread,
whose quality grew constantly worse.

The prisoners had to work twelve hours a day. Even without
speaking of the demoralizing effect of the executions, everything was
done to exhaust the individual to the utmost, to change a multitude
of young men into invalids pledged to an inexorable death. What
was worse was the moral conditions which were systematically
infamous. At the summit of the concentration camp world stood
the SS. They had all the rights, all the powers. Below them was the
multitude of deportees. They had no rights whatsoever. Neither
the right to life, nor the right to a minimum of human dignity—no
more rights than have livestock delivered to brutes.

What Père Jacques had seen in Neue-Breme was not the result
of chance, the excesses of a guard who happened to be particularly
evil and insane. It was only the first applied case, before his very eyes,
of a society systematically organized on the basis of perversion. The
aim of this society was to reduce the mass of inmates to the worst
physical and moral abjection until they died of it in total despair.

First of all this mass of inmates was carefully classified. Next to
his registration number each deportee was rigged out with a colored
triangle sewed on his clothes. The triangles were:

Red for political prisoners, including a letter giving the initials
of the nationality of the inmate. There was even a special classification for Soviet prisoners of war.

Blue for the Spanish Republican refugees who had come to France after 1936, later enrolled in labor battalions of the French Army, and who had been taken prisoner in 1940.

Violet for German conscientious objectors, most of whom were Jehovah's Witnesses.

Pink for homosexuals condemned as such.

Black for the "a-socials," that is to say, those who had tried to evade work laws, gamblers (bookmakers), and, above all, gypsies.

Green for common criminals sentenced to prison under German, Austrian, and Polish law.

Finally, in place of the triangle, a yellow star for the Jews. Even here they were forced to play the role of pariahs among pariahs.

In addition, certain inmates among the political prisoners had the right to be classified in a certain supercategory in reverse, indicated by the initials N.N., that is, "Nacht und Nebel," night and fog. They were automatically forbidden to receive any packages, any mail. They were to disappear from the world without leaving the slightest trace.

In no sense was it the aim of this detailed classification to separate in fact that which it had so well distinguished in principle. It was exactly the reverse. The system made distinctions at first only in order to mix the elements later. Already they had mingled the nationalities in the camp in such a way that the obstacle of languages and mentalities made of this multitude not a body of people, but a confused mob incapable of cohesion and unity. It was an immense Babel.

The political prisoners were mingled even more systematically, as were the black-market operators, the religious objectors, the sexual perverts, and the common criminals because of this deliberate will to create confusion and contempt among them in an atmosphere of degradation and corruption. When the Nazis sorted out people it was only for the purpose of pushing the system to the extreme limits of evil. They organized an intermediate echelon between the SS troops and the multitude of the enslaved, the so-called "kapos." They were a species of corporals and foremen who had jobs as secretaries, barracks and room overseers, factory and yard bosses. In the eyes of the SS these kapos had no rights and no power, for they were recruited from the mass of slaves, but they were used as watch-dogs against their comrades, as guards of the worst and most vicious kind. One might have supposed that having come from this mass of deportees, and belonging often to non-German or even anti-German nationalities, they would serve as buffers and mitigate the treat-ment somewhat to the advantage of their fellow nationals. Here too it was just the contrary, and for a double reason. The first was that the kapos derived all kinds of advantages from their new situation, but this situation was precarious. Their personal security rested only on the additional terror that they inflicted on the mass of inmates. The second reason was that the Nazis had specially recruited them from among the dregs of the camp, preferably among criminals, sexual perverts, and political prisoners.

Thus the terror and the degradation were permanent. Even when the SS were sent elsewhere, the kapos were there to relieve them. With the tacit or overt complicity of the Nazis, there flourished a veritable international gang of brutes, psychopaths, and traffickers in evil who exploited the misery of the mass of prisoners for their personal profit. The Nazis had a whole court of "pets"—scroungers, paid informers—and they stole, bludgeoned, and killed with im-punity.

For every day inmates were openly murdered under the most trifling pretexts. Starvation was not enough. The SS and kapos vied with each other in this mad race to murder. Prisoners were hanged, asphyxiated in the gas chamber, shot, clubbed to death, riddled with submachine guns, kicked to death, killed by having their heads held in buckets of water until they drowned, shoved under glacial showers, or kicked off the hill into the quarry below. And prisoners were also killed merely by the constant standing around outdoors, in rain and snow, hour after hour during the endless roll calls.

Today in calm and deserted Mauthausen one can scarcely be-lieve that such an accumulation of crime and monstrosities had been possible. And how would one believe it when one rides in a pleasant train coach toward the museums of Vienna, when one skis in the Tyrol, when one looks at the bright and shining green bell towers of Linz, the city's busy streets, its flower gardens, its peaceful strollers, and even when one climbs through the quiet countryside toward the heights of Mauthausen. But there, placarded on the walls of the camp, one can see the immense enumeration of the dead.

In round figures: 32,000 Russians, 30,000 Poles, 12,000 Yugoslavs, 5,000 Italians, 3,000 Greeks, 700 Belgians, 8,000 French, 12,000 Hungarians, 6,000 Spanish Republicans, 4,000 Czechs, 200 Austrians, 1,500 anti-Fascist Germans—in all more than 120,000 dead.

This is the official figure, the admission furnished by the lists seized in the administrative offices of the concentration camp at the moment of liberation. A total of 120,000 men officially exterminated, the great majority of whom were young and in good health before becoming prisoners; 120,000 men assassinated in three years, 120,000 men out of about 200,000 deportees.

But these figures are much lower than the reality. They do not include either the Soviet POW's, the Jews, or the deportees assassinated at the moment of their arrival, before being registered. There can be as many dead after a great battle, but here they were exterminated in cold blood. In ordinary life it is the normal men who incarcerate the violently insane, and if they sometimes fall into inhuman brutality, there is no limit to this in a topsy-turvy society in which it is the violently insane who incarcerate normal men.

Mauthausen was a nightmare as horrible, as incredible as the nightmares one dreams, but it was a nightmare which the deportees lived through in a waking state.

The bright glare of the searchlights, which divided the walls into blinding white frames of light, indicated not only the extravagant precautions taken by the masters to see that no slave escaped them; it was not just a strange way to lend a fantastic aspect to these walls, it was the sign of everything that dominated the entire life of the camp: the glaring exposure of the worst instincts which are ordinarily hidden in the dark depths of the human being.

The worst nightmares imagined by the Marquis de Sade were realized here. Mauthausen, like all its rivals, was not only a "society of crime," it was at the same time a society of madness and rage.

Later in Güsen, one of the sinister satellites of Mauthausen, Père Jacques was to tell his friend Maurice Passard, secretary of the Federation of Metal Workers, "We must keep both feet on the ground. It is not really possible that anyone can treat men this way." He not only wanted to say that it was morally inadmissible, but that it was not believable.

The reaction of scientists was the same. Jacques Bergier, a chemist and a former assistant of Professor Helbronner, declared: "Mauthausen—Neue-Breme? Their primary characteristic was to be completely improbable. . . . Daily we saw incidents like the following take place: at Melk, another satellite of Mauthausen, the camp commander walked through the barracks and as we were wondering what he was cooking up he suddenly shouted, 'Greeks! All I see here are Greeks! Send all Greeks to the crematory!' This same personage stopped a French deportee and asked him, 'What do you do here?' 'I am the chief interpreter,' replied the deportee. 'Ah, very good!' and the camp commander split his head wide open with a series of blows from his bludgeon. The same commander came into a block late at night, turned on the lights, and noticed that the feet of a deportee were sticking out of his blanket. He tucked him in and left."

A scientist of world-wide reputation, Professor Heim, the museum director, in his memoirs published under the title *La Sombre route* gave multiple examples which show to what an extent the barbarity of the system was psychopathic. How else explain the flower beds in Güsen in front of the leprous barracks, the sick whom one cared for and killed, the deportees who were given showers and disinfected in order to be sent immediately to lie down on straw mattresses crawling with vermin? Or again the completely insane story of the SS man who at the risk of his life leaped into the water and rescued a deportee who was drowning. Several minutes later this same SS man mowed down the same deportee with a burst from his submachine gun because the latter, exhausted, marched too slowly.

All the testimonies run along the same line. Witness again the case of Doctor Jobst described by François Wetterwald. This Jobst, an SS man from the Sudetenland, was the head doctor in Ebensee. He especially hated the French, but he had put two French physicians in charge of the technical administration of the infirmary and defended them against all attacks. One night he himself killed a prisoner who was late for roll call. Two nights later he came to the infirmary in person after work to bring an antidiphtheria serum for two sick Jews. He forbade any nursing of tuberculars, yet for six months he obtained for some of the sick milk, butter, sugared porridge, foodstuffs that were never given to deportees, even the sick ones. (*Les Morts inutiles*, p. 105.)

All medicine is a desperate struggle against death. In war there is a frightful mockery in the contradictory struggle of cannons and ambulances, yet at least one operates logically on each side of the line of fire. What was particularly psychopathic in the extermination camps was to see the killers organize infirmaries and the doctors organize first nursing care and then murders. Personal friends of Père Jacques like Professor Heim, Maurice Passard, Jean Cayrol, and M. Godlewsky (another survivor) showed further to what point of sadism the mad fury of the tortures extended. "The new arrivals," Godlewsky said, "were ordered to undress outdoors no matter when it was, day or night, in summer or winter, in good weather, rain, or snow: likewise those who were about to leave for another camp. The well or the sick were completely undressed and had to wait their turn outdoors to go under the showers.

"About four hundred deportees, I believe, arrived from Auschwitz. They were very quickly classified outdoors, then an SS man came up and looked at the heads of those who seemed a little less exhausted. There were about eighty whom he put to one side. Then the others were immediately ordered to undress. It was freezing that day, the ground was covered with snow. They stood there two or three days waiting their turn under the showers. Finally they went down to the shower room but instead of hot water, the attendants ran ice-cold water. Several whose hearts could no longer hold out died under the showers, others left the shower room completely naked and wet and again they had to wait outdoors two or three hours. There was a second, then a third shower. I don't know whether a fourth shower was necessary. Their bodies were thrown into the courtyard, the cadavers as well as the living and the dying. They were collected next day to be brought to the crematory."

On another occasion he spoke of the method of assassination widely practiced at Mauthausen: the inmates were forced to throw themselves from the height of the great quarry which was about sixty-six to eighty-seven yards deep.

A young Jew, about twenty years old, jumped and was not killed. Why? Because he had fallen on the bodies of others and the shock had been cushioned. He had broken only some ribs or an arm. The SS forced him to climb the stairs—containing eighty-six steps that had been cut into the ock—and to make a second jump, this time in an area cushioned by no corpses.

The abomination was general, systematic, cultivated at all levels: "I can never recall the arrival of a group of young Jews in September, 1944, without a shudder of horror," said Abbé Barbier. "The block chiefs were there and assisted with undressing. Any poor boy of ten or fourteen who wanted to live had to lend himself to all the caprices of his masters."

Repressed on the one hand, homosexuality had been elevated to the dignity of an institution on the other. From the moment in Neue-Breme when the inmates had seen Lieutenant Schmoll take his children to see the most revolting spectacles, it was clear that the system of the camps, the cruelty and the perversion, formed an inseparable whole. And everything the torturers inflicted on their victims turned against themselves and inexorably degraded them.

St. Florian, the oldest Augustinian monastery in Austria, rises almost midway between Linz and Mauthausen, overlooking the

southern banks of the Danube. Founded in the fourteenth century, it was entirely reconstructed in the eighteenth. Situated on a
knoll, the St. Florian monastery with its immense façade, its red
roof and bright green bell turrets, is as beautiful as a palace in the
open countryside. It is one of the marvels of baroque architecture.
It would be pointless to detail its treasures, except for one: the
admirable paintings of Altdorfer.

From the artistic point of view his paintings of the Passion of
Christ and of the martyrdom of St. Sebastian are pure masterpieces
of the Danubian school. But when one has seen Mauthausen,
pierced the frightful silence that reigns there, and heard the testimonies of the survivors speaking in the name of dozens of thousands of the martyrs of Mauthausen on the northern bank of the
Danube, the splendid paintings of the monastery on the southern
bank cease to be museum objects. What the genius of Altdorfer
froze in a motionless beauty the clamor of Mauthausen revealed
without pity in all its sordid abomination.

The hardened soldiers who felled Sebastian with their cudgels,
the one who mocked Christ with a reed, the one who lashed Him
like a madman, those who spat in His face, the one who placed a
painful crown of thorns on the head of Jesus of Nazareth, all these
are the comrades-in-arms of the torturers of Mauthausen.

And Christ, exhausted, bleeding, mocked, crucified between two
thieves, condemned for an alleged attempt against the sovereignty
of the emperor, is the brother in suffering and in abjection of all
the tortured of the concentration camps.

The gloomy assembly area of Mauthausen is silent today because
it is empty. Altdorfer's sumptuous paintings in the monastery of
St. Florian are also mute. The barracks are gray and indifferent, the
paintings are frozen with a motionless beauty. Everything is still
being done to smother the voices of the victims. Even without
mentioning the lies that the executioners still invent to "justify" or
excuse their crimes, time hangs heavy with all its weight of oblivion
and confusion. The most unimpeachable reminder, the most arrest-
ing images are steeped in the infinite silence of time past in which

are engulfed side by side the cry of the killer and that of his victim. The tourist who passes by Mauthausen and St. Florian will see only the gray remains of a military camp containing monuments to the dead, and museum paintings. In truth, he will see nothing and will pass by like a blind man if he does not understand with the whole fiber of his being what transpired here, if he has not listened with all his intelligence and all his heart to the voice of the survivors of Mauthausen and, in the same way, to the voices of the martyrs who signed with their blood the account of the death of Jesus of Nazareth and His resurrection.

Père Jacques had Mauthausen before his eyes during that glacial night when he paced up and down through the snow beside his friend Augé, but he had also spent years of his life studying and meditating on the narratives of the Gospel, and while he experienced the horrors of Neue-Breme and Mauthausen to the depths of his being, he understood the Passion of Christ as never before. It is often said that the saints were converted to a passionate love of Christ on seeing a crucifix bleed before their eyes. It is not absolutely necessary to imagine strange miracles or to assume that such things are hallucinations. They were overwhelmed through their hearts. But why should the heart deceive? They ceased to behold the crucifix as an object of art and inert piety, they felt the suffering of Christ throughout their being, as if they were before Him, on the earth of Calvary, just as the father, the brother, or the son of a deportee victim of Mauthausen cannot look at that huge, somber place without shuddering.

Certain people lose their faith thinking about the horror of human sufferings, but in the glacial night of Mauthausen, sharing all the horror of this abominable world which closed in on him from all sides, Père Jacques plunged heroically to the very depths of faith. It was with the same look that he beheld his thousands of comrades imprisoned with him in Mauthausen that he contemplated Christ on the Cross.

"Priests are needed in prisons," he had said to Père Philippe when he was in the Fontainebleau jail. And they were needed first of all to

share the worst suffering, the worst abjection, just as Christ had
shared it. But the quarantine block was no more than a station on
the way of the cross of Père Jacques. To what sector now would this
monstrous marshaling yard for slaves send him?

On the evening of May 18, at the end of almost a month of confinement, the deportees of the quarantine block were again marched
off to the showers (hygiene always!). Again they were shaved from
head to toe. The brutes who used the clippers pulled out as many
hairs as they cut. Then they were again lined up in columns in the
roll-call area and, released from quarantine, they were assigned to
different kommandos.

Güsen, which is about three or four miles upstream from Mauthausen along the Linz road was the only satellite camp which in
turn had three others in its orbit. They adjoined each other, but
were separate and were called Güsen I, Güsen II, and Güsen III.
Père Jacques was assigned to Güsen I.

On the map Güsen is almost directly opposite St. Florian on the
other side of the Danube. It is about six miles as the crow flies.

"It was then that I was separated from Père Jacques," said Captain
Petrou. "For me and for all those who had drawn close to him, it
was the loss of a brother and a little bit of ourselves. He left proudly,
stoically, restoring our hope by his words of comfort, his bearing,
his faith, his goodness."

"When he left," added M. Augé, "Debailly, a real Communist,
said to me, 'What a misfortune that he is not staying with us. I take
off my hat to him, he's better than all of us.' "

But at the same time Père Jacques found other old friends and
the first one was Michel de Bouard. They had already seen and
lost each other again in Compiègne and Neue-Breme. It was a joyful
reunion.

"Père Jacques was as calm as usual, and very much the master of
himself," Michel de Bouard recalled. "We exchanged some news,
and then I told him of my intention of making a vow to go to
Lourdes if I ever emerged alive from this ordeal, or attending Mass

and receiving Communion twice a week for as long as I lived. He thought for a long time, then he answered, 'No, you must not tempt God. The greatest proof of trust that you could give Him is to accept, from the depths of your heart, that His will be done, no matter what it be.' These were his exact words. I have often thought about them since, and I understood that in the circumstances in which we found ourselves this was certainly the loftiest expression of a total faith. Once more he made me clearly feel and understand, in the full light in which he lived, that which I had barely felt, and then only confusedly."

This time it was their last encounter.

5 Welcome to Güsen

It was still a world of barracks. Row after row of gray boards, small blocks of squat, ramshackle one-story structures, and the chimney of the crematorium. It was still the same ugly and bleak world peopled with wretched men. This was Güsen I.

In contrast to Mauthausen which was situated on the top of a hill, Güsen was located in a hollow, but it was the same sordid universe.

At the time Père Jacques arrived at this new enclave of the concentration camp world, Professor Heim, of the Museum of Paris, was in the infirmary of Güsen I. Nobody will ever describe the crossing of this threshold as Professor Heim has done, who with his own eyes had seen what Père Jacques was to see on the day of his arrival: the unbelievable mixture of the leprous and of beauty which was Güsen in the fair season.

"When one came back to the Güsen camp during the summer months (and in the spring it was the same), this camp where twenty thousand men lived in an area one hundred and fifty yards wide by three hundred long—one saw well kept beds of ornamental flowers —dahlias, petunias, violets—encircling the barracks, and scarlet runners climbing over the windows. A colorful garden framed the entrance to the blocks. Sometimes flagstones, carefully placed, formed a circle around the barracks as in an old-fashioned garden. There was a freshness of freely flowering plant life about the place. But what was behind this abundance of flowers? Triple-decker bunks—two feet wide for two, three, even four men—covered with a thin straw mat saturated with urine and dung, coverlets in shreds, crawling with vermin, and permeated with the purulent matter dripping from the wounds almost all of us had. The men? Their jackets were in tatters, a gap in the back patched with some sort of checkered material, their trousers were worn through at the seat and split as though by a knife, exposing the knees. The soles of the shoes were full of holes, cracked, tied to the foot by a string. Socks were rare, underwear stained, shirts smeared with dried blood were worn without being washed or changed for two, three, four months at a time, contaminated as they were with pus and blood, with the small red spots left by flea bites and scabies." (*La Sombre route*, p. 14.)

Sad at heart Père Jacques passed through the portal of this next circle of hell. Was this not at last the lowest circle? The natural hollow between hills in which Güsen lay, was this not the deepest dungeon from which nobody was to get out alive? Mauthausen would not surrender its slaves except to cast them into the last of the forsaken places. And what could he do in this ultimate anti-chamber of death? At Neue-Breme, Père Jacques had been able to exercise a certain influence over the sinister Hornetz and bring some ray of tenderness into the horror of the infirmary. But here, amid this mass of twenty thousand men, incessantly harried by a band of torturers, how was it possible to hope that an inmate might succeed in even the smallest undertaking?

Père Jacques's heart was wrung before this abyss of suffering he had entered. What would it be possible for him to do all by himself? What could he do here even for comrades who with their last re-maining energy morally and physically resisted the machine which at all costs was set to crush them?

Then, in the depths of his soul, in that intact and untouched part of him, inaccessible to despair, he began to pray. With the help of God everything is possible, even the impossible. At this moment, as though he intensely desired a mediator, he turned to the young girl who one day had written, "I will spend my heaven doing good upon earth," St. Thérèse of Lisieux. She was from Normandy as was Père Jacques. He was fourteen when he had first heard about her, and it was she who had inspired his desire to become a Carmelite. Long ago he had gone on a pilgrimage to Lisieux. Through the iron grille at Carmel, he had spoken with Céline and Pauline, two sisters of Thérèse. He had read and reread the autobiography of Thérèse, *The Story of a Soul*, the only book he had requested in two secret messages he had sent from the Fontainebleau prison. It was she, the Carmelite of Lisieux, who had led him to the Carmelite monastery at Fontainebleau. Was she not the patron saint of the school? Was it not again up to her to show him the way at this tragic hour when he entered the demoniacal monastery of Güsen?

From the bottom of his heart, Père Jacques murmured this prayer: "St. Thérèse of the Infant Jesus, I come to this camp. I give you full liberty as to the manner in which I shall be received, but I dearly wish to have a sign that you receive me in this camp, a sign of your protection over me."

How the convict guards would have laughed if they had heard him!

And, how wrong one would be to think that Père Jacques was betraying the heroic ideal which he had placed above all else a few hours earlier when he had been talking for the last time with Michel de Bouard. Père Jacques was not asking to have a safe life, or even a respite. He knew what reception was customarily reserved for newcomers each time they descended into a lower circle of the concentration camp hell, and he asked for no attenuation of this frightening reception. But it was at this very time of being "welcomed"—however terrible it might be—that he asked for a sign from Thérèse. He knew *The Story of a Soul* too well to ask for anything else. Thérèse had not once prayed that Pranzini, condemned to death, be pardoned by the President of the Republic, but rather, with his last breath, that Pranzini show a sign of love for Christ before dying. He knew that Thérèse, far from asking for respite from her own sufferings, had no other wish but to make of these an offering of her love to the Lord. He knew that the key word of the agony of Thérèse, at the age of twenty-four, was the cry: "I do not repent of having devoted myself to Love." Had not Père Jacques, too, desired to devote himself to Love when he had been prepared to run the risk of giving asylum to the hunted, when he refused all plans to escape, when he had desired to leave with the convoy for an unknown destination, when, at Neue-Breme, he had remained with the sick at a time when even the strongest men had asked only for a chance to escape. Absolute love in absolute sacrifice. This is what the life of Thérèse signified, and this is also the meaning of the destiny of Père Jacques. He prayed to Thérèse to protect him and give him strength.

Père Jacques's only weakness was to beg a sign of this protection in heroism. But this was an exquisite weakness, for it shows that Père Jacques, despite his prodigious energy, remained human. For if he was a support to others, he himself also had need of support.

Père Jacques was now in Güsen.

He was assigned to Block 17, one of the many dismal barracks where men were packed together, preys to vermin, blows, and infamy.

Suddenly, at 7:00 o'clock one evening, somebody entered the barracks. It was an old inmate of Güsen, an engineer named Henri Boussel. He questioned a few of the Frenchmen present, asking whether they knew a certain Lucien Bunel among the newcomers. He was referred to Père Jacques. Immediately, Henri Boussel went to him: "I told Père Jacques," said Boussel, "that one of my comrades had told me about him and that I was very happy to greet him. . . . This privilege fell to me because I had been a student of the Christian Brothers. One of my first duties was to welcome him to the camp."

A welcome to the hell of Güsen.

Père Jacques did not doubt for a second that this was the sign he had been waiting for, but he did not tell this to Boussel. He did not admit it to him until several months later.

However, Boussel lost no time. An hour later, he returned bringing Père Jacques a few small provisions.

The appearance of Henri Boussel, his first words, his first gesture of help, this was the finest and most beautiful of welcomes in the midst of this sinister world. But tomorrow? What would happen tomorrow?

6   "We Shall Take Care of Him"

Thrown into the midst of this army of slaves who toiled all day long at Güsen, Père Jacques was assigned to one of the most difficult work companies, the one constructing a reservoir near the Güsen quarry. Twelve hours of grueling work every day under the constant threats of the SS officers and the kapos who showered the men with blows, including fatal ones, under any pretext at all.

The rest of the time, it was the same intolerable regimen: endless roll calls, food below the subsistence level, endless inspection of the pallets, odious examinations for fleas, and always a shower of blows from the "gummi," the terrible rubber truncheons of the guards. Even at night there was no surcease unless one could sleep: the emaciated bodies were packed one against the other, gnawed by vermin and tormented by wounds that never healed.

But the little sign that Père Jacques had awaited from Thérèse was there, nevertheless, just as he had recognized it on the first night of his arrival at Güsen.

Day after day, Henri Boussel continued to intervene. Each evening he took Père Jacques with him to his quarters, Block 7, Room 3. It was in one of the most protected parts of the camp, because the chief of quarters, a German political prisoner, behaved like a human being toward the other deportees. Moreover he spoke French and had a special esteem for Frenchmen.

Every evening Henri Boussel invited Père Jacques to have some additional soup with him and his closest friend, Gaston Passagez, another engineer who was a little older than Boussel and who had been his chief in Paris.

But Boussel wanted to do much more than this and while Père Jacques was rapidly exhausting his energies at hard labor twelve hours every day, Boussel actively pursued a double project.

It was not by chance that Henri Boussel had learned of Père Jacques's arrival. He had learned of it through an act of fraternity. The meeting on the evening of Père Jacques's arrival at Güsen was not only the first contact in a new friendship. Behind this gesture of a single man was the whole secret fraternity of the camp. It had learned of Père Jacques's arrival and had procured for him a better place in the prison in order that he might accomplish his mission as a man of God.

Père Jacques recognized the sign from St. Thérèse from the very first. The more time passed, the more the signs were to multiply. The heavenly comradeship of Thérèse and the clandestine comradeship in the camp were one and the same in his destiny at Güsen.

The same kind of pandemonium reigned in Güsen as in Mauthausen. Everywhere were the SS, the kapos, starvation, and murder. Here, too, the crematory burned day and night. Here, too, was a Tower of Babel where every language and all national prejudices were in conflict. There had been many Russians but they had been massacred en masse. There were still Poles, Czechs, Spanish Republicans, Frenchmen, anti-Fascist Germans, men of all kinds and conditions.

The Poles formed the largest group; some six thousand out of twenty thousand inmates, whereas there were only a few hundred Frenchmen, perhaps four hundred at this particular time. The Poles were not only the most numerous, they had also been there the longest. Years before, they had begun to populate the concentration camps—before the invasion of France, before the hammerlike bombardment of England by the Germans, before Hitler's armies attacked Russia, before Japan attacked America, long before the war had become one great planetary holocaust, the Poles had already begun to enter the camps. The Poles of Güsen nourished a deep resentment against the other nations which, once again in their history, had allowed them to perish. And they were not alone. The Czechs also had been abandoned. The Spanish Republicans who had taken refuge in France now found themselves under the heels of the SS. The first French who arrived at Güsen were looked down upon by the other deportees.

The situation was made worse by the fact that the Poles, as greatest in number and the longest "in residence," held most of the responsible positions. They were "the inside masters of the camp," according to Professor Heim. In the eyes of the SS they were nothing, but they enjoyed an immense power over their fellow prisoners. They were the kapos, foremen of the road gangs and the workshops, overseers of the blocks and the dormitories, keepers of stores, office clerks. In camp slang, they were the sort called "top dogs." They had within their reach a thousand ways either of helping or crushing their fellow inhabitants in this hell, where at each moment the life of a man hung by a thread.

The Poles, the top dogs of Güsen, were no better than the frightful collection of sadistic brutes and degenerates who extended the raging mania for violence of the SS to the ranks of the deportees themselves. Naturally such elements had been selected from among the dregs of their respective nations. Here as elsewhere a subterranean struggle prevailed between the "greens" and the "reds," that is between common criminals and the political prisoners. The SS showed a natural predilection for the "greens": in this twisted world, it was not only desirable to mix the common criminals and the political prisoners, but the "greens" were actually put in charge over the latter. In this atmosphere, green ceased to signify hope but had come to symbolize degradation and despair. It was not by mere chance that the SS elected that those in charge wear a dark green emblem which resembled the color they themselves wore. But the system was not perfect. Everywhere the "greens" were torn by rivalries. The strength of the political prisoners, by contrast, lay in their fraternity, the solidarity of their point of view, their capacity for selfless dedication. They helped one another and as much as possible they supported one another in trying to wrest the key posts in the camp from the common criminals. Here and there, little by little, the best and the stanchest emerged, came to the top after a silent and terrible struggle.

At the same time the atmosphere gradually changed. The French became more numerous. In the camp they showed their desire to resist in a heroic way, and the news that filtered through the camp gave proof of the part taken by the French in the over-all assault against Hitler's fortress. Contacts were established between the French and the Poles, friendships became stronger. In the beginning there had been too many terrible clashes, too many atrocities committed by Polish kapos, and too great an unreconcilable opposition between the two extremes formed by the blocs of French Communists and the Polish bloc which was largely anti-Communist, for any general unity to be possible. Nevertheless an attempt was made to bring these two extremes together in a pure fraternity which knew no bounds.

It was in this way that Henri Boussel, a French engineer had become the friend of Valentin Pientka, a Polish lawyer.

Working in the office which received the lists of new arrivals and which assigned them to the different work details, it was Pientka who had first singled out the name "Lucien Bunel" and the notation "priest."[1] He at once informed Henri Boussel.

"All you have to do is to find him," Pientka had said, "and then we'll look after him. Find out what his situation is and how he happens to be here, since his category doesn't belong here."

In his book on Père Jacques, Père Philippe asserts that 522 French priests and religious were victims of the Nazis during the occupation. Of these, 152 were killed on the spot, and 370 were deported. But there were few priests in Mauthausen or in its annexes. At Compiègne Père Jacques had encountered Abbé Barbier and Père Riquet, both of whom were to be sent to Mauthausen, but Père Jacques was to see Abbé Barbier for only a few days, in the quarantine block. Later, he was to meet others, notably the Abbé Michaud, a curate

[1] Or rather, "ecclesiastic teacher."

from the Ardennes, and also a priest from the Haute-Vienne, but it seems they were separated again very soon afterward. So many were the encounters made by Père Jacques in his way to the cross and so many are the gaps among the ranks of the survivors, that it is not easy to track them all down. There were also frequent errors, deliberate or not, in the prisoner lists, and priests were not always known by everybody as such any more than were all the Communists, all the Jews, or the true identities of members of the resistance. In this multitude, agitated by outrageous upheavals, men came and went like phantoms. At first, according to Boussel, as soon as the priests were singled out as priests they were immediately destroyed; later on they were shipped out to be imprisoned at Dachau.

Thus, when Père Jacques arrived, there were barely more than four or five priests, all Polish, in Güsen I. Among them only one, Père Ludwig, showed an interest in the French inmates. Obstacles of language, mentality, and culture, contributed in separating even the French Catholics from the Polish priests. In the case of great numbers of the men, physical exhaustion helped to reinforce and intensify this separation. Moreover, the priestly ministry could be performed only in utmost secrecy. To violate the interdiction against it was to risk torture and death at any moment; it was to add one more pretext to the innumerable reasons for being destroyed.

Pientka's intervention was decisive from the point of view of the religious resistance within the camp. Pientka, Boussel, and their friends swung into action in every possible way to get Père Jacques out of the block to which he had been assigned and to relieve him from the hard-labor detail. Without them, Père Jacques would have been condemned to perish within a very short time.

Terror ruled everywhere in this labyrinth of hell. But within the numerous segments of which it was composed, the possibilities of physical and moral resistance varied greatly according to the work, to the mentality of the kapos, and to the level of those who shared this wretchedness.

The first block to which Père Jacques had been assigned was as infamous as any one of them. But Boussel's was very much better because of the personality of the overseer, a German political prisoner, educated and humane.

The hard labor to which Père Jacques had been condemned in the quarry was the worst detail in Güsen. There were other kinds of work—taxing, interminable, exhausting, for hideously undernourished men—where one could hold out longer, where the overseers were of a better type, and the workers themselves especially picked. The most important among these relatively sheltered sectors of the camp was the factory, a small-arms factory, situated just outside Güsen I. It was an annex of the Steyr industry which was scattered all over the suburbs of Linz.

At the factory prisoners also worked twelve hours a day, but they had a roof over their heads against the ravages of bad weather. They were still at the mercy of an SS officer or a maddened kapo, but the requirements of the machinery and the assembly line curbed the brutalities. The presence of Austrian civilians was also not without certain influence and bit by bit an élite group of prisoners had been assembled there. Conditions were also less miserable from the point of view of food. It was still wretched, but ersatz coffee and sausage, supplements of bread and soup, which were available to the factory workers, could be of the utmost help during these months when the least weakness was enough to make one go under.

It was here that Boussel, aided by Pientka, wished to bring Père Jacques so that he might survive for his own sake and for the sake of others.

The bitter ransom involved was that one had to work in an arms factory which made rifles and machine guns for the Nazis. Once again, the system operated only to increase the most demoralizing subversion. The political prisoners could not help but shudder in revulsion at the work they were doing. Their very heroism was being mocked to the last degree. But it was true that the system also mocked itself. Many of the factory workers were full-fledged specialists, and the throng of these deportees, each of whom spoke only his native language, was far from permitting a high output. It goes without saying that the art of sabotage was habitually practiced: fragile key parts such as rifle sights were easily knocked out of line. During this summer of 1944, moreover, the inmates knew that the final assault was being prepared. They could not guess how long it would take, and if they indulged in the illusion that the time would be short, it was but an additional reason to make them think that the weapons they were making would soon be turned against the enemy.

Moreover, Güsen offered no choice, except among equally revolting alternatives. To be handed over to common criminals or to political degenerates meant to be every moment at the mercy of the worst.

"Life at Güsen," Louis Deblé said, "was a continual straining of oneself not to go under, as the guards would have wished. Each minute was one of flagrant injustice, the triumph of brigandry, of pederasts who crushed you with their arrogance. This injustice perhaps also exists in civilized life but it is clothed in many forms. In the camp it appeared in all its hideous nudity."

It took four weeks of behind-the-scenes effort to transfer Père Jacques from the quarry work to the factory. Here in hall No. 3, he was assigned to running a rifle grooving machine. The work was still too hard; it required standing up for eleven hours a day, not to speak of roll calls, and Père Jacques had developed pulmonary edema. For a while Boussel thought of taking him in with him in hall No. 7, but he gave up this plan. The best he could find for Père Jacques was the "End Kontroll" where the bores of the finished products were checked. Here the work was less fatiguing and the operator was seated. Père Jacques would be near Gaston Passagez and other good comrades. Furthermore, there was a lot of going and coming because of the nature of the work, so that he would be well placed to see many people.

Pientka readily agreed, though in a practical way the transfer depended on an Austrian engineer who was the personnel director, but who offered no difficulties.

Thus, three weeks after entering the factory Père Jacques was transferred to the End Kontroll. At almost the same time he moved to Block No. 7, dormitory No. 3, where Boussel and Passagez were also lodged. He was as sheltered as it was possible to be.

How he intended to take advantage of this, remains to be told.

7   The Previous Good Friday

On stormy days, one sometimes takes shelter under a great oak. Its thick branches provide protection from the downpour. But once lightning begins to strike, one is far from sheltered. On the contrary!

This was more or less the kind of shelter Père Jacques had found in the world of the concentration camp. He had done it knowingly, but he could not have known what he was risking.

At the factory, Père Jacques sat in front of a table in the End Kontroll room. On the table were four or five rifle bores whose calibers had to be checked. Every day a stock of four or five hundred gun parts were delivered to him for inspection. The job was no sinecure. He was there twelve hours at a stretch with a break for "lunch." This break was supposed to last an hour but it was often shortened to twenty minutes by the length of roll call. Nor for that matter did it take twenty minutes to finish the meager fare.

His friend Gaston worked on one side of Père Jacques, and another friend, Passagez, a Navy lieutenant, on the other. Farther down the line were other friends, Louis Deblé, a student from Paris, and Elie Maurin, a Communist.

"The absence of a permanent kapo, of noisy machines, the temperature which was relatively comfortable even in winter, the possibilities of keeping oneself clean," said Louis Deblé, "permitted peace of mind, meditation, and if one were careful, long conversations with French comrades on control duty, or even with those who worked in the halls who could come in to sit down next to us for a moment."

208

In the same way dormitory 3 in Block 7 was a haven. Boussel's bunk was the upper one. For the time being, in this dormitory at least, they had the good fortune of being no more than two to a bunk. When the place next to Boussel was vacated, he procured it at once for Père Jacques. The adjacent bunk was occupied by Gaston Passagez and Marcel Plasiat, a Communist worker for the City of Paris, who was also the best of companions. The corner was the quieter because the German political prisoner, their dormitory overseer, abstained from the odious bed and "flea" inspections, which in many another block served as a pretext for the worst sort of sadistic hazing.

On Sundays, this same overseer treated all four to leftover soup because he regarded them as his French friends and because, unlike the Poles, they never received packages from their families. Pientka also made a contribution for the same reason. Pientka received the regular prisoner's ration like the others, but at noon at the factory he was allowed to finish the leavings of the SS officers. He did not refuse his ration of soup because of this windfall, but he put it carefully aside so that his comrades might profit. He hid it under his mattress and at night he passed it to Henri Boussel who shared it with Passagez, Plasiat, and Père Jacques.

By evening the soup was cold and there was no way of heating it. In normal times it would have been impossible to look at it, much less to swallow it. At Güsen it was an infinitely precious gift.

This double shelter, the factory and the block, was nevertheless a precarious one. At any moment, there might be an eruption of the SS or the kapos; submachine guns, revolvers, clubs could "speak" without any warning. And the kapos handled the bludgeon with a death-dealing skill.

The goings and comings between the factory and block, the roll calls, were so many moments of peril for one was again thrown in with the herd of inmates at the mercy of the pack.

Sickness was a permanent threat. The lack of food, exhaustion, vermin, the long motionless standing for roll call in all kinds of weather, all contributed to ravage and undermine the organism in a permanent way. Everywhere there were countless victims of boils, carbuncles, pneumonia, and endemic dysentery.

Those who could no longer hold out were "hospitalized" in the infirmary. But it was a miracle if anyone came back. Nothing gives better proof of the black subversion that prevailed in this concentration camp world than the atrocious twist given to the word infirmary—"the dream place."

The infirmary at Güsen consisted of five blocks. Block 28 for fever cases and incurables, and block 31 for dysentery cases had the worst reputations.

"Block 31," testified Louis Deblé, who was with Père Jacques in the End Kontroll, "was reserved for those suffering from terrible diarrhea which often turned into dysentery. The only medication, when it was available, was charcoal; the only remedy, diet, which obviously was not a remedy in our state of weakness. If at the end of two or three days, the diarrhea had not been arrested, the sick were sent to a special small room called the 'Bahnhof' (station) where they were left like animals, completely naked on straw which their evacuations rapidly converted into manure. It was sprawled on this manure that they lived their last days, their last hours. One of my comrades succeeded in getting out of this hell alive, and it was he who gave me the following details: at night, when it was time to sleep, there were horrible arguments and brawls among these men, reduced to a level lower than swine, over the few stained blankets that had been given them. And at noon, there were the same vicious scenes over the soup that was left in the center of the room in a cauldron."

Should not anybody who, by chance or by the intervention of a network of friendly support, was the least bit sheltered from this savagery, should not such a person make every effort to spare himself, to economize his strength, to take as little risk as possible, while waiting for the hour of liberation?

Wouldn't this have been the wise course to take in this summer of 1944 when on June 4 French troops had entered Rome and when the thunder of the D-Day debarkation had exploded on the shores of

Normandy on June 6? Victory was approaching. The men at the camp knew it. The news cut through all barriers and the nervous irritation of the prison guards confirmed it all the more.

But Père Jacques was the last to wish to lie low while awaiting the end. For him, this could be nothing but a time for action. He had not wished to come here for any other reason.

He even spoke of it in a way that astonished the others.

"The first time that I saw Père Jacques," Louis Deblé recounted, "was on a summer evening, 1944, June or July, I think. Cayrol had introduced me to him; the gentleness of his face, the depth of his eyes were as striking as the words he addressed to Cayrol: 'Well, I see quite a few people here with whom one might accomplish something worth while.' I wondered what worth-while thing this valiant schoolmaster might have in mind to do here! The more so, as he worked at the quarry. He would find it hard enough trying to save his own skin."

Now that Père Jacques was out of the quarry, and had joined Louis Deblé at End Kontroll, he wanted to profit from it only to serve others, to give to others the increased strength, the calm and the secret freedom that he himself had found.

Of what it might cost him to devote himself to others, Père Jacques had shining proof.

As the days passed by he made more and more new acquaintances among the French. In addition to Boussel, Passagez, and Plasiat, he met Professor Heim at the infirmary, Commandant Bondon, condemned to hard labor in the camp, the Communist Passard, Louis Deblé, the student in End Kontroll, Jean Cayrol, the poet, belonging to the group of young men from Bordeaux who were at Güsen. Most of them had been here since the spring of 1943, after long stretches at other prison camps.

They all talked to him about Père Gruber, especially the younger ones like Jean Cayrol and Louis Deblé, for without Père Gruber they would not have held out. For a year he had saved them from starvation. One must understand what it meant to spend twelve months at Güsen, and the hunger there, in order to appreciate what an extraordinary feat this was.

But Père Gruber was gone.

An Austrian, the former director of the Institute for Deaf-Mutes at Linz, Père Gruber had been imprisoned under some sort of pretext. Oddly enough, he had landed at Güsen as kapo of the Museum. For in this camp which included a crematory and a brothel, there was also a museum to preserve mineralogical specimens and archaeological remains which the deportees dug up in the many land-grading projects on the banks of the Danube, ancient waterway for commerce and invasion. It was a privileged job, the more so since Père Gruber was only a few miles from his home and often received food parcels from his sister. Père Gruber was fifty years old or over, small and rather plump. He was better placed than anyone else for holding out until the end of the war, provided he was cautious.

When great numbers of French prisoners began to pour into the camp, Père Gruber took advantage of his privileged position to help and encourage the German and Austrian inmates, whether they were common criminals or "politicals." It was a violation of orders, but still not a crime.

In May, 1943, near the terrible quarry, Père Gruber met a very young Frenchman, exhausted and terribly emaciated. This was Jean Pelletier, better known as Jim. Père Gruber spoke French, he was a lover of France, and he spoke with Jim. He immediately procured extra food for him. Jim did not want to profit from this alone, selfishly; so he told Père Gruber about his twenty other comrades from Bordeaux, all under twenty years of age. Père Gruber did not hesitate. He arranged for these starving boys to have additional portions of soup. And he added bread and sweets from his personal store. He did even more: thanks to his secret connections he had them all transferred from the quarry to the Steyr factory, particularly to the End Kontroll where Louis Deblé had preceded Père Jacques.

"The 'Gruber Organization' was in full swing," Louis Deblé recalled. "In December [1943], a dozen or so of the French each received at least a quart of soup and four ounces of bread from him every evening. And on Saturdays, sausage, margarine, honey, sometimes even a slice of meat."

"Père Gruber was a prodigious man," Jean Cayrol adds. "The day he found me, I had no more than forty-eight hours to live, I was so terribly hungry and cold. I was barely clothed and at the end of my strength. I was working at the quarry. 'He needs urgent help,' Père Gruber was told. 'Cayrol is one of the most urgent cases.' Then he brought me five quarts of potatoes mashed in water. I called a friend and the two of us finished it in five minutes. Père Gruber had tears in his eyes.

"He was a small, round man, always smiling, with wonderfully blue eyes, very alert. We called him Papa Gruber, and it's true that we owed him our lives. He was an absolutely unbelievable person. He never lectured us on religion. I never saw him pray. Sometimes he would say simply: 'Don't think, just eat,' or 'Cayrol, first eat, then think about your soul.' If you judged this in terms of a well fed man today, you would completely misunderstand. Père Gruber above all wanted us to eat, because we had nothing to eat, and it was he who brought us enough to subsist. So necessary was it for him to repeat this that, from time to time, he would go to the infirmary and, with maternal patience, would spoon-feed the sick who no longer even wanted food, who lay waiting for death as a deliverance. To refuse to eat was suicide and abdication. To eat was the primary and most elementary form of resistance. This shows how right Père Gruber was. Yet, at the same time, the meaning of his words was quite the contrary for he valued the soul above all else when he risked his life to find something for us to eat. His phrase seemed to be materialism itself; in his mouth it was pure heroism."

In the early months of 1944, the "Gruber Organization" became more and more fantastic. It fed thirty-five and perhaps as many as fifty deportees, almost all chosen from among the younger ones, who secretly gathered every day in the lavatory of Block 12. Père Gruber would bring in fifty quarts of soup.

"Every Sunday," Louis Deblé said, "we would join him and have a talk; he would give us what news he had, while his mischievous little eyes roved about on the lookout for danger. Then he would take a loaf of bread, a second, a third, a square of margarine, a jar of jelly, from his pockets and his face would wrinkle with laughter at the ecstatic look in our eyes."

"One day he brought us a brioche," Jean Cayrol added. "At Güsen, this was unimaginable. I had a perpetual impression of the miraculous with him."

"He really was our salvation," Louis Deblé continued, "a messenger from heaven in this Nazi hell. He looked after everything, he himself carried rations to those in the infirmary; he took it upon himself to replace our shoes when they were worn through. . . . We would laugh in good humor when we were with him and quickly finish off our extra ration before returning to our respective quarters."

Père Gruber stopped at nothing. He went so far as to send postal cards to France giving news of these young men. The messages were very short, discreet, but absolutely forbidden. How was he able to manage all these enterprises? This was the most unbelievable part of his prodigious adventure in charity, for neither Père Gruber's personal friends, nor packages from his sister and an aged aunt could have supplied him enough for his large-scale operation. The secret arm of Père Gruber was certainly cigarettes. Whoever received help from him had to promise not to smoke and Père Gruber, by various means, had amassed an enormous stock of cigarettes which he bartered in every possible and imaginable way. When this proved insufficient, he had even a better idea. He got hold of some money and would pay bribes, for example, to have young men transferred from the quarry.

"Once," Jean Cayrol said, "he gave up his watch to save one of us."

But he paid for all this with what was most precious of all, his own person. In order to save this young Frenchman and many others, he was up to his neck in illegalities. He constantly ran the risk of being denounced, but he carried on, nevertheless.

For quite a while Père Gruber remained optimistic; it was his nature. He used to say to those he helped: "Don't forget my address after the liberation; you'll come to see me at Linz and we'll have a celebration." But he saw how the war dragged on. He doubted he would be able to last it out, especially under the improbable conditions in which he lived, helping these young men to survive. Then, as though it were a final message and as though he had a foreboding that quite a few among these youths would outlive him, he said: "Remember, what I do is for the sake of Austria."

Suddenly, April 4, 1944, on Tuesday of Holy Week, when Père Jacques was just becoming acquainted with Neue-Breme, Louis Deblé and his friends heard the news in the End Kontroll.

Père Gruber had just been arrested and thrown into a cell from which nobody had ever come out alive.

That evening in the camp, after work, they assembled in the lavatory of Block 12. Before his arrest, Père Gruber had had time to prepare their extra ration of soup which they had been receiving daily for months. With heavy hearts, they drank it. They were desperate, filled with anxiety. What would happen to Père Gruber? How would they manage without him?

"Jim did everything possible to get some food to our benefactor," said his friend Deblé. He could not get to him for three days. Père Gruber was locked in the cell without food or drink, and tortured each day by the commandant of the camp himself, Seidler. On Friday, April 7, Good Friday, at three o'clock in the afternoon, we Catholics in the End Kontroll, Polish and French, observed one minute of silent meditation. I glanced at Jim; he also was evidently thinking of Père Gruber, and it is the only time, I believe, that I ever saw him cry. At this very time, by an extraordinary coincidence, M. Gruber was dying from the beating administered by Seidler. We were told about it that night in the camp: on Good Friday, April 7, 1944, martyred, as had been our Lord Jesus Christ, twenty centuries earlier.

Nobody had succeeded in getting to him. The case of Père Gruber had been considered a serious offense by the Nazis because charity was an abomination in the death camp. And for an Austrian to give

succor to Frenchmen was seen as a "betrayal," and for this reason
the head of the camp himself had taken charge of the matter as
being one of utmost gravity.

After his execution, the Nazis spread the rumor that Père Gruber
had committed suicide. Doubtlessly they did this to try to dishonor
his memory, to dishearten his friends further, and to make them
believe that he had given in to despair and to remorse over his
"criminal" activity. The executioner always seeks to dishonor his
victim. By a curious dialectical compensation, the more unjust the
condemnation, the more it is seasoned with dishonoring circumstances. Christ was condemned as "blasphemer" and "rebel," Jeanne
d'Arc as "heretic, one relapsed into heresy"; so how could the Nazis
have resisted the temptation to try to make the inmates believe that
Père Gruber was a suicide?

Moreover, they had the cynical impudence to offer exact details:
"He hanged himself in the cell at the same hour as Christ died."

This was the supreme mockery against Christ and Père Gruber. It
was also a clue to their lying and manipulation.

"Our overseer, an aging Austrian, shrugged his shoulders," Maurice
Passard said, "when he heard somebody say that Père Gruber had
committed suicide as the Nazis claimed."

To be sure the body of Père Gruber was found hanging in the
cell, but this was a manner of execution esteemed among the Nazis.
And on all sides, the walls of the cell were spattered with blood.

It was Holy Week. Early in Passion Week, the Nazis had tortured
Père Gruber for being guilty of having revived the charity of Christ
in the concentration camp. Nothing more was necessary but the
final execution. That they had expressly chosen three o'clock on
Good Friday was not in the least surprising. And they made it
perfectly plain that they were aware of the coincidence. They could
have done it on purpose, as a supreme mockery of the Faith. But
here again, in this very mockery, as in charity and martyrdom, Père
Gruber joined hands with Christ.

The testimony he had given of charity had been of such an impressive nature that the Communists of the camp shared the grief of his death with the Catholics.

On Easter Sunday, as a gift from Père Gruber, a friend brought bread and onions to the young men he had protected. Before his arrest, Père Gruber had put aside a little supply so that together they might celebrate the Resurrection.

Père Gruber was dead. Père Jacques had come to replace him.

8   "I Thank Thee, O My God"

At Güsen, Père Jacques's day was as carefully lined out as a sheet of paper ruled for music. There was no respite from the routine of the block, the factory, the going to and fro, the interminable roll calls in the assembly area.

In the morning between waking and roll call, and in the evening between "meals" and curfew, it was possible to circulate a little more freely from one section to another and to meet with comrades who lived in another block and worked in a different place.

In the block, at the factory, in his going and coming, Père Jacques had but one thing constantly on his mind—to take advantage of the slightest possibilities offered for accomplishing his mission.

"We got up," Henri Boussel said, "between 4:45 and 5:00 o'clock. Armed with towel and soap, Père Jacques made his way down the stairs to the washroom in undershorts. Naked, he scrubbed his body, even in extremely cold weather. I reproached him for it; it had been obligatory at one time, but with discipline somewhat relaxed it was now up to each one's 'good will.' After Père Jacques had washed, he would come back and promptly say: 'Pass me the bowls.' Then he went for the 'coffee,' handing me the towel and soap. Several times I said to him: 'Père Jacques, there's no rush, get dressed; at least put your shirt on, we'll have the coffee later. We still have three-quarters of an hour left.' He would not listen. One day, I said that after all this wasn't the moment to affect English ways, and that at home, as it were, we could change to shorts and sit down to lunch in informal dress. But his way had become a habit."

Père Jacques, who had shivered from cold during a retreat at la

218

Trappe, was training himself to withstand the most severe temperatures in this camp which were glacial in winter and where, as might be expected, there was no heat of any sort for the prisoners. Each morning Père Jacques was in a great hurry. For, each day during these three-quarters of an hour of free movement, he would disappear to visit the sick.

"I was sick and you visited me," Christ said when he gave the decisive words of judgment. This was the first, almost monastic Rule in accordance with which Père Jacques made use of his time.

"Dressing quickly, Père Jacques went every morning to the infirmary," Gaston Passagez reported. "Very often I went with him to sow an encouraging word, to bring the comfort of good news to block 27 where so many comrades, afflicted with ulcers, tuberculosis, exhaustion, lay almost lifeless on their pallets. You should have seen Père Jacques's gentle smile reflected in these livid faces, as though in a mirror."

Stealthily they would slip the sick inmates whatever they had been able to bring. Père Jacques always managed to put aside a piece of bread or other food the evening before. Often they would have to hide in order to make the visit. While a friend kept watch a few steps ahead, Père Jacques signaled to the sick through the windows and gave them absolution.

"The first time I saw Père Jacques in May, 1944," Professor Heim recounted, "it was through the window bars of block 27 of the Güsen infirmary where I lay on a pallet, my arm split open by primitive surgery, in a raging fever, waiting for a smile of comfort to come from heaven. It was he who brought it.

"Every day, morning and evening, for three months, Père Jacques came with our friends, Jean Cayrol, Henri Boussel, Gaston Passagez, to give me his word of encouragement, the news which his own ardent hopefulness made all the more vivid, which shone the brighter with his faith in an early victory. His secret visits in the early morning when it was still dark were the only refreshment available to the sick and from this miraculous source I drew stamina for victory over a fatal weakening." (*La Sombre route*, p. 71.)

When Père Jacques returned to the block, he would extract from beneath his thin mattress a small book that had been carefully hidden: a breviary, a missal, a New Testament, or an *Imitation of Christ*. He was not supposed to have books, particularly works as "subversive" as these. Since he had left Compiègne, he had been stripped of everything he had been able to save. But upon his arrival at the camp, when the Poles learned he was a priest, they got these books for him from one of those piles of booty stolen from the new arrivals. The missal was water-stained, the other books in much the same condition, but to Père Jacques these were treasures: the Word of God which down through the ages had passed through so much tragedy. When he read the breviary in the morning, it was not simply to carry on the pious, customary practice of priests. It was rather to plunge himself into the pages of the Gospel, into the epistles, the Psalms of David, the pages of the martyrology; it was to be strengthened from the source of the supreme sacrifice since at every moment Père Jacques, in flesh and blood, was making the way of the cross, and could expect an end like that of Père Gruber.

He read and meditated for a few precious moments.

There was one more thing to be done and this he did every morning, in the company of Boussel and Passagez, in the courtyard before the roll call.

On June 9, 1895, a prayer was composed by a young girl of twenty-two: Thérèse of the Infant Jesus, the Carmelite of Lisieux.

Thérèse called this prayer: "The offering of myself as a victim of holocaust to the merciful love of God."

In the religious life of the Jews of the Old Testament, holocaust was the most absolute of sacrifices, that where the victim on the altar was entirely consumed by fire, as an offering of expiation and thanksgiving.

It was thus that Thérèse desired to offer her life.

Père Jacques could repeat each word of this prayer which Thérèse had lived out, for this is what he sought also—absolute sacrifice, and from the same motives.

"O my God! O blessed Trinity," Thérèse said, "I desire to love

Thee and to make Thee loved. . . . I desire to fulfill thy will perfectly. . . ."

Père Jacques had no other desire than to accept totally the will of the Lord in an act of absolute trust. He had once said this to Michel de Bouard in Mauthausen.

"In a word, I desire to be a saint," Thérèse continued, "but I feel my powerlessness, and I ask Thee Thyself to be my sanctity."

Père Jacques knew that there is no sanctity but from God and a man becomes a saint only insofar as he mirrors God and submerges his will in the divine will. When he was in the army, at the time of a retreat at the Trappist monastery at Soligny during a furlough, he had carefully made the following note in his personal journal: "The Curé of Ars hoped for nothing from himself but awaited everything from God."

"In my heart I feel immense desires," Thérèse wrote further, "and it is with confidence that I ask Thee to come and take possession of my soul."

The love of God filled the whole life of Père Jacques; his heart was not split in two with one part for God and the other for his fellow prisoners, but was one. Christians or not, he loved them all in the love of God. He did not separate what Christ has proclaimed as one when He said that the two great commandments, the love of God and the love of one's neighbor, are but one.

"I cannot receive Holy Communion as often as I desire, but Lord, are not you All-Powerful? Dwell in me, as in the tabernacle, do not ever leave me. . . ."

During the lifetime of Thérèse, even the Carmelites could not receive Communion daily. At Güsen, Père Jacques was almost always deprived. He knew what the cost is to a heart burning with love not to partake each day in the eucharistic repast.

"I would console Thee for the ingratitude of the wicked. . . ."

There are happy periods in history when this message may seem exaggerated; Père Jacques, who day after day witnessed the atrocities of Güsen, knew how much this message understates the truth.

"And I beg Thee to take away the liberty to displease Thee. If through weakness I sometimes fall, let Thy divine gaze immediately purify my soul, consuming my imperfections, like the fire which transforms everything into itself."

Père Jacques did not think about being perfect. He renewed his request to God to accomplish all within him so that he might remain equal to a task that surpassed human strength.

"I thank Thee, O My God, for all the graces Thou hast granted me."

Père Jacques thanked the Lord for the years of life, austere and happy, that He had accorded him in the past.

"Especially for having tried me in the crucible of suffering."

Père Jacques had desired to remain a captive. He had desired to share the sufferings of captives, and after everything he had endured in Güsen, amid this hideous misery exposed to his sight on all sides, and anticipating the worst, he gave thanks to God for having plunged him into the depths of this universe of terror, because here he shared the sufferings of Christ and of his brothers, because here he could transmit a ray of the love of Christ.

"I do not wish to store up merits for heaven, I want to work for Thy Love alone, with the single goal of pleasing Thee, of bringing consolation to Thy Sacred Heart and of saving souls whom Thou wilt love eternally."

Heavenly "rewards" have nothing in common with pleasures and baubles ordinarily called rewards, and "merits" in the eyes of God are other than those ordinarily crowned with awards of virtue, for God alone knows their true worth. The only "merit" is to devote oneself to the love and will of God and the only "reward" of love is love itself.

"In the twilight of this life, I shall appear before Thee with empty hands, for I do not ask Thee, Lord, to compare my works. All our justices are tainted in Thine eyes. Hence I wish to wear the cloak of Thy justice, and receive from Thy love eternal possession of Thyself. I wish no other crown or throne but Thee, my Beloved."

When you have fulfilled all that which is written, Christ said to His disciples, you will say simply: we are useless servants. Only the

Pharisee counts up his merits, all that he has given in time and money for good causes and the satisfaction of a good conscience. Père Jacques, who had given everything, did not boast of this for a second. Empty hands on the Day of Judgment? One is not certain whether one understands these words in the mouth of Père Jacques, and of Thérèse. Is this mystical folly? Is it an excess of modesty? But the light shed by the parables of Christ leaves no room for equivocation: we can give nothing to others which we have not ourselves received from God, be it material goods, strength, intelligence, courage, unselfishness. But what we all egotistically keep for ourselves, Père Jacques, like Thérèse, wished to surrender to God. The earth gives back only the wheat that has been planted, but she returns it a hundredfold. Thérèse gave everything to God, in this world and the next, in order to find only the love of God. Père Jacques humbly wished to walk along the same road: he wished to ask God for no earthly or heavenly good except God Himself.

"Thou canst in an instant prepare me to appear before Thee. . . ." This was true. At Güsen it was hideously evident.

"That my life may be an act of perfect love, I offer myself as the victim of holocaust to Thy merciful love," Thérèse had said, "begging Thee continuously to consume me, allowing the floods of infinite tenderness which are contained in Thee to overflow in my soul so that I thus become a martyr to Thy love."

An act of perfect love, this was the key message of St. John of the Cross, who said that this act was worth all good works put together. Père Jacques had read and meditated on these words from the time of his first retreat at Avon. They were among those which helped to make up his mind to become a Carmelite. He had chosen the path of Carmel as the way of perfect love.

To die a martyr, this surely is what Père Jacques was embracing in Güsen. He was not a masochist who enjoyed suffering; he suffered from suffering, as does every normal man, but he would not resign himself to undergoing it blindly, as one gives in to a terrible and insurmountable fatality. In his daily and tragic life, he desired to radiate love in spite of suffering and, if he was to die there, he wanted

PÈRE JACQUES

this death, however abominable the torturers made it, to be the greatest sign of love that he was able to give, as death on the Cross was the greatest sign of the love of Christ.

"May this martyrdom, after having prepared me to appear before Thee, at last let me die and may my soul, without delay, soar to the eternal embrace of Thy merciful love. . . .

"I wish, O My Beloved, with each beat of my heart to renew this offering an infinite number of times. . . ."

Père Jacques and his friends repeated this prayer every morning in Güsen.

"Until the shadows shall have vanished. . . ."

In Güsen the tormentors were still firmly on their feet, their rubber truncheons still struck efficiently, and the submachine guns shot real bullets. On the German frontiers, the enormous war machine mounted by Hitler still offered fierce resistance. But no earthly power is immutable, it is established in time, that is to say on shifting sands. Peaceful Normandy which had been witness to Thérèse had now vanished like a shadow, and at this very moment in Güsen the power of the executioner bore down with all its weight in vain, for it also was in the process of vanishing like a shadow.

"May I declare my love over and over, face to face, eternally. . . ."

This had been the last cry of Thérèse. It was the cry of the Apostle John at the end of the Apocalypse: "Come, Lord Jesus, come!" If Père Jacques had not continuously lived in faith, in the presence of the Lord, his whole life would be incomprehensible. But the Lord remained invisible for Père Jacques as for us, and faith aspires only to go beyond itself, at the entry to this new world in which we shall see Christ before us as did the disciples long ago, but this time eternally. What Père Jacques most desired was to live with Christ, in faith, despite the unleashed terror; to join Christ, later on, visibly, with all those whom he loved. And he hoped for this without faltering or reservations. It was to God he aspired to give his life, but for the sake of everyone.

The prayer of Thérèse of the Infant Jesus is so long that it has not been cited here in full. It is so long that I wondered whether Père Jacques really recited all of it. His friends have stated that it was indeed the whole prayer that he said every morning, lovingly pronouncing each word.

But it is true that Père Jacques did not know it in its entirety. It was not he who had taught it to his two Christian friends in dormitory 3. He had known it for a long time, he had certainly retained its main theme of absolute love in absolute sacrifice. He had surely read, reread, and remembered certain passages, but he did not know it by heart.

This I did not know. But I did wonder what unusual circumstance could have brought Père Jacques to commit so long a prayer to memory, however great his fervor had been for the young saint of Lisieux. When I asked about this, Gaston Passagez revealed the secret.

"It was I," he said, "who taught Père Jacques the prayer of St. Thérèse. He himself was amazed that I knew the prayer by heart. I had not always known it. But I was arrested in November, 1941, and incarcerated at Fresnes. In my cell, I was visited by Abbé Stock, a priest from Luxembourg of the Foreign Missions, who was the prison chaplain. He was an admirable man; many of the prisoners remember him with immense gratitude. He gave me a copy of *The Story of a Soul* by St. Thérèse. I admired this saint, I read and reread her book and memorized her prayer of offering. It is long, but remember that in prison there's no shortage of time to learn things by heart. I never forgot it, and when Père Jacques came we spoke of this prayer and the three of us, Père Jacques, Boussel, and I, started to say it together."

This, too was a sign from St. Thérèse that Père Jacques could not have foreseen.

9   All Day a Parade of Visits

In winter the morning roll call took place at six-twenty, and work was supposed to start at seven. (In summer both began an hour earlier.) The prisoners then fell into file five abreast in groups of one hundred and they were marched to the exit gate, in the direction of the factory.

Once outside the gate it was no more than a hundred or so yards to the factory, but this included a flight of steps which, although they were short, Père Jacques had nicknamed "Calvary." It was necessary to race down the steps because the SS lay in wait on each side, hitting out at random with their arms, shovels, cudgels, gun barrels, anything that fell to hand, the way a brute strikes animals to amuse himself.

After escaping from this ambush the men had to regroup in haste, each one in front of his workroom. A fresh count was made, then the inmates went to their jobs and set to work at once.

Père Jacques's first appearance in the End Kontroll which Henri Boussel, with Pientka's help, had taken such pains to obtain for him, was far from pleasant: "From the first day, Père Jacques received frequent blows from the gummi, the rubber truncheon. Big Karl, the kapo of the shop, had come in suddenly, cudgel in hand, and for no particular reason he had started bludgeoning the first to enter. Père Jacques," Louis Deblé recounted, "had just been assigned to the end of the room, near the door. I had turned around at the sound of raised voices and I can still see our comrades rushing forward to escape the blows. Père Jacques alone stood still, turning his gentle and astonished regard on the red-faced madman clubbing and roaring at everyone in sight. This constant composure and calm in the midst of commotion and hot-headedness was certainly one of the most characteristic qualities of Père Jacques's conduct in the concentration camp; I liked being near him because his attitude forced one to remain calm; just to talk with him made the camp seem to vanish."

This, however, did not help Père Jacques himself to avoid heavy blows from Karl's gummi. But he managed to retain an air of complete indifference.

"The workday had begun. It was spent checking the parts, in rejecting and discarding as many as possible, and also in sabotage," Gaston Passagez said, "and Père Jacques was a past master in slowing down production."

From a technical point of view he still required a period of apprenticeship, but as for "wasting time" he knew to perfection all the favorite tricks of the most backward and recalcitrant pupils.

Moreover, circumstances were in his favor because except for an occasional dangerous intrusion, such as those from Karl, the two engineers near him, Austrian civilians, Haugenauder and Petrak, shut their eyes to a good many things.

But if Père Jacques slowed up factory production, he was far from wasting his time. He talked a great deal. He made use of the slightest opportunity to chat with the young Frenchmen in End Kontroll, the former protégés of Père Gruber. He talked for all the world as if he were not at Güsen but at St. Joseph's in Le Havre or at the school in Avon, trying to give encouragement to one of his pupils.

"As soon as I arrived," Louis Deblé said, "Père Jacques would smile and he would enter at once into a lively discussion of a subject that interested him, which he doubtless had just been thinking about: 'Louis,' he would say, 'do you know the Fontainebleau forest?' or 'What do you think of secondary education in France?' He was surprised to learn that I did not know Gide—'A mystic seeking his proper course,' he called him, and, while I held a calibrator in my hand for appearance' sake, he, while still checking his work,

would explain his views at length on teaching and on the moral education of children, a subject especially dear to him. One day he said:
'I make my third-year students read Dr. Carnot's *In the Service of
Love.*' Another day, we'd talk about all the great classical and romantic writers; he characterized them in concise, exact words, often
in terms of paradox: 'As a matter of fact, Louis, compared to the
sixteenth and twentieth centuries, the seventeenth was rather in-
ferior.' These ideas, expressed so simply, would leave me stunned.
Meanwhile the hours and days passed, and you ended by forgetting
where you were."

Paradox! This word again became a characteristic of Père Jacques's
life. He had been paradoxical in Le Havre, in Avon, and now he
was still being paradoxical in Güsen. At least he seemed so, for what
today is paradox, often may become a verity tomorrow. Père
Jacques appeared paradoxical each time he shook the pillars of the
temple of classic culture, each time he touched on social divisions
and stratifications, whenever he dreamed, without ever being able to
realize the dream, of having his pupils know workers' families, and to
be able to enter the children of workers in his school. One could see
how he had impressed the young and offered them a new road,
fresh approaches. Nevertheless it is true that he sought paradox for
the pleasure it gave him. "You never quite knew whether he was
speaking seriously or not. He had a keen sense of humor and always
kept a straight face," said his friend Passagez. Even at Güsen. If,
however, he used paradox when he discussed serious subjects such
as education, labor, and communism, it was not to amuse himself; it
was that he understood and wished to make comprehensible the
drama in question and knew that it was first necessary to break
through the crusty surface of routine ways of thinking. He always
tried to face the issue squarely. Since he spoke with clarity, and since
his life answered for his words, he never faded off into the equivocal.

But the mischievous pupils whom he might have come across
would have had a good laugh, had they not been moved to tears, to
see how adept he was at clandestine reading in this black den of
Güsen. He even set an example of how to do this for the others.

"He had managed to get books to read from the Poles and Spaniards and let me borrow them," Deblé continued, "if I promised to be very careful. We would put the book in the partly opened drawer of the table where we sat and used to read leaning our elbows on the table, holding a gauge in one hand and gun barrel in the other. In this way, thanks to Père Jacques, I read *Extracts from Rousseau* ('The Profession of Faith of a Savoyard Vicar' was the subject of long parleys), *New Lecture on Human Understanding* by Leibnitz, which he asked me to summarize and comment on orally."

The Nazis believed they had stamped out thought. What are words before a club? What is human thought in the face of a machine gun? But Père Jacques imperturbably continued his profession of teacher and found this wonderful student who not only read but took it upon himself to study.

In the drawer, beneath Mauser gun parts, were hidden the writings of one of the most illustrious German philosophers. In this camp of twenty thousand prisoners, in this infernal Babel amidst the din of machinery, of polyglot cries of fury and pain, where death was ever on the prowl ready to strike, two French convicts, clothed in rags, barely nourished, half-opened their worktable drawer and discussed the ideas of Leibnitz.

"I had questioned just what this brave schoolmaster could possibly think of doing here that would be of interest," Louis Deblé had said the day of Père Jacques's arrival. Now he understood. Despite everything and against all odds, Père Jacques was continuing his work of educator. The Nazis sought to debase man to the level of beasts; Père Jacques sought to raise him up, to raise his sights as he had done in times of peace. The Nazis did everything possible to demoralize; Père Jacques did everything possible to fortify the spirit. The struggle to cultivate the intellect was in itself an act of moral resistance. Louis Deblé fully realized this: "Often in the course of a day, I felt the need to turn and watch him there, at the other end of the room: he was either working, checking the parts one by one with rapid gestures but without haste, his eyes always cast down, immersed in profound meditation, or he would be reading, his head

bent over the table drawer. Or he might be engaged in a discussion
with one of the French, Spanish, or Polish workers come to take
intellectual refreshment from his words. . . . All day, in the inspection room, there was a file of young Catholics or militant Communists, French or foreigners, with whom he liked to talk and whom,
moreover, he generally got to agree with him. For nobody understood better than he the serious social problems that would arise
after the war. . . ."

This was not without its risks. One could not defy the tyranny of
the camp with impunity and if Père Jacques was able to withstand
the "chastisements," which were not spared, he was nevertheless
dangerously "in error."

"This continuous parade of French deportees, most of whom were
already doomed, caused frequent comments from the chief tech-
nician in charge of the control room, according to Passagez. In fact,
one day Père Jacques received a terrible beating from the boss, 'big
Karl the Austrian,' as we called him, and in spite of the avalanche of
blows he retained his calm expression and looked upon the miserable
wretch with an air of indifference."

Père Jacques, however, carried on his task all the more arduously
and those who knew him took advantage of any chance they had to
stop off to see him, in passing.

Boussel had been right. The End Kontroll, under the very nose of
the Nazis, served as a clandestine salon for conversation. Père
Jacques talked to all kinds of people, Christians and non-Christians.
Sometimes the End Kontroll served as a confessional, without prie-
dieu, grille, or curtains. From the top of his cross, near the cross of
Christ, a thief who had been crucified at the same time had suddenly
poured out his supplication full of love toward Christ crucified who
gave him this reply: "This day thou shalt be with me in Paradise."
The deportees could no more fall to their knees than could the thief,
but their hearts overflowed with love and Père Jacques answered
them surreptitiously and with a pardon full of the love of Christ.

At noon after the brief meal, there was a moment of calm for the
inmates because the Nazis took their time eating. Père Jacques

swallowed his soup very quickly, ate a piece of bread, then disappeared to a place a short distance away, between two barracks. There were always several Poles waiting there for confession. Père Jacques had learned a little Polish for this purpose.

In the afternoon, he would talk again with those who dropped by for a chat, hear confessions, and raise their morale.

From time to time, during a quiet interval, he seemed to be drowsy, and it may be that he was overcome by fatigue and lack of nourishment.

"Père Jacques, so you're taking a little nap—you're dreaming?" Gaston Passagez whispered to him one day.

"I am much farther away than that," he had answered.

This was not the first time.

Before he had been assigned to the End Kontroll, when he worked at a lathe in one of the factory halls beside Julien Jacques, who also operated a lathe, the latter looked up one day and noticed that Père Jacques had stopped working.

"Visibly, he was elsewhere. I cried out to him: 'Wake up! Where are you at this moment?' He looked at me and said: 'In Paradise.' We burst out laughing. But he was a believer, a true one."

The inmates left their jobs at 6:00 P.M. and assembled again outside for another roll call. At 6:45, they left for the barracks in ranks of five in groups of one hundred, and once again they had to run the formidable gantlet of the stairway. In the camp, they returned to their respective blocks for their meager supper.

More or less protected as he was from standing the humiliating inspection for fleas and of his straw mattress, Père Jacques could have taken some time out for a little rest. Instead he used the time to steal out between the barracks to join those whom he had not been able to see at the factory. Again, he made a furtive visit to the sick, then, hidden by the uncertain shelter of the corner of one of the blocks, he once more heard confessions and gave consolation. This had to be done in secret, without attracting attention, and in all weather. In the beginning it had been summer, the weather was mild, but Père Jacques did not remain in the block even when it rained. And when winter came, the long and severe Austrian winter, Père Jacques would stay outside, even in the snow. It was there that the men sought him out, sometimes at the last minute before curfew.

One evening, a young Pole urgently wanted to see Père Jacques. It was cold, it was raining, and an icy wind blew, but the Pole waited, peering at each approaching figure.

"He was expecting somebody [he himself told the story to Joseph Wadseck], but this person was apparently not coming, probably because of the bad weather. The rain increased and the wind whistled loudly, carrying the smell of human flesh burning in the crematory. The constant smell of burning flesh, the horror of things taking place around him made him recall his past life. He reflected.

"Yes, I must confess, I must ask forgiveness from God! This was why he was waiting there for the priest. The boy was about to go, when he saw a figure walking rapidly in his direction. Probably this was Père 'Zak' whom he had met a few days ago. Père Zak, after a greeting, explained his delay; he was late because of work. 'You haven't eaten, have you?' 'Twelve hours of work without eating,' the priest answered. 'You must be hungry then, and you're completely soaked. Go to the barracks to eat and get a little rest,' the boy said. 'I'll make my confession tomorrow.' 'No, my son,' the priest replied, 'man must work not only for his body but also for his soul. Let's not argue,' he said smiling. A moment afterward, at a few paces from where I stood, near the enclosure with live wires against which many had thrown themselves out of despair, there stood the boy, bareheaded, Père Zak beside him. The boy confessed with deep penitence; he felt a great relief and contentment of heart. His eyes fixed on the priest, he listened attentively to the advice and directives given by his confessor.

"Had they both forgotten the cold and the drenching rain? They had also overlooked the most important of all: the red lamp hanging on the wire, a sign that the SS had retired to the inside of the camp. Woe to us if they caught any of us performing religious rites which were rigorously forbidden in the camp! After the necessary counsel,

Père Jacques gave the boy absolution and left. The boy remained there a moment longer thinking of the great and ardent work of the Father-Apostle."

Other evenings Père Jacques would give little talks while hidden in the shadows behind a block. Such talks involved new perils because of the block overseers whose surveillance had to be foiled at all costs. Père Jacques was not the only one to do this. All groups who wished to maintain morale organized such clandestine talks, particularly the Communists, the Protestants, Professor Heim, and a few others. Père Jacques spoke most frequently to small groups of young men, giving them catechetical instruction, conferences on the clergy, and on social reforms to be made in France after the liberation. Young Communists came too, and he answered their questions in a very friendly way. He explained the aim of the monastic life to them.

"He even held these little conferences with Communist groups," said Henri Boussel.

"He helped many of the younger ones," declared Jean Cayrol, "who otherwise might have been undermined by the promiscuity of the foul dormitory in which we slept. I asked him to give some of my vacillating comrades something like a course in religious instruction or, more precisely 'talks about the sacraments.'"

"How many conferences he held in the dirty attics, full of vermin, in blocks 6 and 7!" added Gaston Passagez. "And whom did he have for an audience? Communists, young for the most part. The subject matter? The training of adolescents, education of youth, Christian marriage, love in all its beauty, the Gospel adapted to our life in the camp, social morality, and many other things. These lectures were to leave an indelible memory in the minds of those who heard them. . . . While many of us lay exhausted on our pallets of wood shavings after the distribution of food, Père Jacques carried on his day until nine o'clock when the lights were put out. He ate his meager meal in the dark, a meal which Boussel had prepared for him by crumbling bread into the soup or blackish water, so that the priest, already ill, could not take out any bread to give to others.

"Then night would fall, bitter night, when the prisoners slept, packed together, tormented by vermin, the night of dreams and of slumbers interrupted by the terrible diuretic power of the soup which obliged them to get up in the most extreme cold, a night, in short, that brought no real rest.

"And on the following morning, about six o'clock, Père Jacques would begin all over again as he had the day before."

10 "He Gives Away Days of His Life"

The large crates, filled with gun parts to be checked, were first delivered to the End Kontroll, and then sent to the warehouse. They were carried on the emaciated shoulders of inmates dying of hunger and exhaustion. Père Jacques was always ready to get up and volunteer to take the place of the most feeble when their turn came.

"I noticed more than once," Henri Boussel declared, "that when I came in to see him unexpectedly, he would often say: 'Henri, wait just a minute until I carry that crate, I'll be right with you.'"

Everything said about edifying lives, all the litanies on the tireless devotion of one man to others that seem legendary, unbelievable, or at least dated, inseparable from myths of long ago—all this took place every day before the very eyes of the inmates of the camp in Güsen. With all that Père Jacques accomplished regularly each day, his life was filled to the bursting point. But he wanted it to overflow. When there is a flood of distress, there must also be a flood of charity.

A cause of great misery at the camp was the dirty, tattered clothing that could give no real protection during bad weather.

The Pole Theophilus, who was in charge of the linen room, was goodness itself but he could not supply everybody, since there were so many in need. When Père Jacques found a comrade in the greatest want, he did not send him to Theophilus, but went there himself to intercede for him.

The French shoemaker, Dubois, was no less solicited from all sides. Père Jacques literally harassed him: "I tried to satisfy his needs to the best of my ability," Dubois declared, "calling to his attention the fact that he himself was in dire need. But he would at once hasten to the care of everybody around him, seeing only their physical and moral suffering, neglecting himself."

Money was extremely scarce in the camp. Like the other inmates who worked at the factory, Père Jacques received a bonus; it was a mere pittance—one mark or fifty pfennigs every two weeks. Cigarettes were the real media of exchange, and they had considerable value. Père Jacques carefully stored them away, with voluntary contributions from a few friends, and this way he managed to buy clothing for those most in need.

But there was never enough of anything. In winter, especially, no one thought of anything but of getting enough warm clothing to survive. Père Jacques did not even attempt to clothe himself better, vital as it was.

"If we got a woolen sweater for him or a muffler," said Paco, the Spaniard, "he would say: 'Others are more unfortunate than I, give it to them. I'm not in need,' and he continued to wear the same clothes, a striped shirt, worn trousers, and underwear of the very poorest quality."

"Sometimes," Passagez said, "he would have on a good fatigue jacket or jersey. But never for long."

One very cold day a young Frenchman, sick and inadequately dressed, was obliged to work outdoors. Then and there Père Jacques took off his pullover and gave it to the young man, an act witnessed by Wadseck the Pole.

The situation was no less tragic with regard to food.

"Hunger tormented us," Abbé Barbier said. "The obsession with it even extended into our nightmares; we would suddenly awaken, completely debilitated morally, for our dreams were of but one thing: copious meals where the most succulent roasts were served, followed by elaborate desserts running over with cream. . . . Abruptly, reality would face us. It was a moment when death was near; cost what it might, we had to find something; a potato, a clove of garlic, a handful of dandelion greens is enough to save a man from death for one day.

. . . Even during the day our conversations revolved around cooking and recipes. Menus, this was the main topic of our conversation. One seemed to feed on what one had eaten in the past or would eat on one's return home. O, the psychosis of food! Here the stomach was the axis of life, the constant preoccupation."

This hunger ruined and corroded the body without surcease; it was a torture that kept up hour upon hour, during months and years. One dare not imagine the battles among the dying in the Bahnhof over the smallest scrap of food. But there is no less horror in this peaceful scene which Jean Cayrol saw with his own eyes: "Every morning an enormous pile of warm ashes was removed from the crematory furnace. I saw prisoners roast potatoes in them."

This sight strongly affected Père Jacques. Pity was stronger than hunger in him. He loved his neighbor more than himself.

He was not the only one. Undoubtedly the greatest nobility of the inmates who withstood this horror was their ability to deprive themselves—and at what price—in order to save their comrades. The more violent, the more interminable the physical necessity, the greater is the moral force capable of controlling it. If words were not so inadequate, we could make it clear that this is the very essence of sacrifice. To deprive oneself of a part of one's food, when famished, is not simply to give a material thing, it is to give of one's own life to save another. "Greater love than this no one has, that one lay down his life for his friends," Christ said on the evening of the Last Supper. Güsen was a world purely bestial in appearance where, apart from the will of the guards, material necessity alone dominated. Yet the prisoners, all prey to the most stringent privations, practiced self-control to the point where they accepted privation for the sake of one another. The chains of material necessity were not broken thereby, but what did not serve to nourish one, served the other. In the brief moment when an inmate took food from his own mouth to give it to another the purest strength of the soul was revealed, invisible and more powerful than any tyranny. Without formal ritual, this setting aside of food, this privation, this gift, was the very essence of sacrifice revealed in all its heroic beauty.

There were numerous little groups who, moved by a sense of national fraternity or a common set of beliefs, aided one another.

Air Force Captain Bondon, who had been deported to Mauthausen in March, 1943, with other comrades, belonged to the oldest French group at Güsen. They had taken part in building the small Steyr factory attached to the camp.

"Being officers," he said, "two of my comrades and I refused to work in a factory producing arms. We had ourselves assigned to the 'kommando wagen-wagen,' that is to say, we became human truck horses. Equipment was often most primitive in the camp, and much of the transportation was done by harnessing a wagon to twelve men. We transported everything: bread, garbage, material of every sort. Naturally, when we carried bread we made good use of it. But not for ourselves alone. We formed a group to help the others and it was in this way that I met Père Jacques. We synchronized with him to organize our efforts in mutual aid."

The Communists had also organized a system of solidarity. They would get together by twos and threes to keep another of their comrades going. On the rare occasion when one of them received the remains of a package, most of which had already been rifled by the SS or the kapos, he would keep only a third, handing the rest over to the group, according to Maurice Passard, who had been responsible for their unity.

Passard added the following, which is no less significant: "In Güsen there was a strong solidarity. There were no clashes, no rigid groupings, as occurred in other camps."

By his example, by his rejection of all partiality, by his fraternity regardless of belief, Père Jacques went to the source of this heroic mutual aid and gave it a new impetus.

"He united several of us," M. Bonsergent said, "Captain Ange Gaudin (Yves), Buchsensutz (the pastor of Montbéliard), Professor Heim, Maurice Passard (Mickey), myself, and a few others whose names I have forgotten. By groups of four, we would select a comrade particularly tired and thin, we would each put a little aside from our soup and bread, a small supplementary ration which was enough to sustain him. This example was followed, in fact, by the entire kommando, lasting for several months until February, 1945, when rations were further reduced. I could name several Frenchmen who owe their lives to this system. . . . Aid was given without partiality and Père Jacques himself kept a list of the names of members of the different groups and of those who received their help."

Elie Maurin, who worked beside Père Jacques in the End Kontroll room, was one of the most active members of this group. He described very clearly how it functioned.

"Our first encounters were difficult. . . . But this was of little importance, however, for with our hearts and souls set on the same goal, the distance between us was quickly overcome and a Christian and an atheist became fast friends in the kommando.

"He organized relief for those undergoing greater hardship than we were, and I supported him at once. Often, he would say: 'What a pity, Elie, that you are not one of us, you act like the best of Christians.' And invariably I would reply: 'I have my conscience which I think is clear.'

"He baptized me Brother Prolo [for proletariat], in the sweat of prison.

"Jacques! What integrity! What loyalty! This apostle had nothing but virtues. There was a time when he was on the point of death as the result of refusing to eat his meager pittance in order to save the lives of some youths who were sick. He was a living example of abnegation, of renunciation of self, of unfaltering devotion to his fellows."

At Güsen it was not very difficult to leap the barriers to a friendship of this kind, for among the French there was the deep feeling of solidarity mentioned by Maurice Passard. The more serious obstacles arose out of national peculiarities. Between the French and the Poles an entente was difficult. The differences in language often aggravated this basic difficulty in understanding. Very simple signs can be found to designate essentials, but this rudimentary language excludes confrontation between human beings. One of Henri Boussel's greatest advantages was his ability to speak several languages, especially German. It was a means of understanding the Poles and of being understood by them since almost all of them came from the zone annexed by the Germans. A cordial and fruitful interchange had sprung up with Valentin Pientka. Its most obvious benefit was quickly to extend Père Jacques's sphere of action so that his warmth could reach more people.

The devoutly Catholic Poles in the camp were quite ready to respect and aid the priest, simply because he was a priest. Still, they would not have thought of going beyond this. Père Jacques disclosed a truly evangelical vision of Christianity to them. Then, even though they were obstinately labeled once for all as "Reds" by public opinion, the Spaniards—unhappy refugees of the Civil War, relentlessly pursued everywhere by misery—sincerely welcomed Père Jacques.

In the finest spirit of international cooperation, the Pole Wadseck and the Spaniard Lopez, who from time to time obtained extra rations, would invite the French Carmelite to share with them. They would offer him their treasures: a little bread and sausage, a little cold soup left over from lunch.

"Quite often," said Henri Boussel, "Père Jacques arranged to have somebody else take his place."

The same thing happened with the Spaniard Paco who himself told the story: "The food problem was very difficult, for the daily ration with no supplements gave a man fourteen months to live, at the very most. Let us imagine that one of us shared his portion or helped with his regular ration to relieve others already failing. This man then is sharing his life. He is giving away the days of his life. So it was with Père Jacques.

"During a certain period, upon his return from the factory, we had him come every evening to our block 24 so that he would have some hot soup. This was in the winter of 1944–1945; it was all he had to eat between noon and curfew. One of the young Frenchmen, Hubert, who worked harder than others, was exhausted and weak. Père Jacques noticed him one cold morning, went up to him, and asked if he were sick. 'No,' the youth replied, 'I'm not sick but I'm cold—only a cup of black coffee at 5:00 A.M., and now to have to hold out until noon—I can't keep it up any longer.'

"That night Père Jacques was very sad when he arrived at block 24, his nose red from the cold. 'What's the matter, Père Jacques?' I asked. After a moment of hesitation, he answered: 'My dear Paco, I can't come here evenings any more, I can't be at ease, I can't eat when other French prisoners do not have enough to eat. It would disgrace me.' And he told us about the encounter that morning. Nothing could change his mind. We had to give in and the thin soup that had been his mainstay between the midday meal and 9:00 o'clock at night was thenceforth given to the young Frenchman who is still alive today. . . ."

Frequently it was Henri Boussel who tried to make Père Jacques eat something more but he came up against the same protest: "He would eat only half of his share or none at all, because he gave it to the sick or to the younger ones who needed it more than the rest. As a general rule, Père Jacques wished to receive the same quantity of food as the others and rejected any special privileges. Whenever I urged him to accept additional food to regain strength for the sake of the common good of all Christianity within the camp, he used to say, 'I have no right to have more than others, because I am a priest and I must set an example.'"

Thus, to be sure of not taking too much, he would take less.

But there was no end to it—it was an infernal circle. Hunger and exhaustion continued to increase. No donation was ever enough. Occasionally, you had the horrible feeling of having deprived yourself in vain when a man to whom you had given a portion of your own meager rations would die nevertheless.

At times, to save a sick man at any cost, Père Jacques had no other recourse but to beg from the "top dogs," the Poles holding down the "good" jobs in camp and who received food parcels.

To grasp the full audacity of this begging (even though these men were not themselves the executioners), one must know how things were prior to Père Jacques's arrival. One day, Gaston Passagez and a few other French inmates were watching the Poles peeling apples

which they had just received. The French prisoners did not even dare
to ask them for permission to pick up the peelings, so great was their
fear of a brutal retaliation.

But Père Jacques dared to beg from the top dogs for the sake of
his sick. And they gave him what he asked for!

"Nobody," said Paco, "ever saw him taste anything they gave
him. He took it all to the 'dream house,' the infirmary."

11   The Audacity of a Leader

Not everybody liked Père Jacques.

He wanted nothing but to serve, he practiced devotion to the point of heroism, he effaced himself as he had done at Compiègne when he let the others eat at the small table while he perched on a corner of the bed. He would get up to do another's job for him as in the End Kontroll, or, as in the block, in the morning when he went out for the "coffee." He bore all patiently, including the blows he would occasionally receive in the camp "in order to endure purgatory on earth." But, at the same time, he was a leader.

In the camps the Nazis had really succeeded in crushing all the ancient privileges of caste, function, and academic status. The worth of a man was no longer judged by labels, but by what he was intrinsically and, above all, by his moral strength. This made Père Jacques all the more a leader.

His devotion was contagious—admiration for him aroused a wish to share in his work. But this was not enough for him. Père Jacques did not ask to be admired; he wanted everyone to cooperate with him. He knew how to judge and to censure.

"I was struck by the man from the first moment I saw him," Gaston Passagez said.

Almost everybody, if not all, had the same impression when they encountered Père Jacques.

"He was energetic," Passagez continued, "very headstrong, on occasion even abrupt, but with a sense of humor. He didn't like half measures. He also had an extraordinary talent for appreciating a man with great qualities."

"He was a leader," declared Professor Heim. "He exercised enormous influence. He was very good, but very firm, even severe, yet he knew how to be indulgent when necessary. He was not a political man, but a psychologist. He would have played an important role after the war had he survived."

Yes, he would have played an important role after the war, agreed his Communist friends, because he had both knowledge and understanding.

"From the very start," Jean Cayrol added, "I saw that Père Jacques was an extraordinary man: the Pascalian nose and burning eyes! He was capable of rash imprudences. At Güsen, he wanted to seek out the commanding officer to tell him, 'You simply can't continue to treat men in this way.' We prevented him by explaining that it was absurd to make such an attempt, that he would simply get himself slaughtered without the least benefit to others."

But he was not moderate when the question of Frenchmen who were a disgrace to their compatriots came up.

"Père Jacques," according to Boussel, "had been quite outspoken with those Frenchmen, who, in view of their position, should have helped their comrades and did not do so. He had accosted them openly, which had resulted in an altercation with X. Père Jacques had courageously told him what he thought of him and of the evil he was doing. Père Jacques had vowed to meet him again in France and X, so he said, was going to inform the priest's superiors about certain matters and at the same time vindicate Frenchmen who, he claimed, had suffered because of Père Jacques."

This man's assertions in no way deceived the deportees who saw Père Jacques deprive himself every day for the sake of all, while X sat back and took what profit he could.

This was not the only case. If under the inhuman conditions of existence in Güsen there was extraordinary self-sacrifice, falls from grace were just as extreme. Père Jacques did not keep his eyes devoutly lowered.

"Uncompromising with regard to principles, he knew how to apportion blame," Abbé Michaud was to say when he arrived at the camp during the final months. "He would listen with an inscrutable expression on his face, then his answer would come out concisely and clearly. It was simple. It was right. You knew you were talking with a direct and frank person."

From time to time Père Jacques had to face terrible dilemmas, notably in the organization of mutual aid.

"What difficulties," said his friend Professor Heim, "there were in establishing a hierarchy based on equality, in making a selection of the most worthy, or those most exposed to death, or the youngest, or the oldest, with so little bread for so many mouths! Occasionally he sensed misunderstandings, jealousy. He overcame this by patient explanation. He had to make a choice and in this lay the drama of his conscience."

He encountered many other difficulties.

If one sees the wonderful generosity in the "invitations to dinner" extended by the Pole Wadseck, the Spaniards Paco and Lopez, to Père Jacques, one will also understand what extraordinary courage it took for him to decline these invitations for the benefit of someone else. He not only renounced a food supplement, he had to take infinite precautions not to wound his friends' sensibilities. But he knew how to dare this and did it gracefully. But what could be more difficult? It was nothing more than transforming the gift of friendship into a gift of pure charity, without a distinction between persons.

"It was a question of making use of the relations he had established with the Poles, the inside masters of the camp, who often resorted to Père Jacques's pastoral ministrations," Professor Heim continued. "With dignity and rash boldness, he accomplished his priestly duties among them because this he had to do. But over and beyond this, he extracted for his own, the French, favors which he distributed among them: a better jacket for one, a pair of good shoes for another, and for yet another an additional ration of soup or a piece of bread. But he had to be cautious and this was hardly part of his temperament, for he was full of verve, trust, and selflessness. It was to the priest that certain Poles in high positions made their gifts of food, and when they learned that it was not the priest but other French prisoners in the camp who were benefiting from it, they sometimes withdrew their aid." (*La Sombre route*, p. 72.)

Through Valentin Pientka, the best elements among the Poles had sought out Père Jacques when he arrived at the camp. And Père Jacques returned their kindness in the most admirable way, by helping those among them who had not yet understood how to open themselves to a charity that is not private, but to true charity.

Wadseck, Lopez, and Paco were admirable examples. For they magnificently understood and they had graciously accepted the exchange of guests as Père Jacques had requested.

But there were yet greater difficulties.

"He developed particularly close relations with the Communists of the camp, not as a tactic, but out of sympathy. A dependable reciprocity was established. He, I know, always showed the greatest charity toward them, and they in turn felt a very strong attachment for him." (*La Sombre route*, p. 72.)

Henri Boussel described the difficulties that arose as a consequence of these friendly relations.

"He had acquired great esteem in Communist circles to the point where certain Polish Catholics said: 'But Père Jacques is a Communist, he goes to the Communist meetings,' and so on. These were Catholics who could not see beyond the end of their own nose. . . . To such charges Père Jacques had replied: 'The word of the Gospel is not for those already within the household, but for those who must be led in from the outside.'"

However, he never propagandized. Père Jacques believed first of all in the grace of God, then in example. He gave instruction in the faith only to those who requested it. If a man were converted, he was careful not to broadcast it, for Père Jacques was not a man to take the credit for a conversion, or to exploit it for his own glory.

12   The Bread of Christ—in Secret

There came a night when the dementia of the Nazis reached a climax. A festive night in hell.

The landings in Normandy and the offensive in Poland had started months before. The gigantic battle was in its last phase, but this phase seemed to be interminable. Paris had been liberated, but in the infernal pit of Güsen the terror did not slacken and the coming of winter intensified the suffering.

Christmas approached.

And Güsen celebrated Christmas.

"The most flagrant and amazing contradiction I have ever witnessed, without a doubt," Louis Deblé recounted, "was the ceremony that took place on Christmas, 1944, under the direction of the very assassins who bludgeoned us. At nightfall, everybody in the blocks had to report to the roll-call area and make a circle around a candle-lighted fir tree. Here with bared heads they listened to hymns sung by Germans and Poles, by those thugs, and all this in subzero weather. Let him who can give an explanation. As for me, I spent twenty-five months in Güsen and there are still certain things which I have not yet been able to grasp."

It was a festival the executioners offered to their victims, a cruel festival, a delirious mixture of glitter, singing, and glacial cold, a rejoicing that was an affront. It was a festival of the big lie which replaced the commemoration of the birth of Christ by the feigned veneration of the fir and winter solstice, it was the reply of hell to the message of Bethlehem: "Peace on earth to men of good will."

But, in the shadows, in secret, the inmates had prepared their own Christmas.

"Christmas Eve was approaching," said a Polish friend of Wadseck. "Snow had fallen all the previous day. The camp was covered in a magnificent mantle of white.

"American planes had bombarded the electric plant, consequently there were no lights. We were temporarily relieved from work, so we had time to prepare the Christmas tree. Early Christmas Eve morning, there was a great stir and bustle in the block, the parish of the curé of Güsen (this is what we called him), with a great many people coming and going. Some came for confession, others for reports, interviews, and so forth. So at the end of the day Père Zak was very tired.

"Nevertheless, he could not rest because on that day he had to make an appearance at several places among large groups of Poles, first at the Christmas Eve celebration where there was a tree for children from twelve to seventeen years old of whom there were about four hundred in camp, then at the Polish crèche, then at a festival of stars in the infirmary. At eight o'clock, in barracks 18, a moving celebration took place. Père Zak received the profession of faith from a Russian, a convert to the Catholic Church. Then Père Zak distributed Communion to the large group of prisoners. Yes, the priest had worked hard, and by the grace of God, his work was fruitful. He worked to bring everybody nearer to Christ, with all his heart; he helped in preparing an evening of Christmas carols. There were fifteen nationalities: among them French, Polish, Czech, Belgian, Italian. There were moving moments when all shared the white bread, and embraced one another while singing Christmas carols in their diverse languages. I shall always remember this evening. Père Zak was very popular with all the nationalities. . . ."

That night, in prisoner's garb and in secret, Père Jacques celebrated the Mass of the Nativity. Never had he been closer to Christ who had been born in poverty, on the straw of a stable.

"Père Jacques knelt before his bed, and with what sacred vessels! Chalice and paten made from gun parts and also a breviary whose leather binding had been slashed by an SS man. During the Sacrifice I was but a few inches away from Père Jacques. Never will my eyes again see such concentration, such contemplation—it moved me to tears," said Gaston Passagez. Whence came the consecrated Host during the Mass? From a Polish seminarian who had preserved and hidden it since 1940. The wine? From outside the camp, from no other than the priest of the town of Güsen, separated from the camp by a series of barbed-wire fences.

Père Jacques again celebrated Mass in secret on January 1st, 1945, and distributed Communion.

It was the beginning of the most terrible year in the camp.

More and more swiftly the war was moving toward a dénouement. The Russian armies were pouring into Poland and Hungary, the French, English, and Americans were advancing in Belgium and Alsace. Everywhere the Wehrmacht was losing the initiative. Victory marched with giant steps, but the Nazis were putting up a desperate fight. Doubtless they were counting on the staggering success of their secret weapons to reverse the course of the war, even at the last hour. They already had the V-1 and the V-2. Were they not hoping to put an atom bomb in the scales?

However rapid the march to victory, the situation in the camps dragged on and became increasingly worse.

January, 1945, was marked by such terrible restrictions that two thousand of the twenty thousand deportees in Güsen died.

In February, eighteen hundred died. From the beginning of the year there had been a hecatomb of the young, dying from consumption. But now even men who seemed more robust could no longer hold out.

All at once the solidarity of the groups collapsed. The famine had become so acute that it was no longer possible to maintain groups of four volunteers capable of depriving themselves daily to sustain a weaker man.

This same month, all priests in the camp were picked up and transferred to Dachau. The most contradictory rumors were spread in connection with this move: some said the Vatican had obtained a relative clemency for the priests and that they would benefit from a less harsh treatment in Dachau, others that this was a measure of reprisal because of a revolt in which the Hungarian clergy had participated. In any case, Père Jacques was passed over since he appeared on the lists as "ecclesiastical teacher." He could have had this rectified by the Poles. In fact he was advised to have this done, for he could not find a camp worse than Güsen where the horror of the situation was increasing. In comparison Dachau was reputed to be a "rest home." Père Jacques refused to make the slightest effort to leave and everybody knew why: he wanted to stay with them.

It was during this period that Père Jacques confided his closely guarded secret to Henri Boussel: how he had prayed to the young Thérèse of Lisieux before entering the camp, and how he was sure his prayer had been heard when Boussel made his extraordinary welcome. After months at Güsen, confronted with the incessant aggravation of suffering and anguish, he repeated this prayer aloud to his friend.

In March, the inmates were the prey of a raging famine, but stirred by rumors of victory which infiltrated the camp along with an avalanche of false news. But their physical strength was giving out and twenty-two hundred dead were counted at the end of the month. If this continued, none of them would see the liberation.

Père Jacques celebrated Mass again during this month.

"With a great deal of trouble we had been able to get hold of a little wine and the Host," said Henri Boussel. "I myself had made the arrangements with a civilian with whom I was on good terms: he kindly agreed to see the parish priest of Steyer. The priest thought it was a trap and refused to give anything. Finally, thanks to friends who worked in another place, we managed to obtain a little wine from the priest of Saint-Georges and hosts through a Pole who served as veterinary. Père Jacques said a secret Mass in the linen shop of the brave Theophilus who supplied us with the underwear we needed. We had made a grotto inside the stacks of clothing. Immediately after the morning reveille, the time for going down to the washrooms, there was a half hour when everyone was busy in the interior camp. Having alerted each other the night before, we got up a little before reveille, and dressing quickly we went at once to the linen shop where Theophilus expected us. We entered surreptitiously and Père Jacques began the Mass; we were twelve in all. Everyone, of course, received Communion. In addition Père Jacques consecrated the Host which he took to Passagez and two other comrades who had remained in the barracks. The celebrant had absolutely no accoutrements and used a small glass for a chalice; the missal had been procured by Valentin Pientka. In fact it was he who kept the linen and chalice used at this Mass, and he still has them in his possession.

"Had we been caught," Henri Boussel added, "we most certainly would have been executed. They didn't need any more reason than that!"

On the seventh of this same month, at night, in the depths of these hideous barracks another memorable event took place.

"Until the day I die I shall remember," Jean Cayrol said, "that evening, alas, so short compared to the long precarious hours we were then living through, when with Boussel and Passagez we celebrated the feast of St. Thomas Aquinas with slices of black bread buttered with 'table margarine.' For a few minutes, thanks to Père Jacques's solicitude that the Spirit blow over us, we had communed together through prayer. Thanks to our common faith, to our mutual friendship, to our nearness to the Cross, that evening we again found an oasis of peace, which remained with us despite all the corrosiveness of war around us."

Easter fell on April first of that year 1945. At the approach of Holy Week the fervor of the Christians in the camp increased. Confessions multiplied and it was not singly but in groups that the inmates came to Père Jacques.

"On the roads of the concentration camp," said another friend of Wadseck, "one saw small groups of men who were waiting for Père Jacques. The poor prisoners came there after their work. Père Zak too.

"The circle of Père Zak's close friends stood guard at various points, carefully keeping an eye out for the Gestapo. Meanwhile, Père Zak went from one group to another, giving absolution to those who had come to make their confessions.

"Since not everyone could understand French, he gave a general absolution.

"Those who knew French confessed in the usual way. It should be said that the majority who surrounded their confessor understood and spoke French. Even those who did not know it well understood enough, because his serene, smiling face, his clear, penetrating eyes helped them to comprehend. This courageous man needed nothing for himself, in giving himself entirely for others."

There were also the sick who could not leave the infirmary, but they were the last ones whom Père Jacques could forget: "Not long before, block 24 had become the block for the invalids," recounted another of the Polish inmates. "As overseers of the block the SS deliberately chose thieves, bandits, delinquents: men without feeling, men who could assassinate with pleasure, and who actually did murder our poor invalids with poison, by beatings, by drownings in a vat filled with water. . . .

"The other prisoners, seeing these victims of the SS each day, were afraid that any day they too might be put in block 24. Naturally the SS forbade visits to the sick. In spite of this their comrades visited them when it was possible and always gave them help. One of these was Père Jacques, a French Carmelite, who always consoled our poor comrades, always helped them, often gave them half of the tiny ration of bread he received each night. He cheered them up, consoled them, and did everything he could. He was a true priest, he was a zealous confessor, a disciple of Christ. . . .

"Every evening he visited block 24 where there were six hundred invalids, condemned to die. He aided them materially and spiritually by confession. It happened to be Holy Week. Tuesday at 8:00 P.M. had been chosen for the confession of the sick. All our poor invalids, full of joy, awaited our Père Jacques so they could cleanse their souls, their hearts, there in the concentration camp, this hell on earth.

"Unfortunately, at seven o'clock the drunken overseer of block 24 ordered a clothing inspection and obligatory bath so that he could knock the inmates around. Poor invalids! They had been waiting for confession for two days. Two days! They had so looked forward to this particular evening and now all their hopes were destroyed. After the bath, they were ordered to bed at once.

"At eight Père Jacques arrived—as promised—sad because he could not enter the block. He stood in front for a few minutes, not knowing what to do about confessing the sick. He went around to the other side of the block and approached a window. All the invalids saw him. Joyously they rose from their beds to make their confessions and receive the long-awaited absolution. Those who knew French confessed individually, the others received general absolution. The window on which all eyes were fixed had been opened.

"Everybody watched and waited. Père Jacques bared his head, prayed for a few minutes and gave the absolution. The sick cried like children, thanking God, full of joy, without fear."

A few days later they were all assassinated in the gas chamber.

Easter Day was the signal for another atrocity.

The Nazis decided to conduct one of their customary and absurd disinfection operations in the barracks where total disorder reigned supreme. This was the barracks where Godlewsky was lodged.

The inmates had to strip, leave the block while it was being disinfected, wash in icy water, walk across the whole camp, and stand wet and completely naked in the courtyard.

They remained standing there five hours before receiving permission to go inside and dress. But there were only survivors to go back to the barracks, for the courtyard was strewn with corpses.

In the face of all these atrocities, faith remained intact.

On this same Easter, the feast of the resurrection of Christ, Père Jacques celebrated Mass three times. One Mass was celebrated for the Poles. "The Mass was said in the barracks, between the beds. All stood at the Holy Mass," reported one of the Polish deportees.

"The altar was a table covered with a white napkin on which the cross had been placed. Around the table were placed the aliments, the paschal lamb made with pieces of the margarine we had received for Easter.

"Père Jacques stood in the middle of the room, in prison dress, surrounded by the comrades come to take part in the great feast. Two Polish seminarians served the Mass. A lookout was kept outside the barracks.

"'In the name of the Father, the Son, and the Holy Ghost. . . .' Mass had begun. Père Zak opened the missal. All faces were marked by contemplation and attention. Tears were in their eyes, all were crying. The Offertory. . . . The celebrant first raised the Host, then the chalice. The Elevation. Jesus Christ was present on the altar. He was with us and among us.

"'O Jesus, grant us the true resurrection. Grant us also the freedom we so ardently desire. Put an end, good Jesus, to our suffering.'

"Thus did we pray to God on that day.

"At the end of the Mass, all approached the holy table to receive Communion, to take Jesus Christ unto our sorrow-laden hearts. Then the final benediction. The Holy Mass was over.

"After the Mass we thanked Père Zak for all he had done, exchanging with one another warm and cordial greetings on the occasion of this great feast of Easter."

On the same day, Père Jacques again celebrated Mass. This time he was hidden in a most precarious way between a block and the electrified barbed wire enclosure. Afterward, he was to take Communion to several of his friends who had not been able to attend.

"His presence," said Jean Cayrol, "was proof of the living God and, thanks to him, on Easter Day I had the overwhelming joy of receiving the Holy Eucharist from his hands, hiding behind a muddy block. He risked his life to do this."

Indeed he courted death at every moment that he carried on his priestly ministry in the camp, according to Professor Heim, "because the SS did not tolerate the practice of any religion other than that of which Hitler was the god." (*La Sombre route*, p. 73.)

Père Jacques knew this, yet he did not hesitate.

When Abbé Michaud arrived in Güsen on April 5, he made himself known at once to this prisoner who was in no way distinguishable from the others since he wore the same incredible rags and worked twelve hours a day checking gun parts. But Abbé Michaud was carried away with admiration: "When I arrived in Güsen," he said, "I had the opportunity to make my confession to Père Jacques. Twice I returned him the same service. I felt humble before him. What could I say to this man who had infinitely surpassed me in the ways of union with God? He listened to me religiously as though he were listening to St. John of the Cross. I remember the words he said to me after my confession: 'At this time we must rejoice in accomplishing God's will to the very end, to give our lives if He demands it; perhaps it is our vocation.' I turned cold at the words 'give one's life' after eighteen terrible months and so near to the goal! For him it was altogether natural, he was detached, disembodied."

Would Père Jacques see the liberation?

He had found a "good job" at Güsen right at the start, and he had kept it, but he had continually been depriving himself and squandering his strength.

"Toward the middle of March," said his friend Boussel, "I noticed that at nights his cough was beginning to get drier. I suggested he see one of my friends, a Polish doctor, in order to establish whether or not he had a slight tendency to tuberculosis, to which he replied: 'No, I'm not sick, I feel perfectly well, I shall not go to the doctor, it's quite absurd. Besides if I am tubercular, nothing could be done for it.' He continued to expend himself, especially evenings after work when, very tired, he would stay outside in all kinds of weather waiting for friends, comrades to come to him to make their confessions. He fulfilled his ministry even though day by day he felt his strength diminish. In this general misery, he spent himself intelligently, but always at his own expense."

However, by mid-April, according to Abbé Michaud, when asked how he felt, he admitted to a slight fever. During that month Henri Boussel saw him fall twice from weakness. He literally forced Père Jacques to eat a little soup, bread, sausage, in his presence. It was not a remedy, but Père Jacques seemed to be able to carry on.

April, 1945, was the month when from all sides, from the West

and East, the allied armies penetrated Germany at a rate that was
dizzying in the eyes of history but desperately, exasperatingly slow
in the eyes of the prisoners of the concentration camp.

In April there were more than three thousand eight hundred
deaths in the ranks of the inmates at Güsen. Famine was not the
only cause. Once, in block 33, the Nazis beat three hundred deportees to death with clubs. In block 31, several times, they shut in two
hundred, three hundred, six hundred deportees, pasted paper over
the windows, and released gas inside.

They wanted to satiate their murderous rage at all costs and, at
the same time, wipe out the witnesses of their crimes. The extermination race redoubled its speed.

The inmates were convinced that their liberation would not be
brought about solely by outside help, and that if they did not take
measures for self-protection and organize a revolt destined to break
out at the right time, no one would survive. So they worked out the
minute details of their plan for overt resistance.

Very shortly after his arrival in Güsen Père Jacques had been con-
tacted by Maurice Passard, the leader of the French Communist
party in the camp. In fact, Passard had been alerted by a comrade
who had been interned with Père Jacques, that the latter had been
on good terms with the internees at Compiègne, particularly with
one of their outstanding leaders, Auguste Havez.

"Our first interview," Maurice Passard related, "took place between two blocks of the infirmary, opposite the crematorium of the
camp.

"We at once agreed to take as basis of discussion, first, the existing
conditions in the camp to which all were subjected, and second, the
struggle for liberation that continued in France.

"By common accord our first decision was to speak only of that
which concerned us all or which would draw us closer together, and
to exclude all the rest."

Before Père Jacques's arrival the French National Front in Güsen
had been directed by a committee of four, two Gaullist officers and
two Communists. To adjust the committee to include Père Jacques,

it had been reduced to three: one Gaullist, one Communist, and Père Jacques.

Thus, in addition to his many activities as priest and apostle of charity, Père Jacques was also one of three responsible leaders for French resistance within the camp.

"The innumerable committee meetings," Maurice Passard continued, "the common measures to be taken, all these built up an amicable relationship among us which with time gradually became stronger. Père Jacques confided to me the projects he had in mind for later on."

Père Jacques did not withhold these from friends, Communist or Catholic: he had many postwar plans; everything taught him by his working-class childhood, his experience as educator, his Carmelite training, his life in concentration camps was to be used. He did not wish what he had extracted from these years to be lost and forgotten, he wanted to maintain, to develop, within bounds of the possible, the fraternal relationships he had had with non-Catholics, even with atheists. He did not want Christian life to be bogged down in a rut or the candle of faith to be hidden under a bushel.

But, while he took part as a leader in the common struggle, he did not permit himself to be distracted from his primary mission as a priest, for the sake of which he had desired to remain prisoner.

He was fully conscious of this as events became more and more dramatic.

"About January, 1945," Maurice Passard continued, "the bombings and the new Russian offensive caused us to take fresh precautionary measures, chiefly with regard to our plot for armed resistance.

"Plans discussed in the International Committee were carried out. Père Jacques was in full agreement with the measures taken and he added: 'From now on, with regard to all matters concerning armed struggle or military organization, I ask you to take for me all decisions which you Communists judge to be necessary. You realize that for a priest it is difficult to speak of such matters, yet they are nevertheless indispensable and I am confident you will act in the best interest of all.' "

Even at Güsen, while subject to the horror of the concentration camp and participating in the resistance struggle, he was primarily the man of peace, of the peace of Christ.

The end was near and the worst convulsions were to be expected. After famine, mass extermination by gas, massacres of every kind, there was the torture of the underground tunnels.

Here again the insanity of the Nazis was manifest. They had no real intention of protecting the inmates from bombings, not even to preserve them as slave labor, for they were simultaneously being exterminated en masse and their way of driving the inmates to the shelters caused many more deaths.

"As soon as the alert sounded," Louis Deblé said, "we had to quit our jobs at once and assemble in deep tunnels dug by the prisoners into a hillside some yards from the camp. They were to have served as underground factories. On the way there we had to avoid maddened watchdogs and the usual clubbings of the kapos and the SS. Then there was the excruciating task of entering the tunnel by one of the four openings. On each side the SS and the common criminals in charge redoubled their blows, and thousands of men rushed into the entrances, shouting wildly and knocking each other over in a wild stampede to push ahead. Woe to those who fell. They were trampled on by those behind them who in turn were pushed forward by the pressing swarm. Then we waited in these tunnels for hours, often standing, in fetid air that soon became unbreathable. When it was over, the exit was as dangerous as the entrance: each alert cost several men their lives and the loss of shoes to many more. In the last month this was further complicated when the SS walled up three of the entrances, leaving but one. Later we learned this was done with the intention of exterminating all of us by gas. We were saved from this frightful death only by the rapid advance of the Americans."

Professor Heim happened to be near Père Jacques several times during these dreadful mob scenes.

"I would see him during this ordeal going in and coming out, bearing himself in the familiar way: his hands in the pockets of his worn jacket, his body straight, but his face pensive, head inclined toward the ground, a little to one side. His step was quick but not hurried, not precipitate even in face of danger. His whole bearing was replete with a dignity that made me recognize his steady carriage even in a crowd." (*La Sombre route*, p. 76.)

Each time they could, Père Jacques and his close friends arranged to meet in a recess of the tunnel.

"In this fetid atmosphere, with insufficient air, almost in total blackness," said Gaston Passagez, "men just escaped from death assembled to talk over most varied problems, from cryptogamy, dear to Professor Heim, to world-wide travel, politics, mechanics, electricity, and postwar menus sagaciously planned."

"We would gather," Professor Heim continued, "in the back of one of the tunnels in a sort of amphitheater, an oblong depression hollowed from the gritty sand that had been irregularly amassed around the girders seemingly built as protection from landslides, often deadly in this shifty terrain. We reached this immense cave by shoving and jostling our way in the darkness through a long corridor pitted with holes and pools of water. I recall that I realized my state of weakness when I no longer could hoist myself up on a girder where I wanted to sit. A month before I had been able to do it. Now, I simply tired myself by useless effort. It was then that I started to draw, seated on damp earth during the long alerts, in the faint, uncertain light of a swaying lantern, for I had got hold of a pencil and a sheet of paper. It was a joy of discovery for me and this is how I caught in the half-obscurity of this vast tomb the Pascalian profile of Père Jacques." (*La Sombre route*, p. 77.)

13   "We Are Always Assembled Around You"

Suddenly, the first flares of the liberation flashed like lightning in the camp. At the end of April a rumor spread like wildfire: trucks of the International Red Cross had been seen on the road. They had been repatriating the French and Belgians in Mauthausen.

This was the news they had waited for a thousand times. So long had they been waiting for it that it was unimaginable. For two days they could not believe it.

On April 27 the news was confirmed by the secretary of the camp. The French in the camp were officially informed that they were to assemble the following morning to be taken to Mauthausen from which they were to be repatriated by the Red Cross.

Then it was true! The French were exultant. All the others envied them, as they impatiently waited their turn.

On the morning of April 28th, the French assembled. The sick made a desperate effort to stand. Eight hundred French survivors gathered in the assembly area between the dismal blocks. An icy rain poured down on them. Each one received a food parcel from the Red Cross. They immediately began to eat the contents. The Nazis ordered them to stop, to close the parcels, and to line up in ranks to pass in review before the camp commander.

The order was not obeyed. For the first time in this camp where men had risked torture and death for the least infraction or even a mere caprice of an SS or a kapo, a formal act of collective disobedience had taken place.

"The risk of death no longer counted," declared Professor Heim. "The men were irresistibly propelled by another instinct. It was the awful abandon of a starved animal to whom a full bowl is brought. All around the square were hundreds of other inmates, those who had to stay. Dozens of SS guards, standing under the clock, and the camp commander, looking out his window with stupefaction, observed this unbelievable spectacle of eight hundred men devouring food, despite orders, in utter confusion, sugar, meat, preserves, and cheese, filling their hands with powdered cocoa. Empty boxes, paper, and wrappings were strewn over the ground in an unprecedented disorder. But no burst from a machine gun, no revolver shot, no flurry, not even blows from clubs put an end to this spectacle of revolt, this madness, this final defeat of hunger, this wild imprudence." (*La Sombre route*, p. 84.)

In a flash the Nazis perceived the collapse of their rule. But the wretched prisoners who gave in to this explosive hunger were committing suicide without knowing it, without even thinking. Many died from this indulgence in the following few days.

Some shared their parcels with prisoners of other nationalities who had not yet received gifts or orders to leave. Père Jacques and Henri Boussel shared theirs with Pientka, Theophilus, and Joseph.

All those who had the strength to keep their wits in spite of hunger and the collective madness were saved.

"I turned around," Professor Heim adds, "and saw Père Jacques, dignified as always. I knew he had been busy the hour before offering his thanks to the other nationals remaining at the camp, to all whom he owed effective help in keeping one or other of the French deportees alive in the course of this hard winter. . . . He was greatly moved. . . .

"My last vision of Güsen, and the assembly area where so many men had perished, is for me inseparable from the memory of this man, the priest who dominated in this mass and overcame disaster and who in the end gave us victory, the victory of Man over a system born of material power and the lower instincts. The great victor was he who had passed these trials as it is said a salamander passes through fire. April 28, 1945! In our eyes Père Jacques was resplendent in his victory." (*La Sombre route*, p. 86.)

At three o'clock in the afternoon, in a driving rain that soaked through to the bone, the column of Frenchmen set out and the big doors of the camp opened to let them pass.

The fields were marvelously green and the apple trees at the edge of the road were covered with blossoms.

The men marched slowly, at funeral pace. They had no strength left.

Occasionally, one of them fell along the road. This time the Nazis did not finish him off but heaved him into a wagon next to the corpses it already contained.

Ten died in the same time it took the French column to cover the three miles from Güsen to Mauthausen.

When they were about five hundred yards from Mauthausen, the men saw white trucks painted with the familiar big red cross. They saw the trucks with their own eyes, but they could not get in them, they were already filled. The men had to let them go and wait for them to return. It was truly torture by hope. When would they see the trucks again? They did not know. Perhaps tomorrow, but each day this tomorrow was pushed ahead and they never saw the trucks again.

Once again the men climbed the hillside and passed through the large portal of Mauthausen under the monstrous black eagle which was already doomed but which still gripped them in its claws.

They collected in the large courtyard where the roll call was taken and waited in an icy rain that never stopped.

They waited here for four hours. They were not taken into the quarantine blocks until night fell. They were sheltered, but they were crowded together in a hideous promiscuity. Just when they believed themselves on the point of salvation, they were thrust anew into famine, crowding, cold, and revolting filth.

They spent ten days and ten nights of disheartening waiting in this abyss of wretchedness.

"We drew nothing," said one of the men, "for four days except a quarter of a pound of bread (but not for all of them), a sort of dehydrated or beet soup mixture at noon (three-fourths of a quart) and a pint of some juice almost every evening. The mortality was beyond all imagination: four to five hundred died daily (there were then twenty to twenty-five thousand inmates in Mauthausen).

Exhausted, shaking with fever after this whole day spent in the cold rain, Père Jacques rested in a corner of the barracks. A Polish seminarian had found a blanket for him. For two nights he went without his bread ration to give it to Louis Deblé.

"All who have been in a concentration camp know what a mouthful of bread or supplementary bit of soup means to a man near death. They will grasp the full import of Père Jacques's action," said the young seminary student.

During this time, the tenacious Nazis were preparing another mass extermination by gas.

"It is to the Swiss Heifliger, a delegate of the International Red Cross, that we all owe our salvation. For it was his prodigious courage and initiative that made it possible for American light tanks to arrive before the Machiavellian plan was carried out," Professor Heim writes. (*La Sombre route*, p. 88.)

Suddenly, when exhaustion of the prisoners made it impossible to put up any armed resistance against this ultimate atrocity, on May 5 at one o'clock in the afternoon, two American heavy machine guns were drawn up before the walls of Mauthausen.

Thrown into a panic, the guards believed they were faced by the entire American army and they hastened to hoist the white flag.

At once, an immense clamor of joy filled Mauthausen.

The disorder was indescribable. Crematories were destroyed, typhus broke out, there was neither water nor electricity. Some captives, provoked beyond measure, settled their scores with the kapos and lynched them on the spot, while on the ground between the barracks lay corpses and the dying.

The collapse of order was total and the relief was minimal in the face of the enormous distress of thousands of men.

Despite the chaos that reigned and the ravages of death, the

clandestine organization of the deportees reemerged to the surface.
Emile Valley, the Communist who had befriended Père Jacques in
Compiègne and during his first days in Mauthausen, headed the
French National Committee. Père Jacques, although ridden with
fever, rose to fight side by side with Emile Valley to establish a new
order and organize relief. Both were unanimously delegated to
represent the French on the International Committee.

From May 5 to May 9, Père Jacques took no rest, working with
Valley eighteen hours a day. Boussel acted as secretary. Throughout this time Père Jacques ran a temperature of over a hundred. He
was obliged to go to the infirmary. Professor Dessoile and his
friends hastened to give him the best care possible, but Père
Jacques had developed bronchial pneumonia. He was at the end of
his strength.

At this point a nurse, Madame Crespin de la Susse, came on the
scene. Disregarding the inadequate directives of the Allied author-
ities, she had taken it upon herself to bring a lorry filled with medi-
cines, clothing, and provisions to the survivors of Mauthausen.

On Thursday May 10, Ascension Day, Abbé Michaud, who had
also come from Güsen in the group with Père Jacques, celebrated
Mass and gave him Communion.

On that same afternoon of this beautiful day, Madame de la
Susse returned with the lorry and settled Père Jacques inside it on
a stretcher. He said his last farewell to his friends at Mauthausen.
They drove off rapidly toward Linz, the beautiful city with light-
green bell towers overlooking the Danube. Hospitalized in first one
infirmary, then in another at the French camp, Père Jacques at last
slept in a real bed.

The chaplain visited him every day. This was Abbé Gray, a war
prisoner, who did not accept repatriation immediately after being
freed but asked to remain to take care of the deportees.

"From then on," he said, "I saw Père Jacques every day at the
Schiffswerft infirmary where I would bring him Holy Communion.
In accord with his wish, I said no preparatory prayer. As he re-
ceived I simply said: 'Corpus Domini Nostri. . . .' After taking Com-

munion, he fell into a profound meditation and often I would depart
without speaking, leaving him to his act of thanksgiving. He spoke
little before Communion. I would inquire about his health: often
he answered by a sign. I learned nothing about him (that is, about
his past life) or about his friends during these visits. Sometimes I
lingered in his room. I could see that he suffered but he did not
complain. Quite often he made a sweeping gesture with his arms,
lifting them up, then dropping them to signify *total abandonment*.
He carefully thanked everyone who tended him, always with the
comment that they were doing too much for him. . . ."

Abbé Gray belonged to the Mission of France, founded at Lisieux
under the protection of St. Thérèse. Père Jacques barely had strength
left to speak, but how could he not have admired and loved this
last coincidence? It was the supreme response of the Carmelite of
Lisieux.

Henri Boussel, who had brought the first response, was there
also. He had not wanted to be repatriated with the others by air,
but had wished to join Père Jacques and stay near him.

Around Pentecost, that is about May 20, Père Jacques was transported to the hospital of the Sisters of St. Elizabeth, very near
the Carmelite Monastery of Linz. The Prior, one of whose monks
had also fallen victim to the Gestapo, came to visit Père Jacques
several times.

But the end was approaching. Abbé Gray and Henri Boussel remained by his bedside.

On June 2, Père Jacques received Holy Communion for the last
time.

"He was still lucid, but his speech was thick, he could no longer
make himself understood. Seeing him become weaker, I offered to
say the prayers of the dying. He accepted willingly. I read the
prayers aloud. Père Jacques, his eyes closed, joined in with his whole
heart. Several times in the course of the afternoon I suggested a
formula of offering. 'You truly offer, Father, all your life for the
Church, for France. . . .' He understood me clearly and each time
acquiesced by a voluntary and energetic motion of his head. I can

say that he understood perfectly that he was dying, that in full consciousness he offered his life as sacrifice. When the suffering increased, contracting his features, a word sufficed: 'For Thee, Jesus,'
or simply 'Jesus,' would bring back to him complete peacefulness.

"That same night," Abbé Gray continued, "at eleven-thirty, Père
Jacques died very quietly, without a gesture, without a cry, without
a lament."

Nothing had overcome his desire, or rather his virtue, of suffering all in silence. He was the worthy son of St. John of the Cross.

He had clothed the ragged, fed the hungry, visited the sick and
the captives. He had lived according to the letter of the words of
the Last Judgment. He was ready to see God.

It was he who on Easter, in the great city of Le Havre, had said
to the Carmelite nuns: "Why must death be a constant and cherished friend for us? Why must its contemplation nourish our hearts
and make us rejoice? Briefly, in what do the joys of death consist?
Oh! First, before and above all else, it gives us God. Do you think
of this, my Sisters? Suppose that one of you here is taken suddenly
by death. The soul would leave the body and confront God, face
to face; at last it can with all its love spring to God, hold Him,
embrace Him, become filled with Him. Sister Elizabeth of the
Trinity expresses it delightfully: 'A wall falls down and God appears.' "

Père Jacques was reunited with the Lord, but death had separated him from his friends.

And yet!

"Having done everything in his power for the living," said Jean
Cayrol, "Père Jacques has gone to join the dead, all the dead of
Güsen and the other camps, to be among them still in the secret
of the Lord."

For the living on earth, apparently it is all over except in the
faithful and loving memory of all those who were his companions
in the passage through a terrestrial hell and who think: "He died
too soon." Yet did not Père de Foucauld also die "too soon"? He
too was alone in the Sahara. A mere handful of friends kept his

memory alive until, years later, the time came when the sacrifice of Père de Foucauld visibly bore fruit. Like him, Père Jacques consummated his sacrifice in total abandonment to the will of God. When and how will it bear fruit? This is God's secret.

Christians and non-Christians, all who befriended Père Jacques at Güsen and along the Way of the Cross continue to be his friends. They all deplored his death, first out of affection, then because they thought of all Père Jacques might have accomplished on this earth, after the liberation. They sorely miss Père Jacques.

But this tenacious sense of the absence of Père Jacques is nevertheless the irrefutable sign of his indestructible presence deep in their memories and in their hearts.

Professor Heim ended his account with this vibrant affirmation: "Père Jacques, we are still gathered around you."

Julien Jacques, with words just as moving, declared: "In the ten years since I returned from Mauthausen, I have often thought of all my fellow prisoners. But Père Jacques! Not a day passes that I do not think of him."

Those who share faith in Christ and those who do not share it all hold the same opinion: he was an extraordinary man.

"In that world of the concentration camp which showed up the slightest defects in an extremely harsh light," said Julien Jacques, "I found no defects in Père Jacques."

"He never complained," said Emile Valley, his friend in Compiègne and Mauthausen.

"I never heard him complain," said Gaston Passagez who was close to Père Jacques day and night at Güsen, in the factory and dormitory.

"He never complained," repeated Abbé Gray, who cared for him constantly at Linz.

His only thought was to comfort others, to give them what was possible in that hellish universe whose hideousness is unimaginable.

"We lived because we veiled our eyes," said Jean Sculfort, who had been one of his great friends in Güsen. "Père Jacques could not continue to live because he did not veil his eyes. When one saw that human mass reduced to such a state, one said to oneself: these are no longer men. Père Jacques did not see it as a crowd, but saw each individual there as a man."

"Pientka lived in the same block as I," a deportee named Augé said. "I often heard the Poles express their admiration for Père Jacques. In the midst of this camp where food was more important than anything else, he maintained an unbelievable lucidity and freedom of mind. He considered the mediocrity of most contemporary religious art as a catastrophe, and one day he said to me: 'If we can't offer God homage with means proper to our own times, then we are in a state of insolvency.' On another occasion, after one of those demoralizing, cruel, ignoble scenes which occurred daily in the camp, we were talking about paradise, and I said: 'These SS, I think we at least won't find them up there!' He answered: 'You know nothing about it. Possibly they are sick and not responsible.' To be capable of such a view in Güsen was proof of an astounding control in judgment."

In addition, Père Jacques was a man full of humor. Gaston Passagez, who saw him each day depriving himself of food and working without the loss of a moment to fulfill his mission as priest and educator, also told these two stories about him:

"One day when we were talking about cooking, he told me that things had been hard in his childhood, that when preparing beans his mother carefully saved the water in which they had been cooked for soup. I laughed and said my family had been poor also but we hadn't gone so far as that. 'Well,' he replied with a serious air, 'then you weren't economical in your house.'

"He had so much fortitude that he deprived himself of food and insisted that we do the same so as to sustain the weaker ones. On one occasion, I protested a little, saying, 'But, Père Jacques, with a diet like this we'll all die.' I was fifty-one years old then and he answered me and with a very serious air: 'Well, you patriarch, haven't you lived long enough?' "

"It was not always easy to know just when he was joking," said Passagez. "There were, however, certain questions which he spoke of often and we knew he felt strongly about them. He objected strongly to everything that separated the priest from the mass of people. He was always thinking of the future and making plans for it. He ardently dreamed of mingling children from the wealthy and poor classes, of all faiths and points of view, so that they might come to know one another. In his talks, he constantly touched upon the marriage sacrament and the relationships between man and wife. What he struggled for each day, even in the midst of Güsen, was to build a truly Christian society."

"He had an extraordinary faith. It was not a naïve faith. Sometimes he would lash out," Henri Boussel said. "One day, in thinking of the multitude of hideous deaths which occurred every day at Güsen, he said: 'If what we believe is not revealed after death to be the whole truth, this would be the greatest deception that could be practiced on man."

These were the very words of St. Paul: "If Christ has not risen, vain then is our preaching, vain too is your faith. . . . But Christ has risen." This Père Jacques believed with his whole being.